Lao Peasants
under
Socialism

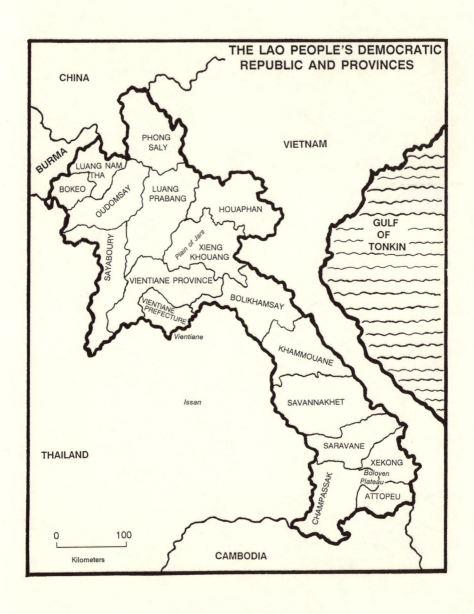

THE LAO PEOPLE'S DEMOCRATIC
REPUBLIC AND PROVINCES

CHINA

BURMA

VIETNAM

PHONG
SALY

LUANG NAM
THA

BOKEO

OUDOMSAY

LUANG
PRABANG

HOUAPHAN

GULF
OF
TONKIN

SAYABOURY

Plain of Jars

XIENG
KHOUANG

VIENTIANE PROVINCE

VIENTIANE
PREFECTURE

Vientiane

BOLIKHAMSAY

KHAMMOUANE

Issan

SAVANNAKHET

THAILAND

SARAVANE

XEKONG

Boloven
Plateau

ATTOPEU

CHAMPASSAK

0   100

Kilometers

CAMBODIA

Lao Peasants under Socialism

Grant Evans

Yale University Press

New Haven and London

Designed by James J. Johnson.
Set in Sabon Roman type by The Composing Room of Michigan, Inc.
Printed in the United States of America.

Library of Congress Cataloging-in-Publication Data

Evans, Grant, 1948–
    Lao peasants under Socialism / Grant Evans.
        p.   cm.
    Includes bibliographical references.
    ISBN 0–300–04598–0
        1. Laos—Rural conditions.   2. Peasantry—Laos—History.
    3. Collectivization of agriculture—Laos—History.   4. Socialism—
    Laos—History.   I. Title.
    HN700.4.A8E9   1990
    307.72'09594—dc20   89–70466
                                                                              CIP

10 9 8 7 6 5 4 3 2 1

The setting up of a collective economy is predicated upon the development of machinery, upon the utilization of natural resources, and of many other productive forces. . . . In the absence of those conditions, the collective economy would not itself represent a new productive force, would be lacking all material basis, and would rest upon merely theoretical foundations. This means, it would be nothing but a freak amounting to no more than the household of a monastery.
—KARL MARX AND FREDERICK ENGELS

Contents

Contents

Illustrations

Illustrations

Photographs follow page 122

Preface

To travel in Laos today is to experience economic and social conditions remote from those of the modern world and increasingly rare in Asia itself. Even in the old royal capital of Luang Prabang one feels cut off from the outside world, and one does not have to travel far from any provincial center before the most minimal trappings of modern industry begin to fade. Plastic bags and buckets become fewer, tin and tiled roofs disappear, nails no longer secure planks of wood, homegrown tobacco is rolled in leaves, cotton is spun under the houses, which are raised on stilts, and the dull thumps of weaving looms are morning and night accompanied by the sound of foot-powered rice huskers. Electricity has been left behind, and even kerosene to fuel lamps becomes increasingly scarce. The radios that now entertain many peasants closer to urban centers while they are re-planting or weeding rice fall silent, and one may catch bursts of a traditional work song. The occasional buses or motor boats peter out and give way to ponies; finally there are only footpaths up steep mountainsides. The isolation of a mountain village in Laos, in the provinces of Xieng Khouang, Sayaboury, or Houaphan, for example, has to be seen to be believed. One sometimes wonders, Do the villagers really know who is in power in the capital, Vientiane?

No doubt when Laos is fully opened to tourism it will be touted in brochures as one of the world's last frontiers, a sort of arcadian peasant society. Such a vision of humans in their "natural" environment, flowing with the seasons, acting according to custom and tradition, so fundamental to the ersatz romanticism that surrounds the *Tristes Tropiques* of travelers, is precisely the world the communist government that came to power in Laos in December 1975 wants to change. Communist regimes in preindustrial societies are, above all, modernizing regimes. They are committed to the economic and social transformation of peasant societies and the natural economy in their attempt to follow the well-worn path of industrialization and urbanization. They have, in the words of Claude Lévi-Strauss, "opted for monoculture,"[1] although they will happily prepackage "tradition" for the tourist trade. Tourism, after all, brings dollars for development.

The developmental tasks faced by the Lao People's Democratic Republic after 1975 were formidable. The country has one of the lowest per capita incomes in South Asia. Its territory of 236,775 square kilometers is sparsely settled by around 3.6 million inhabitants, 85 percent of whom live and work in rural areas and are furthermore separated into perhaps sixty different ethnic groups (maybe 40 percent are ethnic Lao). Barriers to social and economic intercourse are further reinforced by the country's topography: 80 percent is covered in mountains ranging between two hundred and three thousand meters. Thus communications throughout the country are difficult and costly. Laos has one of the lowest road densities in Asia, and important communication routes run up the rivers that flow down out of the mountains. During the wet season many villages are cut off from normal communications, and therefore many live in conditions of virtual economic autarky for at least part of the year. In sum, the country hardly possesses an integrated economy, society, or polity.

This book is about the confrontation between a modernizing regime and the social and economic world of its rural population, which remains embedded in a natural economy. Socialist developmental states have their own peculiar strategies for modernization, collectivization of agriculture being one, and therefore the following pages deal with the problems and paradoxes thrown up in the pursuit of "socialist agriculture." It is the tale of a government on a rapid learning curve concerning the peasantry and socialist development, a curve that in more recent years has intersected with the slower learning curve traced by communist governments and Marxist and socialist politicians and intellectuals elsewhere.

In the late twentieth century, political, economic, social, and intellectual ferment in communist societies is producing more sophisticated and complex analyses of the range of possible and probable socialist developments than ever before. The ferment is going on in both the East and the West, and one of the aims of this book is to contribute to the developing critique of actually existing socialism.

The intellectual lineage of the book descends from anthropology and sociology. I am a card-carrying member of an anthropological association only, which probably makes me a sociological fellow traveler. To many the book's intellectual apparatus will probably seem eclectic, whereas I would claim it is a judicious and logical selection from our store of social scientific knowledge. As C. Wright Mills insisted in *The Sociological Imagination,* a marshaling of the right tools to solve particular problems, not disputes over intellectual demarcation, is all-important.

There is a further problem of style and presentation. Anthropological and sociological discussions of the peasantry, for example, have become very sophisticated and technical over the past decade or so. Inevitably, perhaps, they have also acquired a certain scholasticism, if not occasional obscurantism. In some cases disputes have become intractable, with parties forming into veritable feuding societies. My loose use of the notion *natural economy,* for example, will probably cause consternation in some quarters. I have used it partly because it is one of the common ways the communist government in Vientiane discusses its rural economy and society, but deployment of the concept in the special empirical conditions of Laos also helps illuminate the peculiarities of communism's encounter with the peasantry. I hope my reasons for using it will become clear as the book progresses. Similarly, I use terms like *tribal, primitive, traditional,* and so on fully aware that in some contexts they can conjure up visions of rigid nineteenth-century evolutionism or of a static pastoral past. The contexts in which I have used them makes it clear that they serve stylistic purposes, allowing rapid transitions between main points without a stumbling over neologisms. In this respect I follow the practice of E. E. Evans-Pritchard: "If we have to choose between steering close to the obscurities of everyday speech and the obscurities of specialist jargon I would prefer to risk the lesser perils of everyday speech."[2]

Access to Laos for research has been extremely difficult since 1975, and this is the first major study of rural society there. Until very recently what was happening within cooperatives was considered, in the words of one Lao official, "a state secret." Fortunately for me this official disagreed with prevailing restrictions and greatly facilitated my research. Since beginning work on Laos in earnest in 1979 I have spoken to many peasants and visited many villages and cooperatives in various parts of the country. The research on the villages that are central to the book began in late 1982, when I spent several months surveying the formation of cooperatives in them. Since then I have made return visits of one or two months annually or biannually until 1987. These villages were not far from the capital at Vientiane because it was not possible to do detailed research farther afield. This restriction was in fact an advantage to a study of this sort, however, because, given the importance of state support and backup for cooperatives in any collectivization program, those villages best situated to receive this support should in fact be the most successful. If they are not, then the possibilities for success in remoter areas are poorer still. As we shall see, in the absence of modern technological inputs collectivization is vulnerable to the encompassing logic of the peasant economy. I have changed the names of all informants, but it has been impossible to disguise several key villages.

The following text does not claim to be a definitive study, especially given the difficult conditions under which the research was conducted. Happily, since 1988 political restrictions within Laos have relaxed enormously, and we can look forward to more unfettered research in the future. A second main aim, or hope, for the book is that it will serve as a benchmark for future studies of the Lao peasantry.

Most books are made possible by the generosity of others: Peter Cox took time out from aid work to share his vast knowledge of Lao and Thai peasants; my wife Elizabeth Astbury insisted on clarity and provided companionship; Kelvin Rowley was a continuous source of intellectual stimulation; Paul Cohen and Doug Miles provided early encouragement; many Lao, both in Australia and in Laos, assisted me in my attempts to understand Lao society. I thank them all but still do not have enough faith in *jintanna kan mai* (new way of thinking), Laos's version of *perestroika*, to name them; various occupants of the Mennonite and Quaker offices in Laos also shared their knowledge of Laos with me and provided generous assistance; finally I would like to thank an anonymous reader for Yale University Press for timely suggestions and my editors at the Press, Ellen Graham and Lawrence Kenney. None are responsible for the book's judgments. Unless otherwise indicated translations in the text are mine, as are the photographs.

Abbreviations

ALPW	Association of Lao Patriotic Women
COMECON	Council for Mutual Economic Assistance
CPSU	Communist Party of the Soviet Union
FBIS	Foreign Broadcast Information Service
KPL	Khao San Pathet Lao (Lao National Newsagency)
LPDR	Lao Peoples' Democratic Republic
LPRP	Lao Peoples' Revolutionary Party
NEP	New Economic Policy
NLHS	Neo Lao Hak Sat (Lao Patriotic Front)
NLSS	Neo Lao Sang Sat (Lao Front for National Reconstruction)
RLG	Royal Lao Government
SPA	Supreme Peoples' Assembly
SWB	BBC Summary of World Broadcasts: Far East
USAID	United States Agency for International Development

Lao Peasants
under
Socialism

I

New Socialist Man,

Natural Economy, and

Collectivization

 Speaking at the Fourth Congress of the LPRP in November 1986, General Secretary and Prime Minister Kaysone Phomvihane announced to the delegates that "the new socialist man has emerged." The task of the party was, he told them, to build "a new culture having socialist content which reflects a national and popular character, while building new people, first of all people filled with patriotism, love for socialism, and socialist internationalism, working in accordance with the principle 'one for all and all for one'." The general secretary concluded his lengthy report saying, "The cause of forming the new man [is] the noblest cause pursued by us all."[1]

Mention of the new socialist man by communist leaders prompts instant ridicule from Western commentators. If, however, we scrutinize what a leader like Kaysone means by the idea of the new socialist man we generally find it contains two distinct emphases. One expresses a desire to instill in the population the values and ways of "industrial man," to use the parlance of modern sociology. Thus Kaysone laments the fact that "we are building socialism with the participation of men left by history. . . . They have some weaknesses, such as their insufficient knowledge in management of society, their low educational, scientific and technical levels." Their work patterns evince the "scattered style of work typical of small producers."[2] Such sentiments are thoroughly respectable and would normally be applauded by any Western modernization theorist. The commitment to forging industrial man in Laos has steadily gained ascendancy as the party travels farther from the heady days of 1975 and becomes preoccupied with the mundane, difficult problems of economic development.

It is the second emphasis, fundamentally voluntaristic and concerned with the "moral life" of the people, that is the real target of Western scorn. It implies "cultural revolution," "changing people's heads," or, in Cold War lexicon, "brainwashing." It attacks precapitalist "superstitions" and the cultural "decadence" of capitalism. These "vestiges of the old society," according to Kaysone, are the "cause of negative manifestations in social life." The new socialist man replaces these values with moral rectitude and selfless devotion to others and to socialist edification.

Western objections to this cultural revolution take two broad forms: the first is a straightforward liberal one, which is perhaps not so much concerned with people "changing their heads" as with the fact that it is the party that decides what are the correct moral values to be adopted. It is an argument premised on the State's limited right to regulate individual values. The other objection is more purely ideological in that it argues that socialism is inimical to "human nature." It is an argument which asserts that individuals are naturally selfish and greedy and "look after number one," and therefore only a "capitalist man" is possible, or "rational."

The "commonsense" attractions of this latter argument are powerful. Marxists have often rejected notions of human nature because such claims have generally been cast in a conservative mold. As Marxists they have been concerned with social transformation, whereas human nature arguments have often implied that no matter how you change society the same old human being will always result. Social change for the better is, therefore, a utopian quest. Yet a closer examination of the model of human nature proposed by critics of socialism often reveals that they are advancing the values of contemporary capitalism as universal features of humans. Marx noted this tendency many years ago when he criticized Smith and Ricardo for holding up the individual of competitive capitalism "as an ideal, whose existence they project into the past. Not as a historic result but as history's point of departure. As the Natural Individual appropriate to their notion of human nature, not arising historically, but posited by nature."[3] Marxists and communists, however, took Marx's critique as a rejection of human nature altogether, which led them to a conception of humans as historically and socially infinitely malleable—into socialist men, for example. However, as Norman Geras has carefully argued, rejection of one definition of human nature does not imply a total rejection of the concept.[4] Rather, what is required is the substitution of a different conception of human nature together with a specification of its explanatory limitations.

Social anthropologists and comparative sociologists have been less burdened by these issues (perhaps because they have not been preoccupied with the political results of their conclusions) and have remained simultaneously concerned with both the "universals" of human societies and their cultural and historical peculiarities. Maintaining the dialectic between these perspectives has, however, not been easy. Some anthropologists have fallen into a miasma of cultural relativism that eschews all general statements, while others have been preoccupied with cultural universals, sometimes expressed as cultural or national psychological types. The Lao "national character," easygoing, fun-loving, is allegedly the enduring core of social life and explains the Lao reaction to, for example, socialism, which can be presented as an artificial imposition on this "natural" base. Such an attitude is a favorite of many journalists writing about contemporary Laos. Other anthropologists have been enthralled by the universalistic biological models of humans constructed by sociobiologists, in which culture is an expression of invariant imperatives such as aggressive territoriality.[5] This is not the place to resume a critique of these tendencies;[6] I wish only to register their failure to pursue a research strategy that attempts a dialectical combination of the universal and the particular, and I want to signal my rejection of theories that attempt to deduce cultural and political forms from invariants of psychology or biology.

It is possible, nevertheless, to provide an outline of human nature that contrasts with the so-called common sense of capitalist societies. As a social creature, humans have an enhanced capacity for cooperation and from the beginning have constructed societies because these ensured the survival of the species. Social cooperation has, therefore, been an adaptive mechanism. As *Homo sapiens* we are marked off from other social creatures by our extraordinary capacity to learn and use information with behavior-modifying potential. Sociability multiplies the flow of information and accelerates learning.[7] Thus cooperation, in contrast to the aggressive individualism posited by "bourgeois man," is fundamental to human culture.

It would, however, be extremely foolish to repeat the methodological errors of socialism's critics and try to deduce from this model of human nature a form of social and economic cooperation that allegedly harmonized with it. After all, cooperating to kill other human beings is as natural as cooperating to help them. Whether humans are inclined to do one or the other is historically determined.

The problems of causality and determinism integral to the foregoing discussion are fundamental to another central problem of social science, namely, the relation between social structure and human agency, or the limits and possibilities of human action. Kaysone has also pondered this question: "Man is both a product of society and a subject of history. The new socialist man can emerge only gradually in the process of socialist construction, but ideological and theoretical work does not passively wait until all adequate material conditions are assembled to bring its role into play, but it must take the initiative, step by step and by means of comprehensive and integrated measures, to make an active contribution to the cause of forming the new man."[8] The conundrum facing revolutionary parties presiding over one-party states is the degree to which their own ideological predispositions are shaped or determined by the historical and social conjuncture in which they are forced to act. Parties like the LPRP, being self-consciously agencies of change, run the ever-present danger of trying to force the pace of social change, of voluntaristic leaps from "the realm of necessity to the realm of freedom"; that is, of underestimating objective barriers to change. These dangers are most acute in immediate postrevolutionary periods, in which "will" has recently been seen to triumph, and this gives rise to beliefs that "revolutionary consciousness" is a prerequisite for the solving of social and economic problems. The communist victory in Laos saw a flourishing of propaganda that emphasized the superior morality of the new socialist man. Only as the revolution became institutionalized, or routinized, did this emphasis begin to change.

Arguably the interpretation given to the morality of the new socialist man by the LPRP was strongly conditioned by the Lao social environment. That influence explains the highly traditional and conservative as well as nationalistic cast of this ideology. Reactions against Western fashion, music, and decadent morality, exemplified by prostitution or simply the holding of hands in the street, largely reflected the values of elderly people (whose number included the party leadership), who are traditionally guides in such matters, and the sexual conservatism of village culture. "Capitalist decadence" was rejected in favor of socialist ways, which were interpreted through traditional Lao ways, a process that led to the identifying of nationalist appeals with socialism. Such manifestations of conservative cultural nationalism are not exclusive to communist states and have been found throughout the Third World, especially in immediate postindependence periods or in religiously inspired reactions to the West, such as those in Iran.

The other key anterior influence on party and cadre interpretations of socialist morality in Laos is Buddhism. The concept of the ascetic, selfless person working for a higher existence is the folk model of a good person in Laos, and it is not surprising that this should have been the dominant popular perception of the new socialist man.[9] Indeed, a relationship between the two has been encouraged by the new regime. Speaking to a gathering of monks in late 1976, then–Deputy Premier and Minister of Education, Sports, and Religious Affairs Phoumi Vongvichit said, "The Lord Buddha gave up all his worldly possessions and became an ordinary person with only an alms bowl to beg food from other people. That meant that he tried to abolish the classes in his country and to create only one class—a class of morally conscious people who were respected by other people. . . . We can see now that the revolutionary politics and the politics practiced by the Lord Buddha have the same goals."[10] Thus a quasi-religious gloss was given to socialist policies and thereby there became fixed in the popular mind—especially in the minds of the party cadres in charge of carrying out policy—an idea of socialism as a forsaking of private property (the Buddha's worldly possessions) and selfless devotion to the common well-being of society. Only recently has the government pulled back from this interpretation and acknowledged that "we should eliminate any bias against caring for personal interests."[11]

Despite attempts to bring the Lord Buddha back to the material world in the service of socialist man, Buddhist doctrine provides an unavoidably utopian vision of human perfection. The sources of this utopian vision are not only traditional, but also compatible with certain ideas in Marxist thought. No doubt under the influence of his own training in Hegelian idealism Marx tended to conceptualize socialism as the negation of capitalism or the opposite of capitalism and therefore able to provide the social conditions for the development of a new man. In economic terms this meant common ownership rather than private ownership of means of production and a gradual disappearance of all commodity production and the market as abundance was achieved in a technologically advanced society. Marx wrote very little about socialist society, but in the light of just these speculations by him one can only agree with Alec Nove in his *Economics of Feasible Socialism* that the "little that he did say was either irrelevant or directly misleading" concerning any socialist economy that could exist.[12] Communism, Nove argues, is not feasible because scarcity will always be a fact of life, and the insurmountable difficulties of total central planning in increasingly complex modern economies mean that markets will always be required. It is not surprising, however, that when socialist revolutions are in their most radical phases (which can accompany inner-party struggles) and therefore at their most voluntaristic, revolutionaries casting around for a guide to radical transformation should fix on these end points first set out by Marx. The Red Guards at the height of the Cultural Revolution in China in the late 1960s epitomized this thinking. To these radicals all private property, all market exchanges, all commodity production, and all culture or politics were deemed to have either a capitalist or a communist content. Theirs was a battle between darkness and light. Although manipulated by party factions, this mass movement gave a spontaneously millennial cast to Marx's ideas. Less extreme versions of millennialism can be found in all communist revolutions.

The evolution of much received communist policy and orthodoxy is an accident of Russian history whereby policies developed by the CPSU were transposed into other situations through the dominance of the Soviet Union within world communism. Chinese communism's main features, long vaunted as an alternative model, were in fact drawn directly from Stalinism. And while I believe that Stalinism is essentially a travesty of the main ideas developed by Marx and Engels, their notions about the disappearance of the market and commodity production provided some of the raw material for the fashioning of Stalinist communism. Stalinism in the Soviet Union, and consequently elsewhere, attempted to implement such a doctrine in the midst of acute scarcity while drawing legitimacy for its actions from selected, and sometimes censored, texts of Marx. Collectivization of agriculture was one outcome.

There are, therefore, diverse sources for the LPRP's ideas of what typifies the new socialist man, and they add up to a syncretic ideology fashioned for the purpose of social transformation. This ideology is wielded by a vanguard party that claims to be the source of truth and wisdom. When Kaysone talks of "not passively wait[ing] until all adequate material conditions are assembled" and of the need to act, he is not only rejecting a view that sees politics and culture as passive products of the evolution of the forces of production (sometimes called economic determinism), but above all else is providing a rationalization for the leading role of the party.

At the same time, the idea of the new socialist man is premised on the sociologically acceptable view that human beings change and adapt to new social environments. Change the conditions and you change the person. But, how much? And how fast? People clearly can change quite dramatically in conditions of rapid social transformation. The mountain of information gathered about social change in the developing world over the past half-century has documented the adaption, at times extremely traumatic, of many different peoples and cultures to new values and new ways of living and working. Sometimes this has produced extraordinary cultural inventiveness; at other times, xenophobic reaction, which in itself was a new cultural elaboration. It is also clear that cultures do not change uniformly, as envisaged in the neat models of modernization theory and in the simple determinism of communist theory. Different institutions—such as the family or political leadership—adapt in various ways and at various tempos because societies are complex networks of institutions and activities that are continually acting and reacting on one another. Family institutions, for example, are more subject to biological imperatives than are political institutions. Yet the process is not random, and hierarchies of causality can be discerned through a process of theoretically informed empirical research.[13]

Adaptions and change have a logic that is too complex to be prefigured in teleological ideas like new socialist man. One must conclude that the latter notion is fundamentally nonmaterialist because it attempts to prefigure, regardless of empirical investigation or knowledge, the actual adaptions people will make to their changed material circumstances based on some a priori notion of humans while trying to force on people a particular adaption even in the absence of material change. It has been assumed, for example, that if means of production are held in common new socialist men will selflessly cooperate with one another. This has been shown to be untrue, and one of the aims of this book is to try to discover under what conditions Lao peasants will cooperate or not cooperate and why, without resort to a priori concepts of collectivism, individualism, selfishness, or indeed "happy-go-luckiness."[14] As Alec Nove remarks, "It seems basically reasonable, therefore, to discuss 'feasible socialism' in which human beings are recognizable, similar to those that now exist. Of course, we must take into account any likely or possible changes in circumstances. But that is a different question, the answer to which does not depend on making assumptions about some imaginary New Man, who, in a choice between his own advantage and that of others, would always choose the latter."[15]

Socialism and the Natural Economy

Marxists have tended to conceptualize the main features of socialism as embodying principles that are the opposite of those of capitalism. Full-fledged communism would see the disappearance of classes, private property, the state, commodities, and money. What is intriguing about this vision of communism is the degree to which it approximates the conditions of the "natural economy" that socialists in underdeveloped countries like Laos are committed to transforming.

The origin of this vision of socialism can be traced to the work of Marx and Engels, who, in occasional flights of dialectical abstraction, conceptualized communism as the reappearance in a "higher" form of "primitive communism." In his seminal *Origin of Family, Private Property and State* Engels looked to the work of the early anthropologist Lewis H. Morgan, not only to understand the historical evolution of societies, but also because Morgan spoke of "a future transformation of society in words which Karl Marx might have used."[16] Thus the last lines of Engels's text are from Morgan's *Ancient Society*: "Democracy in government, brotherhood in society, equality in rights and privileges, and universal education, foreshadow the next higher plane of society to which experience, intelligence and knowledge are steadily tending. *It will be a revival, in a higher form, of the liberty, equality, and fraternity of the ancient gentes.*"[17] But how did Engels conceptualize primitive communism? In the same text he outlines the main features of its social organization:

> Production was essentially collective and likewise, consumption took place by the direct distribution of the products within larger or smaller communistic communities. This production in common was carried on within the narrowest limits, but concomitantly the producers were masters of their process of production and of their product. They knew what became of the product: they consumed it, it did not leave their hands; and as long as production was carried on this basis, it could not grow beyond the control of the producers, and it could not raise any strange, phantom powers against them, as is the case regularly and inevitably under civilization. But, slowly, division of labor crept into this process of production. It undermined the collective nature of production and appropriation, it made appropriation by individuals the largely prevailing rule, and thus gave rise to exchange between individuals. . . . Gradually, the production of commodities became the dominant form."[18]

As he does so often Engels here transforms evolution into teleology. Hence the appearance of commodities and exchange prefigure the much later historical appearance of capitalism. But more important, subsequent anthropological research has overturned nineteenth-century ideas of communal property and demonstrated that prestate societies come in many shapes and sizes. Raymond Firth points out that "Marx's antithesis between communal and private is too sharp. . . . He clearly failed to realize the complexity of rights over property, including property in land, characteristic of a primitive agricultural community."[19] One could add that simplistic ideas of egalitarianism were also derived from prestate societies. So the notion of primitive communism has been largely discredited in the West. But as Maurice Bloch has argued, Marx and Engels were misled on this matter by the anthropologists of their day. He also demonstrates that they were to some extent willingly misled because they wanted to counter the arrogant assertions of nineteenth-century bourgeois society that its institutions were both natural and eternal. Thus Marx and Engels "naturally turned to primitive society, as they assumed, like many before and after them, that these societies would offer illustrations of systems as totally different to those they knew as could be found anywhere." They were looking for "opposites to the institutions of capitalism." Unfortunately their legitimate observations on the historical transience of social institutions got "disastrously mixed up" with their polemical interests and "produced a false picture of the idyllic classless community which was later termed primitive communism and then got further confused with the type of society the Marxists were trying to construct in the future."[20]

This confusion has persisted in orthodox Marxism in the party-supervised anthropology of the Soviet Union and other communist countries. Only recently has such orthodoxy been challenged from within. Among Western radical and Marxist anthropologists the notion of primitive communism has not been strong, and therefore their work has rarely asserted an overt connection between precapitalist societies and postcapitalist/ socialist societies. Nevertheless, I suggest that there remains an important subterranean connection.

Attempts by radical and Marxist anthropologists to analyze precapitalist societies in the broader context of colonialism and capitalist transformation of these societies saw a heavy reliance on Marxism's critique of commodification of economic and social relations. This assimilation of Marxism by anthropology has produced some brilliant insights into the way peasants or tribesmen responded to the momentous changes that have overtaken their communities, but, by default, it retained earlier problems. This is true, for example, of Michael Taussig's *The Devil and Commodity Fetishism.* While he explicitly rejects the idea that precapitalist societies represent some "lost Golden Age," his critique of capitalism nevertheless adopts the standpoint of precapitalist cultures in order "to account for the phantom objectivity with which capitalist culture enshrouds its social relations." He says that this vantage point offers only a "negative" critique of capitalism, yet he also emphasizes the "commonality between Marxism and the pre-capitalist hostility toward the flowering of the market economy."[21] Thus even if the notion of primitive communism has been eschewed, a critique of capitalism from the perspective of the natural economy (an economy based on the production of use values) retains the essential polemical and theoretical implications of Marx and Engels's notion of primitive communism. Like socialism, it is conceived of as the opposite of capitalism. This is also clear, for example, in an influential essay entitled "The Destruction of Natural Economy" by Barbara Bradby: "The term 'natural economy' is therefore used to mean those characteristics of pre-capitalist modes of production which are essentially opposed to capitalist relations of production, and which must be destroyed for the development of capitalism to be possible."[22] The examples of Taussig and Bradby are not exceptional.

The paradox for a Marxist-inspired anthropology is that a critique of capitalism from the perspective of precapitalism, rather than socialism, reinforces the idea that socialism is somehow closer to a precapitalist natural economy than to capitalism. The power of its critique is derived partly from the unexpressed presence of a latent alternative: a communism that could painlessly and simultaneously absorb and transcend these premodern societies. The sad irony, however, is that to the extent that modern communism attempts to put in place the features of the natural economy it most closely shares, the greater the direct coercion it must use to promote socialist development. The absence of an anthropology of socialism has, consequently, allowed the confusion mentioned by Bloch to continue at the heart of radical anthropology.

But we require some clarification of the concept natural economy and the extent to which it overlaps with the practice of communism. Of course, the natural economy is largely an ideal type, being a logical extrapolation from the real diversity of the world whose purpose it is to highlight the essential features of particular empirical situations. So, at its highest level of abstraction, the natural economy (and communism) is one in which there is only production for use and in which commodities and money are absent. But except for the most general purposes, or perhaps only very specific empirical situations, this is far too restrictive as a notion of the natural economy. As anthropologists know, a significant proportion of what is produced in primitive economies is exchanged, although the nature of exchange is different from that in a capitalist market. As Marshal Sahlins has argued, it is difficult to isolate any purely economic logic in much of this exchange, which is governed by rules of reciprocity whose purpose is to "establish solidarity between people through the instrumentality of things."[23]

Contrary to ideas of pure, self-contained economies, production and exchange of commodities was common among tribal societies, as was primitive money. A distinguishing feature of primitive money, however, is its restricted range of exchange—a range essentially dictated by social structure. This led Mary Douglas to see these restrictions as "instruments of social policy" designed to protect the social order through systems of rationing and/or licensing, not unlike the policies of the welfare or socialist state.[24] Social purpose and use motivated exchange, and in the absence of the market there was no possibility of objective price formation—once again not unlike the pricing problems faced in state socialist economies. Maurice Godelier observed the following in his essay on salt money among the Buruya: "What counts in group exchanges is the reciprocal satisfaction of their needs and not a well-kept balance of their labor expenditure. . . . Exchange expresses the comparative social utility of exchanged products."[25] In other words, use-values continue to prevail in the presence of money and commodity exchange, and it is, therefore, consistent to call this a natural economy.

Most stateless tribal societies that anthropologists have studied have been transformed this century, usually into peasantries, and most primitive forms of exchange have disappeared in the face of generalized currencies issued by states. Peasants in this context were created out of tribal societies; but of course other peasant societies and markets predated the rise of capitalism.

Peasants have historically participated in market exchanges, the nature and importance of which have changed over time along with changes to the broader social structure. In the process of historical development tribal economies have merged into peasant economies in what Dalton calls peripheral markets "in which a narrow range of produce is bought and sold, either with some money-stuff used as medium of (commercial) exchange, or via barter in the economist's sense (moneyless market exchange). We call these market exchanges 'peripheral' because land and labor are not bought and sold and because most people do not get the bulk of their income from market sales."[26] With the spread of capitalism an increasing number of commodities are bought and sold in the market, including land and labor, and the natural economy is increasingly marginalized but rarely disappears altogether.

Peasant economy differs from tribal economy insofar as demands are made on peasant households to produce a surplus to maintain a state and a ruling class over and above the needs of the household to physically reproduce itself and its conditions of production, and the costs of representing itself in the wider community.[27] This surplus may be extracted either in labor or in kind or, as is increasingly the case, in cash. These demands influence the allocation of labor by the peasant household and how hard its members work but do not fundamentally alter its basic organization in what remains essentially a natural economy. A. V. Chayanov, the Russian economist and rural sociologist who perished in Stalin's concentration camps because of his opposition to forced collectivization, described this peasant economy in his essay "On the Theory of Non-Capitalist Economic Systems": "In a natural economy, human economic activity is dominated by the requirement of satisfying the needs of each single production unit. Therefore, budgeting here is to a high degree *qualitative*: for each family need, there has to be provided in each economic unit the qualitatively corresponding product *in natura*."[28] Such economies are sometimes referred to as subsistence economies. This description expresses the important truth that peasants (like tribesmen) produce the bulk of their basic subsistence needs. The peasant's basic rule of economic calculation is whether there is enough of these basic needs or not, after which decisions will be made about whether to allocate labor to cash crop production (assuming there is adequate land) or whether it will be freed to engage in other money-making occupations on a part-time basis. Consumption needs are socially and historically variable and will play their role in deciding labor outlays, just as labor beyond the satisfaction of subsistence needs will be determined by opportunities for other productive work and the capability to acquire desired consumer products.

Capitalist development and the explicit policies of states and development agencies encourage commercialized peasant production; the result is that more and more on-farm decisions are determined by the market. But in the absence of direct coercion conversion to commercial farming (leaving aside some exceptional colonial situations) has been remarkably slow owing to the logic of the peasant farm and the related demands made on subsistence by population growth and inadequate compensatory price incentives. Nevertheless, widening markets and changing consumer demand do draw peasants into increasing commercial exchange for goods formerly produced and exchanged in local markets, such as cloth, or for new goods, such as portable radios. The peasant devotes greater effort to cash crop production, particularly in gardens, occasional wage labor, or petty trading in order to earn the cash to acquire these consumer items. These activities only occasionally disrupt labor allocations to the staple crop, and more often labor is reallocated from economic activities displaced by commercial penetration of peasant markets, for instance, salt making or weaving. Such activities by members of the household that lie beyond the perimeter of the natural economy remain subordinate to it. In communist societies, however, the line of economic development tends to be somewhat different.

Toward the end of his essay on noncapitalist economic systems Chayanov briefly considers the economic theory of communism, a system that was only just being experimented with at the time he was writing. He compiled an intriguing table of economic categories applicable to different economic systems that shows that the two systems having the most categories in common are the family natural economy and communism. Although only a passing observation, the table is an important guide to the interaction between the peasant economy and communism.

In *The ABC of Communism,* written soon after the Russian revolution and at almost the same time as Chayanov's essay, two influential Bolshevik leaders, N. Bukharin and E. Preobrazhensky, set out the fundamental logic of orthodox Marxism better than anyone either before or since. They asserted, "The communist method of production presupposes . . . that production is not for the market, but for use. . . . We no longer have *commodities,* but only *products.* These products are not exchanged one for another; they are neither bought nor sold. They are simply stored in the communal warehouses, and are subsequently delivered to those who need them. In such conditions money will no longer be required. . . . There will be ample quantity of all products."[29] Leaving aside the important assumption of abundance made by these authors, we note that the predominance of production for use and the demise of commodities and money mean there are striking parallels between this outline and conceptions of a natural economy. There is also a parallel in that society is conceived of as one corporate entity in much the same way as the peasant household is considered to be a corporate unit. The fundamental difference is that the decision-making locus has shifted from the peasant household to "society" (in reality the state and its planning agencies), and, to cite Chayanov, these now decide "where the equilibrium between drudgery of labor and social demand satisfaction has been reached."[30] Moreover, "society" decides that not all that is produced can be consumed by the direct producer, and, according to the authors of the *ABC*, "Part of the work done must always be devoted to the development and improvement of production."[31] Recognition of this fundamental shift in the locus of decision-making led Chayanov to pose several elemental problems for a fully planned socialist economy:

> 1. With the help of which method and according to what principles will the degree of social labor exertion and the required amount of demand satisfaction, as well as the necessary equilibrium between the two, be determined when state production and consumption plans are established?
> 2. By what means is the individual worker to be driven to labor so that he does not consider as drudgery the input expected of him under the production plan and really carries it out in practice?[32]

Chayanov obviously understood the difficulties of the state centrally determining consumer choices and, most important, realized that without economic incentives direct state intervention (presumably coercion) would be required to achieve the fulfillment of state plans. In so doing Chayanov identified a problem that to this day has dogged socialist economies in both industry and agriculture.

The ability of the socialist state to make decisions for the whole of society is seriously curtailed for as long as an independent peasantry continues to exist. It can attempt to draw the peasants into wider economic circuits through trade in much the same way as capitalism, a strategy recommended by Lenin in the early 1920s, when he introduced the New Economic Policy—a policy that has been reinstated in several communist countries, including Laos, in recent years. Or, the socialist state can attempt to suppress all trade, in which case its only alternative, if it is to draw the peasantry into the wider economy, is to directly take over the operation of the peasant farm, which is effectively what collectivization does.

Collectivization of the peasantry is an almost inevitable corollary of orthodox communism precisely because of the latter's similarities with the natural economy. Suppression or restriction of the market by the command economy drives the peasantry back on its own resources and reactivates, out of necessity, forms of self-provisioning that usually die out with growing market exchange. The national economy may shrink and its rudimentary division of labor stagnate. Rarely, however, are communist states in a position to fully supplant preexisting trading networks without drastic disruption of the whole economy. Local markets involving established exchanges between communities in the main continue to exist, while regional and national markets come under increasing control by state agencies. Only extreme coercion, such as that seen in Pol Pot's Cambodia, can fully suppress peasant markets and impose total state regulation of exchange. Few communist states have been able to take such a drastic step.[33]

Increasing state control of national trade and the spread of administered prices gradually robs money of its function as a measure of value and a medium of exchange. Not surprisingly a situation reminiscent of primitive money begins to emerge along with discrete spheres of exchange. For example, state fixing of prices for most basic goods means that peasants will "sell" (barter) rice to the state outlets only if these networks have goods that are useful to them. They will sell their rice at a low price only if they can get what they want at a low price. Money is marginal to this economy. In the peripheral markets money continues to act as a medium of exchange, but shortages force prices up to levels where fewer people are able to enter the market. Blackmarket dealing develops in state-monopolized goods, both local and foreign, a large section of which requires a separate foreign currency to operate. Sometimes foreign cigarettes act as substitutes for foreign money. Finally, state functionaries may be issued coupons to acquire rationed necessities from state shops, and their low wages, which are pegged to official prices, virtually exclude them from the peripheral markets.

If, as is often the case in underdeveloped socialist societies, the state cannot provide the goods needed by peasants in sufficient quantities, and the prices of these goods in the peripheral or blackmarkets are too high, then the peasant has no incentive, for example, to produce rice beyond the household's needs. The logic of the natural economy in this context leads to either stagnation or a fall in production. The socialist state, however, in order to satisfy its needs, requires surpluses to generate economic development and is compelled to take over peasant production and increase the peasants' toil or drudgery (to use Chayanov's term) over that required to fill the latter's needs. Short of collectivization, orthodox communism's adherence to policies derived from the classical vision of communist society serves only to strengthen the peasant natural economy, the very opposite of its stated intentions. Only a socialism that eschews the classical vision can avoid this outcome: that is, a socialism that has more in common with capitalism than with the natural economy.

In Laos the social structure ranges across the full gamut of possibilities, from nonmarket exchange in the remote mountain areas, to peripheral markets, to commercial markets, stopping short of full commercial farming or full cooperative farming. Therefore, in this book tendencies toward or away from the natural economy will be expressed at different levels of inclusiveness, from the peasant household to the national economy. No doubt this procedure will annoy some readers; however, as the argument progresses I hope they will see both its conceptual and empirical usefulness.

A final question should be dealt with, if only because it allows us to rejoin the opening topic of this chapter, socialist man; namely, the question of material abundance under communism, which is so vital to the classical vision of a future society. I noted in the opening section that authors like Alec Nove have effectively criticized the notion of abundance—the absence of scarcity—as a foundation for an advanced socialist society. His position is, as ever, pragmatic: given the complexity of industrial societies and the diverse demands of its citizens, there will always be opportunity costs involved in economic decision making. Socialists may, however, want to respond that he is gauging needs by a capitalist yardstick. This would most likely have been Marx's response, as Agness Heller summarizes: "It is absurd to try to use the current, existing structure of needs as a basis for judging the system of needs which is Marx's precondition for the society of associated producers. . . . For Marx, the complete restructuring of the system of needs in communism is the *sine qua non* for any assertion about the future society."[34] Needs are, therefore, socially relative.

Marshall Sahlins argued an apparently similar case in his essay "The Original Affluent Society." In it he suggested, "There are two possible courses to affluence. Wants may be 'easily satisfied' either by producing much or desiring little." People in certain social structures, notably hunter and gatherer societies, desire little, and not because Economic Man has been "subdued by a cultural vow of poverty" but because there is nothing in their mode of life that makes them desire more. It is a materialist explanation, not a psychological one, and Sahlins concludes, "It was not until culture neared the height of its material achievements that it erected a shrine to the Unattainable: *Unlimited Needs*."[35]

For Marx and Engels the original affluent societies functioned as proof of the possibility of communism at a "higher stage" of human civilization and proof that alternative societies and hierarchies of cultural values are possible. However, it is untenable to extrapolate from conditions in original affluent societies to a supposed stage of advanced affluence under communism because the social organization of the two societies is necessarily radically different. The productive base of the former is structured around a "domestic mode of production," which entails a minimal division of labor. In Sahlins's word, "It offers society only a constituted disorganization, a mechanical solidarity set across the grain of segmentary decomposition."[36] In contrast, the constituent units of any advanced socialist society would unavoidably be large-scale formal organizations that are interconnected, via planning and the market, by virtue of a highly elaborate division of labor (organic solidarity)—despite Marx's vision to the contrary.[37] Like capitalism, such a society would be one committed to technological innovation and economic growth and, therefore, to continually changing needs. Unlike societies of original affluence, modern societies (capitalist or socialist) have no obvious mechanisms for desiring little. It remains to be seen whether any advanced feasible socialism is capable of moderating capitalist culture's often destructive desire for more of everything. Yet it is clear, once again, that conditions of original affluence are no guide to the type of human beings or culture possible in a socialist society.

The Reasons for Collectivization

There are three principal reasons for communist commitment to collectivized agriculture. The first is deeply ingrained in the history of Marxist socialism. Marx and Engels expected socialists to come to power in a situation of fully developed capitalism, which in the countryside meant capitalism had displaced the small peasants with large-scale mechanized agriculture. Like most other thinkers of the late nineteenth and early twentieth centuries they believed the latter typified modern agriculture. As E. H. Carr comments, "Marx and Engels never abandoned their belief in the large-scale organization of production, in agriculture as in industry, as an essential condition of socialism."[38] They simply assumed that socialist relations of production would replace capitalist ones and achieve even further economies of scale in the application of modern technology.

The second emerged directly out of the Bolshevik experience, in which communists for the first time had to contemplate coming to power in a peripheral capitalist, or indeed precapitalist, society in which the mass of the population were peasants. Beginning with Lenin's classic analysis in *The Development of Capitalism in Russia* (1899), communists assumed that peasant society in Russia was tending inevitably toward capitalism and that this was the spontaneous tendency of the peasants. The view was expressed most forcefully by Lenin in 1920:

> Small-scale production engenders capitalism and the bourgeoisie continuously, daily, hourly, spontaneously and on a mass scale. . . .
>
> Abolition of classes means, not merely ousting landowners and capitalists—that we accomplished with comparative ease; it also means abolishing small commodity producers. . . . It's a thousand times easier to vanquish the centralized big bourgeoisie than to 'vanquish' millions of petty proprietors; however, through their ordinary, everyday, imperceptible, demoralizing activities, they produce the very results which the bourgeoisie need and which tend to restore the bourgeoisie.[39]

The continued existence of private property in means of production would, it was believed, produce a class of capitalists in the countryside who were opposed to the regime. If, however, property was held in common, then this process of class differentiation of the peasantry could not occur.

The third reason is that independent peasants are incompatible with a model of socialist planning that has no place for the market. Peasants can disrupt central planning by, for instance, withholding produce from the market or resisting other means of transferring an economic surplus to the state. "Rich peasants" may, furthermore, use their economic power to undermine socialism through price manipulation or refusing to sell their produce to the state. A collectivized peasantry, alternatively, would be integrated into central planning and be unable to resist surplus transfers from agriculture to wherever the state planners saw fit to invest it.

Of all these justifications it is fair to say that the third argument took precedence over the others in the early Bolshevik debates and has done so in communist regimes since then. The state's thirst for funds for economic development, regardless of the interests of individual citizens, provided the broad context for Stalin's success inside the Bolshevik party and for the bloody collectivization campaigns he launched in the late 1920s and early 1930s, which subsequently became the model for communist agriculture. One should not overlook the way this policy option emerged ad hoc out of the debates, the maneuvering and scheming of the 1920s, and the fact that coherent alternative strategies were being proposed, for example, by Bukharin,[40] who had by then rejected the views of the *ABC*. But the logic of state interests definitely favored Stalin in that historical context. As Nove observed, "There is the logic of the one-party state, there is the logic of trying to change society from above, . . . in the name of building socialism in a peasant country. There is the logic of the tough, organized bureaucracy which the party *had* to become in order to carry out those changes."[41] The more gradual "market socialist" option of development proposed by Bukharin would have diluted that logic. Feelings of encirclement by hostile powers encouraged a faster rather than slower pace of change, thus further reinforcing the Stalinist logic.

Because the debate over collectivization is long and complex perhaps it best suits our purpose to outline Paul Baran's cogent defense of it as a strategy of development in his classic postwar study *The Political Economy of Growth*. This work is an inquiry into how different social structures in the Third World utilize economic surpluses generated in the economy. Underdevelopment in capitalist-dominated countries, Baran claims, is a result of the surplus being either taken out of the country by international capitalist firms or squandered in luxury spending by the local elite. As a result there is no indigenous economic development, and the peasants are ground into poverty by exploitation. After a revolution these "parasitic" groups are removed and the previous surplus from industry becomes available for the state to invest. In the countryside, however, the liberated surplus is now absorbed by increased peasant consumption. The "recapturing" and "mobilization of this surplus constitutes the indispensable condition for any development endeavour," writes Baran.[42] But it is no easy task because the peasants remain poor, and any attempt "to seize this increment of their real income for investment purposes encounter[s] embittered resistance." Using taxation as a means of cornering a surplus, he argues, is administratively unmanageable in a peasant economy; while the use of "unequal exchange" (a shift of relative prices in favor of nationalized industry) would discriminate against the poorer peasants in the countryside. However, until the problem of mobilizing an economic surplus is solved, he maintains, a socialist government will be unable to embark on a program of planned development.

For Baran, planning differentiates socialist from capitalist development. In the former, he argues, the apportioning of the surplus between
consumption and investment is determined by rational, conscious decisions, whereas in the latter it is determined by power in the market. Planning is impossible so long as a large and crucial part of the national
output—agriculture in predominantly peasant countries—remains outside the planning apparatus of the socialist government. Thus Baran writes
in defense of collectivization,

> The only way to include it in the general nexus of the national
> economy is by liquidating subsistence farming as the principal form of
> agricultural activity and transforming agriculture into a specializing,
> labor-dividing, and market-oriented industry in which the structure of
> output as well as its distribution between the consumption of those
> who work on it and the surplus accruing to society as a whole can be
> determined by the planning authority, as in the case of other industries.
> Under conditions of socialism this transformation cannot be accom-
> plished except by means of productive cooperation of the peasants,
> through collectivisation of peasant farming. . . . If there were no other
> powerful reasons for the desirability of collectivisation of agriculture,
> the vital need for the mobilization of the economic surplus generated in
> agriculture would in itself render collectivisation finally indispensable.
> By transferring the disposal of agricultural output from individual
> peasants to government-supervised collective farm managements, col-
> lectivisation destroys the basis for the peasants' resistance to the "si-
> phoning off" of the economic surplus.[43]

With the peasants in collectives the state could directly control the amount
of surplus able to be directed into industrial or agricultural investment,
social welfare or consumption.

The other "powerful reason" for collectivizing agriculture, according
to Baran, is that it allows the application of science and technology to
agricultural production, which, he argues, is impossible in conditions of
small-scale peasant farming. Baran is prepared to concede that some
"useful things" can be done to alleviate the conditions of peasant farmers in
underdeveloped countries, such as supplying them with better seeds, better
livestock, cheap credit, and agronomic advice. But, he claims, the "rate of
improvement that can be attained in this way is, however, so small that the
population growth is likely to prevent any appreciable increase in per
capita output. It surely cannot be expected to give rise to surpluses."[44]

Peasant farming therefore is unlikely to provide the basis for a socialist industrialization strategy. Only the use of modern techniques—mechanical draft-power, complex equipment, and chemicals—can expand productivity and supply surpluses for industrialization, and these techniques "are applicable only under conditions of large-scale farming." Baran neither provides much evidence for these claims nor allows for different types of agricultural activity, such as the needs of rice farmers compared with those of wheat growers.[45] But I shall return to these issues in chapter 7.

And yet the ability to inject into agriculture the products of modern science and technology presupposes that a certain level of industrialization has already been achieved in the country. "It would seem we are faced with a vicious circle," writes Baran. "There can be no modernization of agriculture without industrialization, and there can be no industrialization without an increase of agricultural output and surplus." How can the circle be broken? Capitalism could rely on the large-scale transfusion of an economic surplus from abroad for its economic takeoff, and hence imperialism plays a key role in Baran's theorization of the rise of capitalism in Europe. But Baran is forced to rule this out as a possible socialist solution. The alternative he finally adopts is Stalin's "revolution from above," that is, a massive use of force by the state to herd peasants into large-scale collective farms. In the USSR this coercion caused waves of migration from the countryside to the city to provide the workers for industrial projects. Baran's discussion of this process is apologetic. He admits that it "caused a painful drop in the standard of living" but says that "in this it was very much like most revolutionary breaks in history. . . . While the illness that it provoked was acute and painful, it was manifestly an illness of growth: it reached its crisis with enormous speed and yielded to convalescence within a few years,"[46] Consumption, he claims optimistically, had recovered by 1935 and, moreover, collectivization had served its purpose and provided the surplus needed for the crash industrialization program. Baran does not seriously consider the enormous disruption of rural life or the extent of the misery, which "cast a deep shadow over the life of the countryside, of the whole country, for many years after,"[47] or the depth of demoralization in the rural work force.

Baran admits that a surplus could be extracted from the peasantry through collectivization without changing the peasants' tools of production. Then, he writes, "the collective farms might become large-scale latifundia manned by a starved peasantry rather than prosperous agricultural enterprises providing high living standards to their members and large agricultural surpluses for a society as whole."[48] But in such a situation, he says, peasants could not be induced to join or stay in a producer cooperative voluntarily. What he underplays is that they could be made to stay by the use of force, and indeed the collective farms in the Soviet Union did come to resemble latifundia peopled by second-class citizens who were legally bound to stay in the countryside. But in Baran's perspective it seems that the use of force would be short-term. Once the factories were able to supply their goods to the farms and raise productivity, the peasants' enthusiasm for cooperatives would grow (Baran cannot be blamed for the fact that agriculture was starved of investment funds under Stalin and other communist governments, causing poor productivity and making the rural areas unattractive).[49] Certainly, there was significant capital input in the rural sector during the first Five Year Plan through a crash program to supply agriculture with tractors. However, this supplying of modern equipment to the cooperatives, theoretically one of the material prerequisites for their formation, was not a carefully thought out program of agricultural modernization, but rather a consequence of the mass slaughtering of draft animals by peasants resisting Stalin's collectivization drive.[50] Typically, Baran is also prepared to justify coercive collectivization in the interests of long-term "macro-economic rationality" because a radical break with backwardness "could not have been achieved with the consent of the irrational, illiterate, and ignorant peasantry."[51] The following chapters will show the serious macroeconomic consequences that flow from such a dismissive attitude toward the microeconomic rationality of the peasant farm.

As outlined above, Baran's model assumes that the economy has internal access to all the resources it needs. But there are few countries in the world with all the resource endowments necessary for their development, and therefore they must, where possible, enter the international economy. In underdeveloped countries, Baran writes, "the economic structure and the resource endowments are such that economic relations with the outside world represent not merely a highly desirable mitigation of otherwise not insuperable difficulties, but indeed a condition of their very survival." Participation in the international economy may give access to foreign loans, which, in turn, may reduce the need to mobilize all available internal surpluses in the early phases of development and thereby alleviate hardship. Also, the use of foreign loans, for instance, to import agricultural machinery or industrial equipment "may even save the beneficiary country the necessity of hasty collectivisation of the small peasant."[52] It is, he argues, in the interest of socialist countries to participate in the international division of labor, capitalist and socialist alike; he also quite rightly points out that for a long time communist countries were too poor to provide each other with sufficient aid, while the capitalist world erected political obstacles to trade with and aid to poor communist states. Hence they have often been thrown back on the more autarchic strategy, especially in their early days.

Even when these constraints have been mitigated (as they have in recent years especially) and small communist states like Laos are able to get loans and aid from both capitalist and communist countries, other political and strategic factors come into play to prompt the state to launch collectivization campaigns. These are discussed in detail in chapter 3 with regard to Laos. The role of ideology, in its full sense, cannot be disregarded. The fervent nationalism of postrevolutionary regimes makes them susceptible to visions of "self-sufficiency" and concentrates their gaze on internal sources of surplus. Since the rise of Stalin communist leaders have been taught to believe that collectivization is *the* communist strategy for agricultural development. Communist parties have been seen to believe and act upon each other's propaganda; for example, the Vietnamese launched their drive to form cooperatives in the late 1950s partly because they believed false Chinese claims of fantastic productivity gains in rice production achieved by their cooperatives and communes.[53] Such circles of illusion and delusion can, of course, be sustained in a situation in which there is no critical feedback and in which state planners have a strong interest in believing such claims. Delusion is another consequence and cost of the "logic of the one-party state."

The notion that independent peasants are incipient capitalists who will grow in strength and come to oppose the regime is the other key motivation for collectivization. The most convincing body of theory marshaled against this argument was that of A. V. Chayanov. Peasants were not spontaneous capitalists, he argued, because the categories of the capitalist economy were simply inappropriate to the peasant economy. The latter's basic unit was the household, whose dual role as a producer and consumer unit involved it in production mainly for use rather than exchange.

Chayanov's theory of the internal workings of the peasant farm is fundamental to his understanding of the nature of social differentiation in the countryside. Central to his theory is the idea of the labor/consumer balance, which postulates that the area worked and the intensity of work are determined by the active labor force in a family relative to its number of consumers (laborers plus dependents). In peasant agriculture there is a "tendency of land for use to approach family size and composition." This characteristic distinguishes the peasant farm from the capitalist farm: "Any capitalist agricultural unit, its size being determined by a constant and unchanging amount of capital and land area, may in the course of an indeterminate lengthy period (within infinite limits) remain at one and the same volume; but the peasant farm in the course of decades . . . constantly changes its volume, following the phases of family development, and its elements display a pulsating curve." Chayanov is careful to stress that at any particular point in time the family is not the sole determinant of farm size. Other factors may intervene, most obviously population pressure or the existence of outlets for labor through crafts or commercial livestock farming. Land size may be adjusted to family size through various mechanisms, such as communal repartitions, short leases of land, or the sale and purchase of land. He also notes that "where the land regime is not very flexible the relationship between land and family is regulated by a change in the amount of labor hired in or hired out."[54]

The structure and activity of the peasant farm pivot on the production of use-values, as distinct from the generalized production of exchange-values typical of capitalism. This difference determines farm use of land, labor, and investment. Because the peasant farm does not need to turn a profit and at a minimum has only to feed its laborers and dependents, it can run at a "loss," and in this respect it has a competitive edge over capitalist farms. "Frequently, the family farm's internal basic equilibrium makes acceptable very low payments per labor unit, and these enable it to exist in conditions that would doom a capitalist farm to undoubted ruin." In a situation of commodity competition in the market the "ultimate" form of commodity production, capitalism, can be squeezed out by peasant farms in the same line. For similar reasons, peasants also better capitalists in competition for land in short supply and when rents and prices are high. Peasants will pay so-called hunger rents, which are significantly higher than capitalist rent. And so "labor farms . . . are victorious not only in establishing the market price but also in the struggle for land; a clearly marked transfer of land from capitalist to labor farming takes place."[55] What is so striking about Chayanov's formulation is that it proposes a result diametrically opposite to that of classical Marxism.

The last chapter of *Peasant Farm Organization* offers a unique model of social differentiation among the peasantry and a perceptive prediction of the development of capitalism in agriculture. Referring to Russia, Chayanov argues that while some social class differentiation was observable in the countryside, the underlying reason for the heterogeneity of the peasant farms was demographic: "in the depths of the peasantry takes place a series of very complex and tangled demographic processes." The various strands of this tangled process entailed some families dying out, others migrating, and still others dividing into several independent farms. Very small farms were the ones that completely broke down, and the occupants would migrate in search of better territory or to the towns. Among the larger and older farms at the other end of the scale "more than half of them reached full maturity and broke down into a number of new farms." The general pattern, he maintains, is the rising and falling sizes of particular farms: "Before us are two powerful currents. One in which the young, undivided farms with small sown area mainly participate, is rising, expanding the volume of its farms under pressure of family growth. The other is declining, largely due to the dividing of old, complex families." In this model the peasantry is seen to experience considerable social mobility, but if we choose to look at the balance of the respective currents "we get a picture of complete static calm."[56]

Chayanov was writing about European agriculture, which because of its extensive nature (wheat, for example), at least according to some writers, is favorable to economies of scale and therefore to capitalist development and class polarization. Rice agriculture, by contrast, which is common in most of Asia, responds to labor intensity and is "not as susceptible as Western farming systems to capital-intensive economies of scale."[57] Consequently one can claim that Chayanov's theory applies most forcefully to the farming systems of Asia. Francesca Bray claims, "One of the advantages of a 'skill-oriented' agricultural system such as wet-rice cultivation, which provides little scope for economies of scale and depends far less upon capital investment, should be that technological advance does not promote inequalities."[58] Generally she argues that the rice-producing peasant household remains resilient in the face of changes in the broader economy.

In communist societies resilience is likely to be a result not only of policies that reinforce the natural economy, but also, as Galeski maintains, of communist control of state power, which in itself should be capable of arresting any tendencies toward capitalist polarization:

> Abolition of capitalist property entails the socialization of the basic elements in the national economy. As a result the socialist state becomes

able to effectively control small scale production and determine the direction of its development. The socialized economy absorbs both the labor power released from the family farms and the surplus products they produce. The family farm becomes subordinate to the whole socialist economy and becomes a factor in its overall development. As Polish experience demonstrates, tendencies in the direction of capitalist stratification can thus be effectively mastered.[59]

There is little reason to believe that this situation would be any different for Laos.[60]

The relevance of Chayanov's demographic model of peasant differentiation or mobility to today's peasantry has been questioned by one of Chayanov's main defenders, Teodor Shanin, who writes, "Demographic determinants act relatively slowly compared with the current trends of social transformations. The growing complexity, heterogeneity, and changeability of contemporary agriculture and of the peasant ways to make ends meet would make this demographically related model very limited as against the factors which do not enter it: state policies and markets for goods and labor (now worldwide), new agricultural techniques, the extra-village cartelization of supply, demand, and credit, or the social construction of new needs."[61] Shanin does not question the capacity of peasants to survive or indeed, to grow in the face of capitalist or socialist development, but he suggests that the main determinants of peasant mobility and economic effort are no longer demographic. The general accuracy of this observation cannot be discussed here; however, Shanin does acknowledge that the less developed a society is the more salient is the demographic model. In an economy and society like those of Laos, in which the peasant natural economy continues to predominate, Chayanov's observations retain all their force. In fact, his "picture of complete static calm" could have been written with the social landscape of the Lao village in mind.

2

The Sociology of Isolation

"Life in Asia's Shangri-la" was the *Bangkok Post*'s headline for a feature story on Laos in mid-1988.[1] The image is conjured up many times by journalistic and travel commentary. Typically the genre is capable of breathtaking simplifications about Lao culture and society as a "land of smiling, pious peasants" who act in a world governed by "timeless traditions." Such romanticism ignores the political turbulence of premodern Laos, the impact of French colonialism, and the consequences of civil war and revolution in the recent period. Yet, compared with that of many other peasant societies, the basic structure of Lao society has remained remarkably intact during its journey into the modern world.

The small principalities or petty states that ruled in Laos prior to French colonial control over Indochina were centered on Luang Prabang, Xieng Khouang, Vientiane, and Champassak. These were the remnants of a more glorious past in which the kingdom of Lane Xang (Million Elephants) ruled over large parts of modern Thailand as well as Laos during the sixteenth century and in attenuated form in the seventeenth century. By the early eighteenth century, however, it had fractured into three small kingdoms based in Luang Prabang, Vientiane, and Champassak; by the end of the century the kingdoms had become vassals of the newly established Siamese court in Bangkok. The rise of Siam (Thailand) to preeminence in the region can be dated from the sixteenth century, when, as Wyatt points out, coastal kingdoms, in contrast to landlocked kingdoms like Lane

Xang, began to benefit greatly from international commerce. These contacts hastened the centralization of the coastal kingdoms and the creation of social and cultural cohesion.[2] The powerful Thai kingdom of Ayudhya (1569–1767) was succeeded in 1767 by the new and formidable (and still reigning) Chakkri dynasty in Bangkok, which proceeded to establish control over the Lao principalities. A failed Lao uprising against Bangkok over 1827–29 commanded by the lord of Vientiane, Chao Anou, led to the decimation of the aristocracy in that principality and to a lesser extent in Champassak and to the mass deportation of their subjects. Throughout the revolt Luang Prabang remained a loyal vassal of Siam. Consequently when the French took the reins of power in Laos in 1893 they were more or less forced into a position of direct rule in areas south of Vientiane, while in the north they were able to practice a form of indirect rule through the surviving aristocracy. Thus, in the north social relations similar to those in the neighboring principality of Chiang Mai (or even in some respects to those in the ever-strengthening Chakkri dynasty in Bangkok) persisted between elite and peasants.

The crucial difference between Laos and Thailand, of course, was the important transformation of precapitalist social and legal relations between lord and peasant that had been carried out by King Chulalongkorn (1868–1910) and the massive commercialization of agriculture centered on the Thai Central Plain that had commenced in the late nineteenth century. In Feeny's apt phrase, this period saw a transition "from property rights in man to property rights in land" and the accumulation of large areas of paddy land in the hands of aristocrats and state-based officials.[3] No such transformation occurred in Laos.

The reasons for the difference were, broadly, that there was no central state in Laos in a position to carry out such change. Nor had the petty states in Laos been subject to the same strains as the central dynasty in Bangkok. The transformation in Thailand occurred under the twin pressures of an encroaching European imperialism and the usual centrifugal tendencies in such states. International pressures and opportunities forced the Thai state to solve its internal fissiparousness by embarking on a process of political centralization and modernization. The surviving small Lao principalities, by contrast, were neither threatened by internal secession nor capable of resisting outside pressure. Indeed, the French were "invited" by King Oun Kham of Luang Prabang to take over Laos to protect it from Thailand, whose process of administrative consolidation threatened to swallow most of the Lao principalities that are now part of the modern Lao state in much

28

the same way as it had the Chiang Mai–based kingdom of Lanna. French colonialism, which had been seeking every pretext to take over Laos, was only too willing to oblige the monarch of Luang Prabang.

Despite early "el dorado" fantasies the French found in Laos nothing like the Mekong Delta in southern Vietnam that could be turned into a commercial basin or like the Irriwaddy delta the British developed in Burma or the equivalent of a Central Thai Plain. Except for Xieng Khouang, with its plateau known as the Plain of Jars, the Lao principalities were situated on relatively small alluvial plains sandwiched between the Mekong River and the mountain ranges that cover two-thirds of the country. There were few opportunities for Lao aristocrats to transform themselves into commercially oriented landlords wishing to swallow large tracts of land, or indeed for a commercially oriented peasantry to form. In fact, even if a potentially exploitable area had existed its commercial development would have been inhibited by problems of transportation. The elaborate canal system developed in the central plains of Thailand, for example, was vital to its commercial development. By contrast, the railway from Bangkok to the key transit point to Vientiane, Nong Khai, was completed in 1955. Only then could a rice export boom, if it was to happen, have occurred.

The French, like Chulalongkorn in Thailand, abolished slavery and other forms of bondage in Laos (at least formally); they imposed headtaxes and redirected some of the traditional corvée to service the colonial rather than the dynastic state. This strengthening of central administrative control over society was perhaps the most important change the French brought to the Lao social structure. Even so, it was never sufficiently strong to extract a surplus capable of supporting that administration, and the French colonial apparatus in Laos had to be cross-subsidized from its other Indochinese possessions until the end of the colonial era in the early 1950s.[4]

Aristocrats in Luang Prabang continued to live off their traditional domain in the district of Luang Prabang. Collectively the "various members of the royal family own[ed] no more than a few hundred hectares of irrigated rice land."[5] A similar situation applied to the surviving aristocrats elsewhere around Champassak, whereas aristocratic landholdings had all but disappeared around Vientiane. The surpluses received by these aristocrats were consumed unproductively in maintaining the pomp and ceremony and life-style of a traditional aristocracy, which in many ways it remained. It is worth emphasizing, however, that commensurate with the small surplus generated, differences in standards of living between the elite

29

and commoners were not great, as in Bangkok, although all the trappings of rank and social status were strictly enforced. The relative size of their capital cities provides a good index of surpluses generated and illustrates the contrast that existed between Laos and Thailand by the nineteenth century. During the reign of King Monghut (1851–68) the population of the city of Bangkok was said to have reached 400,000 and was reported to be 600,000 in 1900,[6] whereas Luang Prabang at the end of the nineteenth century had between 5,000 and 15,000.[7] Vientiane became the French colonial capital. Repopulated with large infusions of Vietnamese merchants and administrators, it became the largest city in Laos. Even so, a comparison with Bangkok in the mid-1940s further underscores the contrast: the Thai capital's population stood at over 1 million, while Vientiane's was around 23,000. The important point is that surpluses in Laos were not great and were neither generated by commercial development nor plowed back for commercial expansion. Under French colonial protection the petty principalities in Laos were slightly transformed, but essentially were preserved intact. There was no real growth of a landed gentry or of a class of commercially oriented landlords.

The Lao State

Before the era of French colonialism Lao peasants were part of what Wolf calls a "tributary mode of production." That is a form of social organization in which surpluses are extracted from the subordinate population by political rather than economic mechanisms. In conceptualizing this mode of production, he writes, it is "possible to envisage two polar situations: one in which power is concentrated strongly in the hands of a ruling elite standing at the apex of the power system; and another in which power is held largely by local overlords and the rule at the apex is fragile and weak. These two situations define a continuum of power distributions."[8] Historically Lao society has traveled back and forth along this continuum.

It has been argued that the constituent unit of Tai-type societies is the *muang*.[9] Wyatt writes, "*Muang* is a term that defied translation, for it denotes as much personal as spatial relationships. . . . It can mean both the town located at the hub of a network of interrelated villages and also the totality of town and villages which was ruled by a single *chao*, "lord". . . . Tai villages banded together for mutual defense under the leadership of the most powerful village or family, whose resources might enable it to arm and supply troops. In return for such protection, participating villages rendered labor service to their chao, or paid him quantities of local produce or handicrafts."[10] (One might add that in modern usage *muang* can refer to a city or a state, for example, muang Vientiane or muang Lao). These muang were both the building blocks of the occasional more powerful states that arose in Laos and the units into which centralized states fragmented. While these muang were the intermittent vassals of a centralized power, they also established vassals among the ethnically and linguistically distinct groups in the mountains surrounding the alluvial valleys in which the muang were located. At the edge of the tributary system one sometimes had chiefdoms emerging from a "kin-ordered mode of production."[11] The majority of the Lao population were peasants, but peasant society merged into ethnically diverse, kin-ordered "tribal" systems.

Besides peasant labor the other major source of surplus in tributary systems is state control of trade. In precolonial Laos it was slave trading and control of land routes to southern China that provided vital revenue. But the Lao principalities did not oversee thriving commercial routes. When a mission of French explorers reached Luang Prabang in the late 1860s they found English cloth that had come via Burma, Chinese silks, and lacquer boxes and parasols from Chiang Mai. Louis de Carné, one of the members of the French mission, warned against being deceived by "these appearances of commercial life. . . . We found the only money current at Luang-Praban[g] was in the shape of little white shells, strung together. . . . Twenty-five of these strings are worth a [silver] tikal. . . . A tax-gatherer passes through at the close of the market, and levies so many shells from each booth as the king's right; for in Laos there is no difference between the king, the state, the town, and public and private property."[12] Market transactions were peripheral to the peasant economy.

Due to the waxing and waning of the petty states in Laos and poor communications peasants were differentially integrated into political units and therefore subject to various ruling class impositions. Peasants around Luang Prabang have been part of a state system longer than any other peasants in Laos, whereas around Vientiane, for example, peasants drifted into a situation of subsistence autonomy after the sacking of Vientiane by the Siamese (1828) and had virtually reverted to some form of kin-ordered mode of production, except that the Buddhist *vat* at the center of the villages provided a degree of supralocal identification. The various ethnic minorities, on the other hand, were only intermittently integrated into the tributary system.

Only with the coming of the French were Lao peasants and the highland minorities drawn into a relatively stable national political structure. The French effectively formalized the muang structure: in the north they retained the kingdom of Luang Prabang and ruled through its established muang; in the south they directly ruled over colonially created provinces, *khoueng,* which were headed by *chao khoueng;* districts, muang, headed by *chao muang;* and cantons, *tasseng,* headed by *nai tasseng;* below these were the villages, *ban,* headed by a *nai ban* or *pho ban.* Each of these levels, except the village, could correspond to a muang in the old structure, but the more "rational" colonial state was based on clear spatial rather than personal principles. Only in 1946 was the lord of Luang Prabang elevated to the position of king of Laos, and the provincial structure that had operated in the south generalized to the whole country, now divided into twelve provinces. The upper levels of the structure were generally presided over by appointed chao khoueng and chao muang with various claims to an aristocratic pedigree, while the nai tasseng and nai ban were elected positions, naturally with the approval of superior levels.

Relations between the state and the ethnic minorities were also increasingly formalized. For example, the Hmong of Xieng Khouang had previously been vassals of the Tai Phuan in the region, and chiefs, or *kaitong,* had been charged with delivering small quantities of tribute to the chao muang. Following a Hmong uprising in 1896 the French committed themselves to increasing ethnic minority representation in the new state structure, and Hmong nai tasseng were progressively appointed in Xieng Khouang and later in Muang Ngoi, a district of Luang Prabang.[13] Not until the 1930s were Hmong elevated above the tasseng, though the way this was done produced serious political divisions among the Hmong clans on which the communist movement later capitalized. Indicative of relations between the traditional Lao state and most of the ethnic minorities was the fact that many of the latter were called *kha,* or slave. The Mon Khmer–speaking Lamet studied by Izikowitz, for example, were historically under the sway of the Tai Lu and were called *kha.* The French administration formalized Lu power over the Lamet by placing the literate Lu in charge of the local administration. "This had partially unfortunate consequences for the Lamet," writes Izikowitz. "For the slightest misdemeanor they were forced to either pay fines to the Lu in money or goods, or to perform certain kinds of work." In other words, besides collecting taxes for the French the Lu treated the Lamet as if they were part of a traditional tributary state. "Meanwhile the French discovered this, and a Laotic canton leader with French education was installed."[14] Many minorities, however, lived beyond the influence of the traditional state and of the colonial state and have remained independent of modern Lao states, yet there has been a gradual tendency to draw them into the orbit of state influence.

The colonial state raised taxes that were redeemed in either cash or in kind, and it could levy corvée labor. These demands were relatively light and unevenly enforced. Accidents of geography, such as French wishes to push a road through a particular area, could mean heavy burdens for the people there. But, as the French discovered, whole villages would sometimes flee rather than labor on these colonial projects, in which case it was easier to bring in indentured Vietnamese laborers. The groups most affected by French colonial taxation were highlanders like the Hmong, who grew opium. French colonialism established opium monopolies in Indochina as a way of financing its administration, and in 1938 opium accounted for 15 percent of colonial tax revenues.[15] French demands on the Hmong of Xieng Khouang province to increase their production of opium sparked the revolt in 1896 referred to earlier, after which the French decided to work through Hmong intermediaries. Clans led by clan elders with chiefly status were the constituent units of Hmong society, but the ability of heads of particular clans to establish external alliances with the French led to a transformation of chieftainships among the Hmong. From one "in which the chief and his followers are still embedded in kinship arrangements and bound by them, [to one] in which the form and idiom of kinship may be maintained even as dominant group transforms divisions of rank into divisions of class—in fact, using kinship mechanisms to strengthen its own position. In this second kind of chiefdom, the chiefly lineage is in fact an incipient class of surplus takers in the tributary mode."[16] The French supported one particular Hmong clan against others in Xieng Khouang, and when the colonial treasury placed even greater demands on the opium growers owing to the fiscal crisis accompanying the outbreak of World War II, the head of this clan, Touby Ly Fong, was charged with gathering the extra revenue. He "raised the annual head tax from three silver piasters to an exorbitant eight piasters, but gave the tribesmen the alternative of paying three kilograms of raw opium instead. Most Meo [Hmong] were too poor to save eight silver piasters a year and took the alternative of paying in opium. Since an average Meo farmer probably harvested less than one kilogram of raw opium a year before Touby's election [as chao muang in 1939], the tax increases precipitated an opium boom. . . . These measures were applied all across northern Laos, changing the hilltribe economy from subsistence agriculture, to cash crop opium farming."[17] This final statement is wrong: opium was not a cash crop that drew the Hmong into commodity circuits, but rather a straightforward state-enforced tax that among other things bolstered the power of Touby Ly Fong and his clan in Xieng Khouang. This remained basically true after the French disbanded their opium monopolies in 1949 and the trade was taken over first by French intelligence and later the American CIA.[18]

French colonialism brought little fundamental change either to Lao peasant society or to the social structure overall. Roads had been built, thereby easing communications throughout the country (2,258 km of main roads and 2,569 km of secondary roads by 1938), but these were used mainly for purposes of administration and the ferrying of goods between commercial centers, not for carrying commercial relations into the countryside. A nationwide currency had been introduced, but it was rarely used by the local inhabitants except to integrate it into preexisting circuits of wealth exchange. French silver piasters, minted in the 1930s, still adorn the headdresses of women and children among the Hmong and Yao populations in the north of Laos.

Independence

The immediate result of Lao independence (1953) for the peasants was the abolition of the intermittently enforced colonial head tax and thus a retreat of the state. They were taxed only on certain market transactions. The new state did not turn to the peasantry for sources of finance, and the elite did not turn to land as a source of wealth and productivity; rather, because of Laos's strategic location in Southeast Asia, a fabulous new source of sustenance became available in the form of U.S. aid. In the first four years of independence the Lao government received $166 million of aid from the United States, and a further $125 million was programed to establish Lao armed forces. In the mid-1960s the RLG raised "at most about 40 per cent of its national budget through taxes and duties," primarily on trading licenses and international trade.[19] Little attempt was made to tax the peasants.

The traditional aristocracy and their relatives were well placed to reap the benefits of this U.S. aid bonanza, and some of them grew very rich by channeling aid to suit their own purposes.[20] Some diversified into businesses such as banks, airlines, movie theaters, hotels, construction, and transport firms. Yet little of the influx of U.S. dollars cornered by them was invested in productive activities, and much was dissipated in luxury spending. As Jean-Pierre Barbier observed in his study of the effects of foreign aid on Laos, "The local bourgeoisie . . . engaged itself in the commercial sector, notably imports directly linked to aid dollars, while neglecting the secondary sector. Thus in Vientiane, a city far from being 'industrialized', commercial activities employ two times more personnel than productive activities."[21] American aid did not create a viable indigenous capitalist class, but it was a wonderful new source of "tribute" for the traditional elite.

The aid did not create a sturdy, unified state either. USAID's gradual usurpation of governmental responsibilities and division of the country into military regions during the civil war created a peculiar dispersal of state power, so clearly described by Fred Branfman in 1970: "The central government has little influence within these military regions, where the word of the military commander, and of the traditional families supporting him, is law. Indeed the open hostility of all the military commanders to 'interference' by the central or local civilian government is a major political fact of life in Laos. And the rivalries between military commanders and the families allied with them prevent functional collaboration among regions. . . . The colonels who control each district capital regard these posts as opportunities for personal enrichment and jealously guard their domains, which they rule with an iron fist."[22] This recreation of the structure of the dynastic state in outward form was, however, a type of class power that did not rest on the extortion of rents or taxes from a subject peasantry but on the cliental nature of the state. In fact, economically the dominant class groupings were increasingly disarticulated from the majority of the Lao population. They were not a modernizing elite and were neither willing nor able to transform social relations across the breadth of Lao society.

The Lao Peasant World

Lao peasants live in compact villages of around two hundred persons. Sometimes the villages are composed of several hamlets, and often they lie alongside streams or rivers. The majority live in houses constructed of wood, bamboo, and thatched roofs and raised on stilts. Each household usually keeps some domestic animals—pigs, chickens and ducks, or dogs—and cultivates a small garden. Some also tend small orchards. The most important resource in the village is paddy land, which grows the annual staple crop of glutinous rice. Rarely is this land irrigated, the farmers relying on the annual monsoon rains. Rights to paddy land in these communities are governed by the following customary rules:

> The person who clears the land has proprietal rights over it.
> Rights are transmitted by sale, freely, or by way of inheritance.
> It is not an absolute right: prolonged lack of use, gauged according to the type of land use, frees it from all rights. Only continued cultivation and work maintains proprietal rights.
> The strength of one's kinship bonds in the village, however, modifies the temporary character of these rights.[23]

Arbitration of these rights is the province of the village headman. Under the dynastic state all land was deemed to be the property of the monarch, and this practice was upheld by the French, although in practice the state rarely interfered in the administration of village land. Attempts to construct a modern state following independence saw ordinances for the registration of individual land titles introduced during 1958 and 1959, and these titles were held at district offices. Kaufman's study of villages on the Vientiane Plain in the 1950s reported that "disputes over land rights and the division of land are quite prevalent," but it appears that few peasants turned to the state for assistance in these disputes.[24] Another study noted that very few peasants took advantage of having their land legally registered.[25]

The disputes noted by Kaufman were beginning to appear in the more densely settled parts of Laos, but in general the relative underpopulation of the country was, according to Taillard, the key to explaining Lao land-ownership patterns:

> Lao customary rights has a very pragmatic character which is a result of both underpopulation, and therefore weak land pressure, and the organization of the village community which regulates it. It is perfectly adapted through its flexibility to the real variations which characterize the Lao household, permitting adjustments to the number of people who have to be fed (and therefore the available workforce) to the amount of land required. The possibility of clearing new ricefields, or inheriting them, and of renting land in or out, ensures that for all of his life each farmer will have enough land to cover the needs of his household.[26]

His analysis of the Lao peasantry accords well with the analytical framework of Chayanov. In fact all the studies available on the Lao peasantry prior to 1975 show little social differentiation, as one would expect from this model, except as a result of population pressure close to Vientiane.[27] In villages not subject to population pressure land "can hardly be considered so much a criterion of wealth since it is very evenly distributed between households. The village has, therefore, a social structure which is little differentiated because one only has to clear land in order to meet a growth in household needs."[28] This assessment applies to most Lao villages. But in an area close to Vientiane Taillard concluded, "In this very homogenous society social differentiation has begun, determined by demographic and economic growth. Three social groups have begun to distinguish themselves: the poorest households, those who have neither land nor regular incomes from sources outside of agriculture; the wealthiest group, those households which as well as working the land have outside incomes, often from salaried workers; and the third, and most numerous, intermediary group which constitutes the rest of the traditional undifferentiated society."[29] He also notes that these villages have been more closely integrated into the national economy. Yet the changes do not demonstrate a growth of capitalist social relations in the countryside or of peasant indebtedness to oppressive landlords.

Land was not an important source of wealth for the postindependence Lao elite, and consequently there was little absentee landlordism in the rural areas. As we have seen, aristocratic ownership of land had been strongest in Luang Prabang and for reasons of recent history weaker in the provinces of Vientiane and Champassak. Rough estimates offered for land ownership in Vientiane province before 1975 claimed that between 70 and 80 percent of peasants worked their own land, with their holdings varying from one to five hectares. A Lao agriculturalist reported that the largest holding he could recall was thirty hectares, and he thought that perhaps one hundred people had holdings of this size. These figures may be compared with the three largest landholdings in the Thai Central Plain in the early 1960s, which altogether totaled 19,200 hectares, with another eighty-two people owning between 160 and 320 hectares each.[30] Holdings of this size were unheard of in Laos.

The majority of the Lao peasantry continued to live and work in a natural economy until the mid-1960s. The main reason for the existence of a natural economy then, as now, was the poor internal economic integration of Laos due to the lack of transportation routes and lack of year-round access along those that existed. The rugged terrain added further obstacles. Consequently, there was no truly national economy in Laos, only regional economies with, for example, significant differences in prices for rice. The

Lao peasants produced little economic surplus and engaged in little commercial activity. As a result, Joel Halpern noted in the early 1960s, "This makes it necessary for Vientiane, and even a smaller town of less than 10,000 population, such as Luang Prabang, to rely on imports from Thailand. The case of Vientiane might be easily explained since Thai towns with good transport facilities are just across the river, but in Luang Prabang the rice must be brought in by barge over a distance of several hundred miles. The shortage is particularly acute in extreme northern areas where even local government employees have difficulty buying enough to eat."[31] The observation has a distinct contemporary ring to it.

The persistence of a peasant natural economy perplexed American aid donors, as revealed during House Committee on Government Operations hearings in Washington in 1959. Large imports of Western goods were required already in the late 1950s to soak up American dollars and stop chaotic inflation of the Lao national currency, the *kip*. Who was going to buy these Western imports? A Mr. Howell stated his dilemma to the committee:

> MR. HOWELL: The people outside of the small urban areas were practically at a subsistence level and didn't have a latent desire to buy the goods that were coming in from the West.
> MR. HARDY: Do you mean they were the kind of goods that the rank and file of people couldn't use?
> MR. HOWELL: I think, Mr. Chairman, it is a little bit different. In many countries you will find that the people have a perfectly sound idea of what they would like to have. They just haven't got the wherewithal to get it. We found in many areas of Laos they just didn't know the things existed. There was no demand of any kind. They were completely content.

But, he concluded confidently, "Of course, they learn very quickly to want other things."[32]

Supply stimulated demand for previously unheard of items, such as medicines, radios, watches, lamps, clothing, and transport, and peasants close to centers like Vientiane began to produce fruit, vegetables, meat, tobacco, and so on over and above their subsistence needs to trade in the market. In the dry season an increasing number of people migrated to urban centers to carry out some petty trading or wage labor in order to earn cash and buy commodities. Yesterday's luxuries became today's necessities. By Thai standards, however, even this level of activity was sluggish.

For several reasons land pressure began to build up on the Vientiane plain in the mid 1960s. Population growth in the rural areas had been accommodated through the clearing of new land and by the formation of new villages. Much of the Lao peasantry lived on an agricultural frontier, and Laos functioned as a frontier area for landless migrants from the Thai northeast, Issan. Migrant villages began springing up on the Vientiane plain, and because these migrants did not have the support of relatives nor enough wealth they were rarely in a position to immediately clear and prepare new paddy land. Consequently a new phenomenon began to arise in some areas: the use of agricultural wage labor. As a result there was some weakening of traditional agricultural cooperation. Thai from Issan also swelled the ranks of wage laborers, hawkers, and prostitutes in Vientiane itself.

On the other hand, the existence of paid work in and around Vientiane reduced the pressure on the peasant economy to establish new paddy fields for its growing population. In fact outside paid work made smaller plots for some a more viable option than in the past. Sons could migrate or commute to Vientiane to become taxi drivers, for example, and therefore supply some of the cash needs of families in the villages. This arrangement began to sour after 1973 as foreign support for the urban boom began to be withdrawn and the price of imported items began to escalate, whereupon the migrants to the towns were transformed from benefactors into dependents.

The other major pressure brought to bear on the alluvial plains surrounding the lowland provincial towns and capitals was the civil war, which caused massive refugee movements. Thirty-five thousand people relocated into Vientiane province alone in 1971. The ranks of potential wage laborers swelled with this influx; some of the refugees used the support given by foreign aid donors as a basis for establishing new villages and paddy lands, in the process encroaching on land areas and water rights traditionally claimed by established villages. Further, population pressure on the frontier saw the appearance of landless Lao peasants—as distinct from refugees and Issan migrants—in the districts surrounding Vientiane.

Symptomatic of the closing of the frontier close to Vientiane was the disappearance of *hai,* or dry rice fields. It is calculated that even today approximately one million Lao farmers practice some form of slash-and-burn cultivation. This number includes lowland Lao as well as hilltribe shifting cultivators. Around Sayaboury township, to take a typical example from an outlying area, most lowland Lao farmers still combine paddy with some upland rice cultivation. In the districts close to Vientiane this has disappeared, and older farmers reflect nostalgically on areas of forest that in the early 1960s were inhabited by deer and monkeys and now contain village houses and paddies. Slash-and-burn activities, of course, are options for young, potentially landless people starting out in life and necessarily precede the establishment of paddy fields. This option gradually disappeared around Vientiane, and young, landless couples were faced with the options either of migrating relatively long distances to form new homesteads and villages (an increasingly unattractive option in the unstable civil war period) or staying close to home and becoming rural wage laborers, petty traders, or urban wage workers, or often all three.

The important point is that the landlessness that existed was primarily a result of population pressure due to refugee movements and migration from Issan. The closing of the frontier in densely settled areas indeed produced some Lao landless peasants, but landlessness was not a result of peasants being forced off the land by unscrupulous landlords or capitalists. Of course in some cases this happened. Lao military men sometimes used their power, direct and economic, to force peasants off their land and ensconce their own relatives on it—but such instances were exceptions to the general trend.

Inequalities did exist in Lao peasant society, but they were largely a product of natural fluctuations of fortune. Many of those who appeared landless to the cursory observations of an outsider were really young families at the beginning of a domestic cycle that would see them inherit some land in the near future. At the other end, peasants with, for example, five hectares were generally old and on the point of dividing up the family inheritance among those who were eligible. Any consideration of indices of inequality should also take account of the fact that many Lao peasants, because they are on a frontier, practice both upland and lowland cultivation, and hence crude statistics of land area owned or worked, if taken at face value, present an inaccurate picture of relative resource allocation among peasants. The renting of land also occurs among peasants within villages and from different villages. But it is more often related to the needs of domestic groups at various points in the domestic cycle than to landlessness in any absolute sense. Renting and tenancy do not necessarily demonstrate the existence of a permanent class of tenants or a permanent class of landlords or so-called rich peasants. Some landlordism existed in the rural areas of Laos before 1975, but capitalism did not.

The elite that developed in Laos in the twenty years after independence from France was largely a by-product of American intervention in Southeast Asia during the war in Vietnam. Vientiane, like other urban areas in the region, had become for them a relatively pleasant "fools' paradise," disarticulated from the rural areas and sustained by U.S. dollars. Thus when foreign support stopped the elite quickly disintegrated, leaving the communists in control of a relatively intact peasant society.

The Reasons for the Revolution

Communists came to power in Laos in late 1975 largely as a consequence of the wider conflagration in Indochina arising out of the Vietnam War. There was no mass-based peasant discontent directed at onerous landlords on which the revolutionary movement could capitalize. Promise of land reform was not a major plank in the LPRP's program, making its rise to power something of an oddity among Third World communist revolutions. Kaysone Phomvihane spelled out the party's analysis in his one major work, *La révolution lao*: "Elsewhere, to liberate the peasantry in colonial or feudal countries one must (following a universal law) introduce agrarian reform to abolish the feudal regime of land ownership and put into effect the slogan 'land to the tillers'. In our country, however, scattered agriculture took on a natural and autarkic character which was still very backward, and the mode of production was still *pre-feudal*."[33] He goes on to say that although the peasants suffered from some "feudal" exploitation the most important cause of their misery was their use of backward techniques of production. That is, technology, not maldistribution of land, was their major problem. The LPRP's appeals to the Lao peasantry therefore were largely nationalist.

In some respects it was easier for the communist movement to find recruits among disaffected hilltribe groups, who, as we have seen, were most affected by French colonialism. Most important, key leaders among them bore grudges against the French: in the north the Hmong leader, Faydang Lo Bliayao, had been passed over for promotion within the French administration in Xieng Khouang in favor of Touby Ly Fong; the Loven leader, Sithon Khommadan from the southern Boloven Plateau, whose father had been killed in 1937 after resisting the French for thirty years, had been exiled to the northern province of Phong Saly. Both of these men were present at the founding of the Neo Lao Issara (Free Lao Front) in 1950, the precursor of the Lao communist party formed in secret in 1955, and the

NLHS, established in 1957. The movement was commonly known as the Pathet Lao (Lao Nation) to distinguish it from the RLG.

The key leaders of the communist movement were drawn from the same small elite as their opponents in the RLG. Aristocrats like Prince Souphannouvong, later president of the LPDR, joined the movement, as did the offspring of urban-based merchants such as Kaysone Phomvihane. These people were among the few in Laos who had received higher education from the French and therefore were exposed to ideas of modern nationalism. The precise reasons some of the nationalist elite that emerged in Laos in the aftermath of World War II decided to become communists is not our concern here. Some were inevitably strongly influenced by the radical nationalist Viet Minh in neighboring Vietnam, which was led by communists.[34] The Viet Minh and the Pathet Lao were forced to operate from redoubts in the Annamite chain of mountains running along the border between the two countries, and this circumstance made it imperative for both movements to formulate a policy on ethnic minorities that recognized them as part of the Vietnamese or Lao nation. The Pathet Lao's formulation of a credible ideology of mass nationalism distinguished it from the elite nationalism espoused by the RLG and was ultimately a key component of the communists' success.[35]

Education expanded beyond the traditional elite in Laos after 1945 and gave rise to a weak form of bourgeois nationalism. Thus the late 1950s saw the formation of an organization of "young turks" calling itself the Committee for the Defense of National Interest, which was strongly pro-Western in orientation. But, as Halpern notes, it shared many of the shortcomings of the traditional elite; in particular, its declarations never "even indicate that there are peoples other than ethnic Lao in the country of Laos."[36] The various Vientiane regimes never overcame these shortcomings.

Massive corruption in the RLG and army served to undermine its legitimacy in the cities and among many lowland Lao, while massive American bombing of the mountain regions did not endear the RLG to the minorities there. The Pathet Lao grew in strength over the 1960s but was never in a position to topple the RLG. Only the defeat of the U.S. war effort in Vietnam, which caused it to withdraw its support from the RLG, finally led to the latter's collapse and to the victory of the LPRP in December 1975.

It was not internal social change that led Laos to revolution, but America's commitment to rolling back communism in neighboring Vietnam, which in turn made it imperative for the North Vietnamese to support the

Pathet Lao and thence led to U.S. intervention in Lao political affairs throughout the 1950s and 1960s to ensure that only solidly pro-U.S. governments ruled in Vientiane. Thus, because of the foreign policy priorities of the world's strongest state the Lao lost control of their destiny. Large bankrolls of U.S. dollars disappeared into the pockets of the Lao elite and in the meantime kept them off the backs of the lowland Lao peasants. After 1975, however, neither the old elite nor the lowland Lao peasants could go on living in the old way. Change was inevitable.

3

The Campaign and After

Following the communist takeover in late 1975 there was no headlong rush into social transformation of the countryside.[1] Peasants were simply encouraged to adopt "a collective way of life" and to form "solidarity and labor exchange units" through which they were expected to come to appreciate the advantages and necessity of forming cooperatives.[2] A recurring theme from the very beginning was that large-scale collective production would free the peasants from the whims and uncertainties of nature. In its first year the government was preoccupied with establishing a new administration in a country that had always had a weak state. The feebleness of the new government's reach moderated the tempo of change, but it also meant that "rogue" cadres in remote areas could not be stopped from indulging in communizing zeal. Fortunately, instances of this were rare, in contrast to the cataclysm then engulfing neighboring Khmer peasants under Pol Pot's notorious regime.

Apart from attempting to establish a new administration in 1976, the LPDR had to try to revive the Lao economy, which had collapsed following the flight of capital, entrepreneurs, and merchants from the country. It cast around for sources of economic surplus not only to finance itself but also to promote development, yet there was little to be had.[3] The 80 percent of the population that lived in rural Laos were either slash-and-burn cultivators who produced no identifiable surplus or a peasantry that was largely subsistence oriented. Nevertheless, the government tried to introduce an

44

agricultural tax in September 1976. It was unpopular with the peasants, who had not been seriously taxed by the previous regime. The tax was one of the first clear signals to the peasants that the new government planned a new role for them in the country's economic development.

Bad weather over 1976 caused poor harvests and underlined the vulnerability of the Lao rural economy and the country's underdevelopment. General Secretary Kaysone Phomvihane expressed his party's frustration to the SPA in February 1977: "Small-scale production, characterized by rudimentary economy, is still expanding in our country," he said, while productivity remains low; communications are poor, and during the wet season some areas are entirely cut off "from the mainstream of life in the country"; a national market does not exist; and, the "newly established state-run economic enterprises remain weak and cannot genuinely play the leading role in our economy." Worse, they were continually undermined by "economic enterprises run by the capitalists, primarily in trade, based on profiteering and hoarding."[4] Therefore the sooner private production and private trade could be displaced, the better. In the countryside, however, little was done to displace private production. By the end of 1976 only a few thousand people had been drawn into low-level cooperatives in nine of the thirteen provinces, and most of these were located in the former "liberated zone." Yet in the same report Kaysone went on to say, "In the agricultural sector, at present and in the next few years, the revolution is being and will basically be carried out by boosting the production units and labor-exchange units. Under this form, peasants are allowed to retain the right of ownership of farmland, cattle, farm implements and farm produce. However, under the new system the character of independent agricultural production cannot remain unchanged. The change in agricultural production must be carried out in two aspects—the relations among the peasants, and the relations between the peasants and the state" (*SWB*, 6 April 1977). The changes Kaysone envisaged between the state and the peasants involved taxation and their integration into a planned national economy and polity.

The general direction of the government's thinking was clear. It would use all of its available resources to shift the peasantry into a collectivist direction, but there was no hint that they would be administratively forced into collective farms. The policy review foresaw a relaxed pace whereby peasants would be steadily incorporated into low-level forms of cooperation "in the next few years," and it was cautious about the pace of development for existing cooperatives. There were no immediate plans to create giant collective farms, and Kaysone cautioned that it would be "inappropriate" to consolidate those in existence into a unit because management capability for large farms did not exist. But the party and the state had to develop plans for "transforming such cooperatives into socialist cooperatives once conditions permit," socialist cooperatives being those that practice "large-scale socialist production" and in which the means of production are common property.

At the beginning of 1977 the communist government in Laos seemed to be preparing for a slow and steady march toward socialism. It was not in total control of the situation inside the country—its administrative reach remained limited and its control of the shrunken economy fragile. Yet it looked as though the postrevolutionary nadir had been reached and that the situation would improve from then on. However, a concatenation of international and local events soon plunged the new regime into a state of insecurity and finally spurred it into taking strong protective measures. Deteriorating relations between Vientiane and Bangkok, whose extreme right wing regime under Thanin Kraivixien was hostile to Laos and blockaded the country in 1977, was one factor; another was growing tensions between Laos's close ally Vietnam and both China and the latter's ally Democratic Kampuchea. As a landlocked state sharing its border with all belligerents the government in Laos had every reason to feel insecure.

Further, natural calamities during 1977 in the context of rising international tensions caused the higher reaches of the LPRP to contemplate the need for speedier economic and social transformation. A collectivization campaign was not envisaged, but all "leading organs" were instructed to step up their organizational capacity to guide and "promote this movement" of peasants toward collectivization and "steer them along the path laid down by the party" (*SWB*, 5 July 1977).

Moderation and persuasion, meanwhile, remained the party's watchwords. The formation of labor-exchange units, an editorial in the party daily *Sieng Pasason* argued, was a form of organization that would allow the peasants "to get acquainted gradually with labor organization, management, and the division of labor," so that they could move to higher forms of production later. In a sense these forms of collective organization were seen as having an educational function, though the economics of the exercise were not ignored: "The peasants must be helped to score more achievements than they would through their private and ill-organized means of production, and [be shown] that earnings must surpass what they would receive through other means. This will ensure a firm basis for persuading the individual peasants to march gradually toward socialist collective production." Cadres were instructed not to form units that were too large, and the fact that all means of production remained the personal property of the peasants was emphasized—though here the editorial struck an ominous note, saying this property "will not be touched *yet*" (*SWB*, 5 July 1977, my emphasis).

The *Sieng Pasason* editorial also offered cadres working definitions of the two forms of collective labor organizations they should promote:

> The first are unity units. A unity unit is merely a mutual-aid organization that is aimed at gathering labor forces to join in carrying out major works in certain fields. Those who join a unity unit are paid nothing for their labor. This form of collective labor organization is adapted by our party from the notion of "asking a favor," which our Lao peasants of various nationalities have been acquainted with for a long time. . . . The labor-exchange unit . . . is a form of collective labor in which labor is organized and those who engage in labor are compensated. This system guarantees justice and compensation for those who work. The labor-exchange unit can be organized for any type of work or for particular long-term production tasks; this depends on the situation in each locality.

Despite the growing emphasis on collectivization of agriculture in government pronouncements, the rest of 1977 was taken up with attempts to conserve rice and calls for upgrading the country's communications network, the deficiencies of which had been graphically illustrated by the system's inability to transport rice from surplus to deficit areas. The shortages also caused outbursts against middlemen, who were allegedly responding to the shortages of rice and other commodities in the country by demanding higher prices, and led to renewed attempts by the state trade sector to displace private traders. But in the absence of an adequate response by state organizations the cumulative effect of attacks on middlemen was further inhibition of trade and exaggerated shortages.

The economic situation in Laos at the end of 1977 was far from the hoped-for recovery expressed by the country's leaders at the beginning of the year. The only bright spot was the easing of inflation in the latter half of the year, partly as a result of the government's policies, but also because of the easing of demand pressures as commodity aid began arriving and some local enterprises recommenced operation.

On 2 March 1978 Kaysone introduced Laos's first three-year economic

47

development plan to a joint sitting of the SPA and the Council of Ministers. It was not a detailed, Soviet-type plan (for that was impossible at this stage) but a temporary, general framework that specified some physical targets and identified major projects. The plan covered only 1978–80 so that in 1981 Laos could begin a five-year plan in coordination with Vietnam and the Eastern bloc's COMECON, whose member countries were supplying Laos with the bulk of its aid and expertise.

The three-year plan, Kaysone announced portentously, would bring about a "turning point of strategic significance in our country's march towards socialism" (*SWB*, 16 March 1978). While this echoes the name given to Stalin's collectivization drive—the Great Turn—nothing so drastic was in store for Laos, but clearly the Lao leadership envisaged radical changes in their country during the period of the plan. And, although Kaysone's speech was not couched in the strident class warfare rhetoric that preceded and accompanied Stalin's Great Turn, it contained an unusually combative edge. The plan was part of "a decisive struggle since it will settle the question of who wins over whom between socialism and capitalism—a conflict which is developing in our society and is clearly related to the struggle to build large-scale socialist production."[5] Kaysone reminded his listeners several times that the "struggle between the two lines" had reached a new phase, and he placed a new emphasis on the importance of transforming the society's social relations of production. The general tenor of Kaysone's speech stressed the importance of socialist transformation: "The economic policy of our party and state is to use agriculture and forestry as the basis for developing industry. . . . That is why we must first concentrate on effecting socialist transformation in agricultural productive forces to develop . . . and introducing profound revolutionary changes to the countryside in the political, economic, cultural, national defence and peacekeeping sectors. . . . Conditions are ripe in the countryside for rapidly diverting individual production to collective production."[6] The statement strongly implied that the growth targets outlined in the plan could be achieved only by a rapid revolutionizing of agriculture.

Regarding international security, Kaysone's speech reflected grave concern about regional tensions. He observed that relations with Thailand, though improved since a coup against Kraivixien in November 1977, were far from satisfactory and still in flux. But he devoted special attention to the "sad situation" that had developed along the Kampuchea–Vietnam border. He endorsed the Vietnamese negotiating proposals for settling the dispute and implicitly criticized the Pol Pot regime for refusing to negotiate.

Vientiane hoped it could play a mediating role, and Kaysone expressed Laos's "earnest desire" to maintain relations of "special solidarity" among the three Indochinese countries. As the smallest state in the region it had the greatest interest in stability, and Kampuchea's attacks on Vietnam threatened the security not only of the latter, but ultimately of Laos as well. With an eye to this, the LPRP saw collectivization not only as a means of economic security, but of political security as well: "In coordination with the national defence and peacekeeping task," the party leader said, "it is necessary to build a strong administration at the grassroots level by grasping the central task—to reorganize production along collective lines."[7] The ever-tighter interlocking of international developments with domestic decisions finally dictated the precise timing of Laos's collectivization campaign.

The Campaign

The prime minister's Instructions on Agriculture, broadcast on 1 April 1978, emphasized economic reasons for collectivization. They drew attention to the ability of mass mobilizations of "tens of thousands" of people to overcome adversity, as had happened during the previous year's drought, when people dug canals and carried water to avert disaster. The instructions were suffused with voluntarist mobilization rhetoric. They spoke of "launching emulation campaigns to mobilize the entire party, army and people to make preparations to start emulating in order to win achievements in the 1978 production season" (*SWB*, 6 April 1978). It was to be a campaign for "organizing centralized agriculture"; yet these instructions did not launch the collectivization campaign, but rather merely stressed the importance of boosting agricultural production. But, given that the party was convinced cooperatives were the best means of doing this, it is not surprising the mobilization soon snowballed into a collectivization drive.

The first indication that the drive had begun came when Vientiane Radio announced on 13 June that earlier in the month the prime minister had "visited Champassak and Saravane Provinces to inspect and guide production . . . and launch an emulation campaign to set up agriculture cooperatives" (*SWB*, 14 June 1978). Two days later the resolution of the Political Bureau of the LPRP Central Committee calling for "widening the movement to build agricultural cooperatives" was broadcast. It said, "The motivation of farmers to join agricultural cooperatives is a thorough-going revolution in the countryside. . . . We must turn private relations of

49

production into collective relations of production . . . so as to serve the people's lives and the socialist industrialization of our country better." The security and administrative dimensions were also emphasized. Cooperatives would lead to a "strengthening [of] the party's leadership over the countryside" (*SWB*, 24 June 1978). On the same day the guiding document of the campaign, the Provisional Regulations of Agricultural Cooperatives (dated 15 May), was also made public.

The provisional regulations systematize many of the themes enunciated in prior government statements. They claim cooperatives are the best means for modernizing agricultural production while "bypassing capitalism" and provide the foundations for the "laboring farmers' right to collective mastery." The regulations stipulate that peasants must join cooperatives only on a voluntary basis, "without any coercion whatsoever," and that they must practice democratic management. The cooperatives were to be based on villages rather than wider units. And in keeping with the principle of voluntariness members would be allowed to resign from the cooperatives. When they joined, members were expected to contribute their cultivated land and their basic means of production for the cooperative's use. Other types of property were to remain in personal hands, though the cooperative reserved the right to make use of it.

The drive involved local party activists and government officials in a propaganda campaign for collectives. Collectivization was a subject raised at every provincial, district, canton, village, and subvillage meeting. The local officials' agitation was supported by a stream of government statements on the virtues of collectives and advice about forming them. On 10 July the government news agency, KPL, gave an early balance sheet of progress in the campaign: "According to incomplete figures, there are now 180 cooperatives in Champassak Province, 110 in Xieng Khouang, and a dozen in Saravane, Attopeu, Khammouane, Vientiane, Sayaboury, Luang Prabang, Houa Phan and Oudomsay provinces" (*SWB*, 14 July 1978). KPL assured its audience that more and more farmers were joining cooperatives.

Kaysone offered a further progress report at the beginning of August. Initial figures, he said, showed there were now 700 cooperatives in the country, and he interpreted this growth as demonstrating "the spirit of revolutionary enthusiasm" of the peasants (*SWB*, 9 August 1978). Yet while Kaysone spoke of the campaign as the main task of "our entire party and masses at present," his report showed that it was encountering administrative difficulties and being implemented unevenly. In some areas cadres emphasized the politics of the campaign to the detriment of production, while other areas were simply failing to participate in the drive. Kaysone called for more training courses for cadres to overcome these shortcomings, and it was also evident from his speech that the state's administrative structure was not up to the task.

Laos, he frankly admitted, did not possess a unified national economy. It had only a combination of what he called a "central economy and local economies." The "local level is a constant objective structure" in Lao society, and for this reason the new state had to build from the bottom up and from the top down and hope the two structures would ultimately coincide. Kaysone's references to the local level being the only constantly objective structure in Lao society is oddly reminiscent of the "Asiatic mode of production" concept, whose object was societies in which despotic dynasties rose and fell against the background of an unchanging village society. Obviously this was not what Kaysone had in mind, but his formulation does draw attention to the fact that the Lao communist state was precariously seated on top of a relatively autonomous natural economy. The process of integration of state and society, as Kaysone set it out, entailed building down by establishing the provincial level as "an all-round and complete strategic center" that would concentrate on building an integrated provincial economy and government; and building up from the villages, integrating them into the national economy through the formation of cooperatives. This, it was hoped, would facilitate the consolidation of intermediate levels of government. He went on, "In the immediate future, through the process of establishing agricultural cooperatives . . . the district level will be built into an economic unit different from the past, and into a zone in which the three revolutions can be carried out simultaneously in the countryside . . . transforming the district level into the direct leading level for the cantons and agricultural cooperatives" (*SWB*, 9 August 1978). The "three revolutions" refer to relations of production, science and technology, and culture and ideology. Kaysone's formula left unresolved the immediate problem of political guidance and technical inputs to support the collectivization movement, and therefore the movement was in danger of becoming a potential vicious circle. The hiatus between the village and province levels created confusion about just who was in charge of the campaign.

By late August the campaign was overtaken by the second natural disaster to hit Laos in two years. In 1977 drought had struck; in 1978 it was floods. Once again the southern provinces were seriously affected. In Champassak province about 90 percent of the rice fields in the districts along the Mekong and other rivers were reported to be inundated. In Savannakhet province 50 percent of the rice fields were reported to have been flooded. Also in Vientiane and Khammouane provinces rice fields all along the Mekong and other rivers were damaged by floods. The Lao vice–foreign minister told the UN General Assembly in September that the floods had ruined an estimated 125,000 tons of rice and threatened half the population with famine. The international reaction to his appeal was lukewarm, and little aid arrived in the month following the appeal. Everyone not affected by the floods was urged by the government to donate two kilograms of rice to the victims, who were advised to concentrate on subsidiary crops like maize and sweet potato and to "hold aloft the principle of self-reliance." On the other hand, it did not want people to retreat into self-sufficient insularity, and it warned that efforts had to be made to stop peasants from "adopting an attitude of regionalism or partiality in which districts think only of their own vested interests without any regard for those of the country and of the province as a whole (*SWB*, 24 August 1978). Commitment to Pathet Lao, unlike that to the local community, was still only skin deep.

The government quickly recognized the dangers the disaster posed to its plans for socialist transformation. It warned that "reactionaries" would try to take advantage of the country's woes and indicated that in some localities "the enemy has resumed fomenting disorder." The grim situation did not deter the government from its drive to collectivize. It still argued that the "setting up of cooperatives must be regarded as the main task in carrying out all other tasks," which presumably applied to coping with the disaster.

Late 1978, however, was not the most propitious time for a collectivization campaign. As James C. Scott argued in his *Moral Economy of the Peasant*, because Asian farmers court hunger every year they have good reason to be circumspect about outsiders' suggestions concerning new techniques or new forms of farm organization. If these "bright ideas" fail, the peasant's family could starve, and thus it is safer to stick to tried and proven ways. Scott writes, "There is a defensive perimeter around subsistence routines within which risks are avoided as potentially catastrophic," but beyond that perimeter, he argues, the peasant can be tempted to experiment.[8] Lao peasants are generally on the subsistence margin, and therefore 1978 was not, from their point of view, a time for experimentation with cooperatives. Too much was at stake. The government's resolve to continue with the campaign was bound to run into spontaneous resistance.

Official statements at the time gave little indication of the problems encountered by the campaign. Indeed, statements tended to reflect rising confidence. The first official sign that the campaign was not proceeding as smoothly as hoped came in late November, when the text of a 15 October decision by the Council of Ministers was released saying that it had set up a Central-Level Committee to Guide Agricultural Cooperatives under the direction of Sali Vongkhamsao (*SWB*, 21 November 1978). The committee was directly responsible to the Party Secretariat and the Standing Committee of the Council of Ministers. Its function was to coordinate and supervise the campaign, which had gained a degree of local momentum. The party seemed uncertain about what exactly was happening on the ground. It was really a troubleshooting committee established to short-circuit normal bureaucratic channels in order to either direct the drive or gather information on it. Therefore it was, to some extent, an attempt by the center to gain control of what was happening in the provinces.

Despite the formation of the central-level committee, there was no sign that the Lao government would slow its collectivization drive. In a report of February 1979 Kaysone continued to argue that cooperatives were the only way peasant agriculture could overcome natural calamities and achieve food self-sufficiency; he continued also to emphasize the security and administrative dimensions of collectivization. He informed his audience that by December 1978 over 1,600 cooperatives had been set up throughout Laos, encompassing 16 percent of all farming families. The majority of them were in Khammouane and Champassak provinces. Most of the cooperatives were, he said, based on single villages and on average comprised 30 to 40 families. Some were supravillage organizations of over 200 families. "The Pa-ai Canton cooperative in Saravane District, Saravane Province, comprises 226 farming families from eight villages" (*SWB*, 24 February 1978). However, cooperatives of this sort, reminiscent of Chinese communes, were rare and were not encouraged. In his speech to the first National Congress of Agricultural Cooperatives on 24 April 1979, Kaysone warned against forming units that were too large. The same speech fixed targets for the year: "According to plan, an additional 30 to 35 percent of the farmers' families are to join agricultural cooperatives in 1979."

Yet two and a half months later, when the number of cooperatives in the country was said to stand at 2,500, the Central Committee of the LPRP stopped the campaign. A statement on 14 July said, "Efforts to mobilize farmers to join agricultural cooperatives or set up new ones during the current production season should be immediately and strictly suspended while the people are engaging in production in order rapidly and effectively to increase production." The overriding reason for the suspension was that it had become obvious to the party that collectivization was seriously disrupting production. It realized that it could not afford another year of disastrous results, this time brought on by man-made factors. Cadres, according to the statement, had simply concentrated on the numerical growth of cooperatives without ensuring an increase in production. Cooperatives had been rushed together without adequate preparation, peasants had been forced to join, and often means of production such as cows and buffaloes had been expropriated or peasants offered minimal compensation for them. This created serious tensions in the countryside that threatened not only the economic basis of the campaign, but also its intended security benefits. The Central Committee statement went on to say that "enemies" had taken advantage of the campaign's weaknesses

> to infiltrate into cooperatives to create confusion among the people and sabotage the party and state line, thus disturbing the peaceful situation in the country. Because of this, the people, including the peasants, have become discouraged and unhappy, thus seriously affecting and delaying production. Some people have abandoned their farms, turned to other occupations, sold or secretly slaughtered their animals or fled to other countries. This has now become an urgent problem which will create an immediate and long-term danger if it is not quickly, effectively, and skillfully resolved. It will become not only an economic danger affecting production and the people's living conditions, but also a political danger.

It emphasized the voluntary nature of the program and insisted that "those who have already joined cooperatives should be allowed to leave when they wish" (*SWB,* 15 August 1979). In short, the aims of the campaign threatened to backfire on the communist government.

It is difficult to reconstruct the overall situation in the Lao peasant community during the collectivization drive. The evidence suggests that conditions varied considerably from province to province, district to district, and even canton to canton.[9]

Market Socialism

In December 1979 Kaysone announced to an SPA session a major reorientation in the LPRP's strategy for transition to socialism in Laos. Its perspective was long-term and recognized the difficulties of attempting to force the pace of social change. It included a critique of orthodox communist command planning and began an examination of different approaches to socialist economic development, starting with Lenin's famous articles on the New Economic Policy in the Soviet Union in the early 1920s. These argued that the suppression of trade and the private sector in an underdeveloped socialist country was "suicidal," and Kaysone wholeheartedly agreed. Guidelines were laid down for the diversification of the economy and the encouragement of private alongside state trade in an attempt to develop a more sophisticated division of labor and draw the peasants into the national economy. These themes were reiterated and strengthened at the Third LPRP Congress in 1982 and at the Fourth Congress in 1986.

But while private enterprise in the form of petty commodity production, small-scale capitalism, and joint state–private enterprises were given legitimacy and an important place in LPDR economic strategy, the state sector was still to control the "commanding heights" of the economy. The policy shift was not based on any fundamental reappraisal of capitalism. The long-term superiority of socialism over capitalism remained unquestioned. The reappraisal was based on a more realistic understanding of the weaknesses of Lao society and its economy. Kaysone states in his 1986 Congress speech, "We should be aware that the commodity economy, including the simple commodity economy, is more advanced than the natural and self-sufficient economy. Therefore, our state must encourage and develop the commodity-money relationship . . . with a view to turning the natural economy into the socialist-oriented commodity economy." The state will guide the "evolutional process of transforming a multisector economy into the socialist economy."[10] Notwithstanding economic criteria taking a new pride of place in Lao communist thinking and the market being given prominence, the aim remained the socialist transformation of the natural economy.

The seminal document of this policy turn, Resolution 7 (issued in 1979), criticized state restrictions on private trade and argued that the state trading network was too weak to "act as a spearhead in promoting and developing the national economy." Trade was crucial to developing an integrated national economy, creating a viable framework for a more elaborate division of labor, and creating a home market. But, Kaysone said, trade generally had been limited "by numerous complicated marketing management methods, complicated inspection regulations, and multiple tax collecting procedures." Because the state trading networks were unable to satisfy internal demand Kaysone proposed what amounted to a system of subcontracting: "The private trade sector still plays an active role in expanding the circulation of goods within the country. It should be used as an agent for selling goods at retail prices and purchasing farms and forestry products for the state trading service. It should be allowed to operate businesses freely within the bounds set by the state" (*SWB*, 5 February 1980). Alongside state and private traders, he also encouraged the formation of trading cooperatives. But, he said, the state trading service had to aim at capturing the "commanding heights" in the market and "take a dominant role in the four types of markets, namely, national, local, planned and unplanned markets," on the basis of economic competition, not administrative coercion. He was especially preoccupied with the circulation of goods between the countryside and the city, which, he said, was the basis for the "worker–peasant alliance" in Laos. Private traders would have their role to play in the cementing of this alliance.

Relations with the farmers required an economic basis, and supplies of "essential industrial goods" would provide it. "If the state trading service wants to purchase farm products from them, it must contact them directly. Transactions in these goods must be conducted on a fair economic basis. The state cannot coerce them into selling goods to it on whim." The peasants' main economic obligation to the state was to pay taxes.

Previous anxiety about internal security gradually acquired a marked economic emphasis. Security was important for the circulation of goods throughout the country, and the very circulation of goods had a vital security feedback in that people would be less dissatisfied about shortages. Kaysone made this clear in mid-1987: "The enemies have in the past used goods as a tool of psychological warfare. . . . An effective arrangement for ever-increasing exchange of goods between urban and rural areas and between the state and the farmers leads to an establishment of close contacts between the state and farmers. It serves as a firm guarantee for the new system" (*SWB*, 17 June 1987). Thus, the discarding of the trappings of a command economy led to the downgrading of administrative control over the population in favor of economic means for creating popular allegiance to the government.

The government also tried to tackle the vital issue of prices in an attempt to get them functioning as proper incentives and indicators in the economy. Various systems of price regulation, some more extensive than others, were tried. But the most radical reform came in mid-1987 with the introduction of the "one-price system." This aimed at abolishing virtually all cross-subsidization, multiple exchange rates, and administered prices, leaving prices to be determined by supply and demand and mutual agreements between contracting parties in the market. The policy "is applicable to all categories of retail and wholesale goods, purchasing prices of farm products, prices of construction material, prices of transport and services, and rates of foreign exchange" (*SWB*, 4 August 1987).

Elements of socialist market regulation were evident in the government's emphasis on the contract system. Kaysone speaks enthusiastically of the "rich" lessons to be "drawn from the contract procedures in the economies of the socialist countries" (*SWB*, 17 June 1987). Nouhak Phoumsavan, in his Economic Report to the Fourth Congress, insists that contracts provide the basis on which individual enterprises can plan ahead and are crucial for the implementation of "socialist accounting procedures"; therefore "the planning institutions and bodies concerned must help the production and business enterprises by procuring various contracts for them." Contracts are expected to play a vital role in tying nonsocialist sectors into the priorities established by the socialist sector. Nouhak urged socialist trading services "to sign contracts with the peasants so as to make them consistent in their productive activities" (*SWB*, 20 November 1986). Sali Vongkhamsao spelled this out: "As regards the collective economy and small production involving the families of handicraftsmen, private farmers, and the private economy, the state will introduce as its instruments taxes, prices, credits, contracts for selling material to and buying products from them, or the form of advising them to produce goods ordered by the state in order to enable these economic sectors to follow the path of the national economic plan and to implement state laws" (*SWB*, 20 June 1987). In sum, contracts rather than some form of compulsory sales to the state were regarded as the key economic link to the peasants.

The general thrust of Lao government policy since 1979 has been in the direction of market socialism. It upgraded measures to get producers to respond to demand signals that are essentially commercial rather than bureaucratic. This does not mean that the government has abandoned planning. It now attempts to influence the market by using price controls, subsidies, taxes, decisions about resource allocation, and so on. The methods are macroeconomic and are aimed primarily at influencing the calculations made by managers and direct producers rather than instructing them about what they should do.

Collectivization

At the SPA session in December 1979 Kaysone restated the government's commitment to collectivization and gave a predictably optimistic assessment of the recently suspended drive: "Generally speaking the movement has developed splendidly." But, he said, coercion had been used, the "principles of voluntariness" flouted, and peasants' rights abused, leading to discouragement in "some localities" (*SWB*, 30 January 1980). No new drive was foreshadowed: "The direction of our current collectivization task is to consolidate and develop cooperatives, with the former as the main task." In the immediate future attention was to be given to strengthening the organization of cooperatives that had already been formed, not to creating new ones. As shown in table 3.1 there was a dramatic decline in the total number of cooperatives in Laos from 1979 to 1980. The number dropped by over one thousand, and by 1983 the figure was still below the 1979 figure.

The change of economic policy by the LPRP had not led to a revision of its general position on the role of cooperatives in the process of agricultural modernization. Its main policy statements continued to echo earlier positions. At the Party Congress in 1982, Kaysone still spoke of the need to "persuade the peasants to embark on the socialist collective path of production in the form of agricultural cooperatives . . . thereby creating favorable conditions to get the three revolutions under way in the countryside . . . in the direction of advancing to socialist large-scale production" (*SWB*, 1 May 1982).

Despite ideological commitments, however, considerable malaise had set in in the cooperative movement. In a speech before the SPA on 11 January 1982, Kaysone bewailed the fact that "several services at the center have almost forgotten their responsibility in the movement to set up agricultural cooperatives" (*SWB*, 16 January 1982). He spoke in a similar vein at the Party Congress three months later: "Party cadres and members have even now become discouraged and dare not carry out a campaign to mobilize the masses to set up model cooperatives" (*SWB*, 17 April 1982). In response to this flagging enthusiasm for the cooperatives, Kaysone, in

TABLE 3.1. Number of Cooperatives by Province

Province	1979[a]	1980	1981	1982	1983[b]	1984[b]	1985	1986
Phong Saly	73	152	152	156	167	167	167	167
Luang Namtha	59	74	74	74	74	74	74	69
Oudomsay	72	93	93	98	98	111	115	182
Sayaboury	120	44	44	89	129	160	160	154
Luang Prabang	41	44	44	76	82	98	101	152
Xieng Khouang	200	212	212	252	251	251	247	247
Houaphan	155	263	263	274	311	311	318	374
Vientiane Prefecture	—[c]	—	—	63	104	119	167	192
Vientiane	486	101	101	47	71	93	176	242
Khammouane	433	12	12	24	67	99	104	372
Savannakhet	250	12	12	18	53	164	547	579
Saravane	235	18	18	168	107	216	254	314
Champassak	304	306	306	587	587	597	651	659
Attopeu	24	12	12	12	13	19	19	14
Bokeo	—	—	—	—	—	40	40	67
Bolikhamsay	—	—	—	—	—	17	34	76
Xekong	—	—	—	—	—	10	10	120
Total	2,452	1,343	1,352	1,943	2,114	2,546	3,184	3,976

Sources: Cooperative Department, Ministry of Agriculture, Irrigation and Cooperatives, Vientiane.

[a]A. R. Khan and E. Lee, *Employment and Development in Laos* (Bangkok: ILO, 1980), 41.

[b]State Planning Committee, *10 Years of Socio-Economic Development in the Lao People's Democratic Republic* (Vientiane, 1985), 105.

[c]Dashes signify the absence of an administrative area prior to the commencement of the statistics.

classic commandist fashion, set a target: "The objective of agricultural cooperativization in the five-year plan is to accomplish, in the main, the building of cooperatives in the rice planting areas" (*SWB*, 1 May 1982). This statement applied only to areas that cultivate paddy. In other areas, where farmers practice both paddy and swidden farming, he went on, cooperatives should be set up "if good cadres are available and the people show willingness. . . . If conditions are not yet ripe for forming cooperatives, mutual-aid teams can be set up instead." As for areas where swidden farming is dominant, "we should study various forms of collectivization so that the most proper ones can be put into practice."

The year after the Third Congress was one of consolidation—or of slow growth in the formation of cooperatives—as can be seen in table 3.1. But the general direction of policy had not been forgotten, and rural cadres were reminded in 1983 by Sali Vongkhamsao, previously in charge of the 1978–79 campaign and now vice-premier, secretary of the LPRP Central Committee, and chairman of the State Planning Committee, that "collectivization is the sole efficient way to liberate the peasants from outdated agricultural patterns and introduce new and modern techniques" (*SWB*, 11 November 1983). Soon after the Politburo released a detailed review of agricultural collectivization. It went over the mistakes of the previous campaign, acknowledging the dramatic collapse of cooperative numbers, but went on to argue that the lessons learned were being put to good use. The review claimed that the provinces of Houa Phan, Xieng Khouang, and Phong Saly had "basically fulfilled the cooperative program." There was a steady growth in the number of cooperatives, and in 1984 the total reached in the previous campaign was surpassed.

The review singled out cadre training as the key to successful collectivization, and this issue was taken up in a *Sieng Pasason* editorial in early 1984, reflecting a renewed combativeness on the question of collectivization. It perhaps also signaled some retreat from, or misgivings about, market socialism. "In the socialist system," it said, "state and collective production normally encompasses all social products. With regard to the agricultural sector in particular, collective or cooperative production is a decisive factor in social production as well as in the struggle of who will emerge as victor between the socialist and capitalist paths." Cadres, it said, needed to be trained and sent out to lead the formation of cooperatives. In apparent contradiction of the spirit of voluntariness, it dispensed instructions to local officials: "A canton which does not have any cooperatives should set up at least one or two units to carry out production on an experimental basis for future comparison. . . . Party committees and administrative committees at all levels must regard the work of changing to agricultural collectivization as an important task which must be confidently consistently carried out" (*SWB*, 19 March 1989). This was followed in April by Council of Ministers' Instruction No. 022, which urged local officials to establish plans for switching to collective production "without delay" (*SWB*, 8 May 1984). The renewed emphasis on collectivization maintained momentum throughout 1984 and was reflected in the formation of new cooperatives, particularly in the southern provinces over 1983–84, as can been seen in table 3.1. Specifically, an article entitled "An agricultural cooperative is a correct and bright path for farmers" reasserted the correctness of all the earlier key resolutions relating to the collectivization campaign of 1978–79, which, "in spite of inconsistency in development," registered important achievements. The article returned to the theme of "two paths," with a more orthodox political rather than economic emphasis. It stressed that small-scale agriculture was the source of "all forms of exploitation" and led spontaneously in the direction of capitalism (*SWB*, 13 October 1984). Other articles around the same time emphasized the importance of centralized agricultural development, claiming it was "completely suited to the current reality in our country" (*SWB*, 19 October 1984).

Fears and anxieties had clearly emerged within the party about the new economic policies and about the continuing independence of the peasantry, which was perceived, at least by some, to be an imminent threat to socialism. There was, however, no evidence of serious divisions within the LPRP over the objective of collectivization. Rather, the disagreements were over timing and method, although such differences can have significant strategic implications. Yet, although this series of articles had overtones of the earlier campaign, it also recognized that hastiness in the establishment of cooperatives would be self-defeating.

As in the earlier campaign, the articles provided an upbeat assessment of the progress of collectivization. As of June 1984, 37.6% of farm families (which included 35.3 percent of farmland) was said to be in 2,402 cooperatives. Since then the combative tone has largely disappeared from pronouncements about collectivization, giving way to a reemphasis on the economic role of cooperatives.

At the Congress in 1986 Kaysone's political report, in contrast to the sentiment of those in the party who in 1984 appeared to be pushing for a rapid transformation of agriculture, placed equal or more weight on the objective conditions required for transformation to be successful: "Our main shortcomings lie in subjectivism and haste, in our failure to combine transformation with construction, in our inclination to abolish the nonsocialist economic sectors promptly." Cooperatives play a central role in Kaysone's thinking about socialism, and their establishment in "every national economic branch in the initial stage of the transition to socialism is a most important strategic task for the building of socialist large-scale production." But the pace envisaged is comparatively moderate; the organization of peasants into collectives should be achieved "fundamentally by the end of this century."[11]

The process proposed is also important because it contrasts with that of the more orthodox communist centralizers in Kaysone's own party. The new economic mechanism, with its reliance on the market, is crucial to what Kaysone sees as the "worker–peasant alliance" in Laos. That is, the timely supply of goods produced by workers in urban areas to the peasants is the crucial stimulus required for agricultural productivity. As I noted in the discussion of the new economic mechanism, commerce is seen as the most important link in the transition period.

Kaysone's view is also interesting in that he takes a much broader view of cooperative activity than was evident in earlier years, and this new perspective demonstrates a shift away from an insistence on transforming social relations in the sphere of economic production. Thus he sees cooperatives taking a range of forms:

> The best examples in many localities have shown that wherever there are various types of cooperatives in one area, such as supply and marketing, credit, agricultural handicraft cooperatives conducting business in various trades within the framework of a single organizational system, under the guidance of a just management board according to a common plan, good results have been achieved, since it is suitable both to the fairly low level of development of the productive forces and to the actual conditions of our country in regard to cadres and the consciousness of the working people. Wherever agricultural cooperatives are yet to be set up, our decision must be based on the real conditions of each place, and we could possibly set up supply and marketing cooperatives first, then persuade the peasants to take up the collective mode of working, from low to high levels.

The market has been integrated into the LPRP's scheme of cooperative evolution, an approach requiring significant modifications to orthodox communist conceptions of collectivization.

Gauging the quality of the cooperatives that have been formed throughout the country is problematic, and information is scarce.[12] In an interview in 1983 an official in the Cooperatives Department offered the following assessment of the state of collectivization in some provinces: Of the 252 cooperatives then in Xieng Khouang, he said, 30 were considered good cooperatives, 121 middle cooperatives, and 101 weak. By *weak* the official said he meant they were "pseudo-cooperatives. Just cooperatives in name, but really only labor-exchange groups." In Houaphan he said there were 66 good cooperatives, 84 middle ones, and 124 weak ones. In Champassak there were only 2 good ones (out of 587), and the rest he felt unable to classify.[13] A statement from 1984 claimed that the "current number of outstanding cooperatives comprise only 15% of the total throughout the country" (*SWB*, 13 October 1984), while officials in the Department of Cooperatives in Vientiane in early 1987 were prepared to say only that 7–10 percent of cooperatives could be considered excellent. In other words the standard of most cooperatives in Laos is not high. Kaysone offered an assessment in his report to the Fourth Congress: "In the agricultural field [most] cooperatives are still in the low form and the peasants have just embarked on the path to collectivisation, but in general, they are still engaged in the natural economy."[14] In the most successful province of Champassak a report of 1986 claimed that of 94 cooperatives in Champassak district, 4 could be "regarded as model ones" (*SWB*, 13 October 1986). That is, 4.2 percent of cooperatives. An overall assessment given in 1987 claimed Champassak province had "29 'leading' cooperatives and 188 'middle level' cooperatives among its total of 645 cooperative units."[15]

The actual nature of cooperatives in Laos cannot be accurately determined through an examination of general statistics. The issue can be settled only by detailed field studies, few of which are available. Nevertheless it is fair to say that collectivization in Laos has never been as widespread as claimed by the government, and the organization of the existing cooperatives is rudimentary.

The LPRP is very conscious of the fact that it is overseeing a *transition* to socialism, and Kaysone never tires of a chance to remind his cadres of the fact. As he told them at the Fourth Congress, "It would be incorrect to say that our country is not at all a socialist society, and it would also be wrong to say that our society is a socialist one."[16] His multisector picture of the Lao economy underlines its transitional nature. There is, he says, the socialist economic sector, "which exists in two forms: the state and collective sectors"[17] and is weak or poorly developed; the state capitalist sector, made up mainly of joint state–private endeavors, is only "newly founded and is a transitional form"; the small private capitalist sector is dominated by "petty proprietors"; and a sector of small craftsmen and peasants who have not joined cooperatives. He goes on to say, "In brief, in our country at present there are still nearly all the modes of production from primitive to contemporary modes of production mankind has gone through. All of these sectors exert an effect on one another, depend on one another, and remain united in an economy still in the period of transition to socialism. However, they contradict and struggle against one another in the class struggle and in the struggle between the two roads which are evolving in an arduous, fierce, and complex manner." Precisely because the new policies hand over part of the "struggle between two roads" to the market there has been a simultaneous emphasis on the need for a stronger, more disciplined communist party because the LPRP wishes to use its control of state power to ensure that a transition to socialism takes place.

Given the absence of any predominant, dynamic mode of production or class in Laos, the party and the state are in search of a class on which to base itself during the transition period. In this light one can understand why the LPRP sees the creation of cooperatives as "a most important strategic task" in the transition period. Because "with the transformation of the relations of production through the process of agricultural cooperativization there emerges in the rural areas of our country a new class, namely, the collective peasantry."[18] The formation of classes and social groups characteristic of industrial socialism is decades away in Laos, hence the strategic importance of the "collective peasantry" to the party.

Like Lenin in his final articles, the LPRP has found its expectations for cooperatives have been tempered by experience. In a key resolution on agriculture in mid-1988 commandist relations between the state and the cooperatives were firmly rejected "as fundamentally contrary to Lenin's view on the system of cooperation." Citing Lenin's articles "On Cooperation," it called for enrolling most of the farmers in marketing cooperatives and argued that this was one of the "initiatives proposed by Lenin in the search for ways to lead the farmers to socialism, and according to Lenin, the system of cooperation is "'the most simple and acceptable' form for the farmers."[19] As Kaysone told me in late 1988, "Our previous cooperative policy was in the old style practiced by other socialist countries. After some investigations into the actual situation in Laos, we decided to change direction and start from the family."[20] Now the party is prepared to tolerate "various types of cooperation at different levels [as] transitional forms to socialism."[21] Such a policy has the advantage of allowing a great deal of flexibility in practice in the villages through the consecrating of all forms of cooperation, including traditional peasant cooperation, as somehow transitional to socialism. The peasantry's normal everyday actions are in this way brought within the orbit of state-sanctioned action, rather than the peasants feeling that what they are doing is in some way illegitimate in the state's eyes. Whether it will lead to socialism is another matter entirely.

4

Peasant Society

under Socialism

The persistence of peasant society has been a headache for communist governments in the twentieth century. The peasantry are an uncomfortable reminder to communist leaders of the underdeveloped nature of their economy and society and of their precocious attempt to "bypass capitalism"—a formulation whose very coherence derives from the revolution's defiance of classical Marxism's expectation that socialism would be built on the economic and social foundations of advanced capitalism. As if reenacting the archetypical psychoanalytic nightmare, communist governments often appear to be haunted by a "return of the repressed" capitalist stage in the form of a peasant—scythe in hand.

Chapter 1 argued that communists have assumed capitalist class differentiation among the peasantry is inevitable and inexorable, and they have often transferred this prognosis to postrevolutionary society. The Lao communists followed this well-hoed-row. During the renewed push for collectivization in 1984 the following reasons were advanced to demonstrate the urgency of transforming social relations in the countryside:

> If our farmers were to continue to follow the private path of earning a living at random, they would only face difficulties and suffer more privation. As a result of the private and scattered mode of production, the gap between the rich and the poor in society would be widened. This means that those who owned more farmland and capital would

become richer, buying other laborers as their servants. These people would then become labor exploiters. As for those who owned a small piece of farmland or those who had no property, they would have to sell their labor for low prices. As a result, they would suffer more and become poorer. In the end most of our farmers would reach bankruptcy.[1]

In 1987, while promoting the new economic policies, *Sieng Pasason* warned its readers that "the private and individual economic sectors have a tendency to develop towards capitalism."[2]

The possibility of peasant society having its own autonomous logic and perhaps adopting a distinct long-term trajectory under a socialist system has been seriously considered by only a few theorists, notably Bukharin and Chayanov following the first successful socialist revolution. They have had few successors. In the following pages I shall consider the impact of the new communist government's policies on rural social relations in Laos after 1975. Special effort will be made to discern an emergent class of rural capitalists and a rural proletariat.

Devolution after the Revolution

Many of the elite and their supporters, including foreign traders, speculators, and the few extant landlords, fled Laos immediately before or immediately after the communist takeover. But a significant number stayed, though not for long. One of the new government's first actions was to place restrictions on the activities of "capitalists" and "class enemies," namely, the merchants. Their ability to import was severely curtailed; they were prohibited from buying rice and livestock and from conducting interprovincial trade. Restrictions on intermittent peasant commerce and petty traders spilled over from this policy. Unfortunately for the new regime there were no socialist trading organizations to take the place of existing traders. Consequently a substantial decline in internal commerce occurred and quickly forced the peasant communities to retreat to their previous high levels of self-sufficiency. Handlooms packed away many years before when foreign imports became available were reassembled under houses; evenings lengthened as villages drifted into darkness following the drying up of fuel supplies for lamps. A currency change in June 1976 from the old kip to the "liberation" kip reignited not-long-dormant peasant suspicions of paper money and led to a resurgence of barter exchanges. In its battle with inflation the government tried to fix the purchase prices of essential commodities, but continuing inflation made these unrealistic, and it was soon not worthwhile for peasants to exchange any of their produce with whichever traders got through to them. The revolution, contrary to its intentions, gave the peasant natural economy a new lease on life.

Some evidence suggests that a spontaneous "land reform" took place in the peasant communities. The depression of the urban economy following the communist takeover had a number of consequences for the peasants in the districts surrounding Vientiane and other urban centers. Generally it meant fewer opportunities for earning occasional cash income through some form of employment in the cities. The contraction of the urban economy also modified the viability of smaller landholdings. But the job market was not the only element to contract: wages and salaries plummeted. The government admitted that its salary scales were very low and lagged well behind inflation. In this situation earnings from the land became increasingly important. One response was a certain "peasantising" of the city as the government urged the urban population to grow its own food and ministries were instructed to establish gardens for their employees. Rather than commerce fanning out into the countryside, the natural economy began making inroads into the urban areas. But the contraction of the urban economy also led to a reflux of labor back into the countryside, and land rights back in the villages were reactivated. As a result, some families experienced a serious strain on resources, while others—those who held larger parcels of land (five hectares or more)—either sold off portions of it or prematurely dispersed it in fear that if they did not do so they would be accused of landlordism and have their land confiscated. One effect of the revolution, therefore, appears to have been a spontaneous, egalitarian "land reform" without any government intervention whatsoever.

Evidence for this claim is found in the village of ban Hat Kansa, located about twenty-five kilometers from Vientiane. Land distribution in ban Hat Kansa in 1967–68 compared with that in 1983 (fig. 4.1) underwent a general shift downward in the size of landholdings among a group of farmer households whose number had fluctuated only from forty-six to forty-one families over the period. What the statistics from 1967–68 conceal, however, is that 20 percent of the total families bracketed in the zero to one hectare figure are "landless." By contrast, there are no landless in the 1983 list, although there are some farmers with very small holdings. These figures are sufficient to suggest a redistribution of land downward after

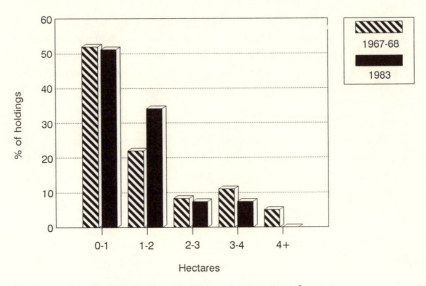

Figure 4.1 Landholding in Ban Hat Kansa (1967–68 and 1983)

1975 and perhaps a premature distribution of inheritance to sons and daughters.

General statistics from the Vientiane Plain on the distribution of land before and after 1975 are provided in tables 4.1–4.3. The first thing one notices about these figures is that they show little evidence of extreme or even significant disparities before 1975. The available statistics after 1975 suggest even fewer large holdings. They do not provide evidence for tendencies toward growing social differentiation in the countryside.

A general breakdown for various areas on the Vientiane Plain in 1973 is shown in table 4.1. If we retabulate the tasseng Bo-O data in table 4.2 into the same categories we get 70 percent of holdings below 1.5ha, 26.4 percent between 1.5ha and 3.5ha, and 3.2 percent above 3.5ha. In tasseng Bo-O there are few large holdings compared with those on the Vientiane Plain in general prior to 1975, many more smaller holdings, and relatively fewer middle holdings. The area Casier Sud provides a point of comparison because it is in the same muang as tasseng Bo-O: holdings above 3.5ha are roughly the same in both areas, but in Bo-O the number of holdings below 1.5ha is significantly higher than in Casier Sud. The figures indicate a general downward distribution of land with more smaller to middle holdings and fewer larger holdings in the villages of tasseng Bo-O. A com-

TABLE 4.1. Comparative Holding Size on Vientiane Plain, c. 1973

Holding Size in Hectares	Perimeter of Tha Deua	Vientiane Plain without Casier Sud	Casier in sud
0–1.6 (0–10 rai)	53%	45%	56%
1.6–3.8 (10–24 rai)	32%	37%	40%
3.8 + (24 rai +)	15%	18%	4%
Total	100%	100%	100%

Source: Ministère du Plan et de la Coopération, *Etude du périmètre de Tha Deua,* Annexe 1, Socio-Economique (Vientiane, September 1973), 44.

parison of tables 4.1 and 4.3 suggests further leveling of landownership after 1975.

Despite the general nature of the figures, the weight of evidence supports an argument for spontaneous rural leveling of landholdings after 1975. The disparities that remained were minimal, and by no means can the situation prevailing on the Vientiane Plain be characterized as an inegalitarian distribution of land implying a class monopoly of means of

TABLE 4.2. Distribution of Land in Four Villages of Tasseng Bo-O, Vientiane Province, 1982

Village	Maximum Size of Holding in Hectares											
	0.5	1	1.5	2	2.5	3	3.5	4	4.5	5	5.5	6
Don Dou	0	0	1	0	1	1	1	0	0	0	0	0
B. Thana	11	19	18	4	4	2	0	0	1ᵃ	0	1	0
Bo-O	5	15	8	10	4	4	4	1	0	0	0	0
B. Nok	16	17	15	6	1	5	1	1	0	0	1	1
Total	32	51	42	20	10	12	6	2	1	0	2	1
Percentage	17.6	29.8	22.6	11.0	5.5	6.6	3.3	1.1	0.5	0	1.1	0.5

Source: Tasseng Bo-O Records.
ᵃThis farmer had become a refugee and the land had not been registered with new owners.

TABLE 4.3. Land Distribution of Rice Farms
in Selected Villages on the Vientiane Plain, 1984

Size of Holdings	Category 1[a] No.	Category 2[b] No.	Total No.	%
0.01–0.50	5	35	40	74
0.51–0.99	5	6	11	20
1.00–1.99	3	0	3	6
1.99+	0	0	0	0
Total	13	41	54	100

[a]Category 1 villages depend mainly on upland rice.
[b]Category 2 villages are paddy rice farmers.

production. It does not demonstrate tendencies toward polarization either. If a land reform program that, for example, redistributed land above two hectares in tasseng Bo-O it would have only a marginal impact on the social landscape there. But land size cannot be abstracted from family size, and a land reform program that arbitrarily decided to redistribute land held above two hectares would probably spark a premature partitioning of family land, that is, it would simply hasten what would happen anyway— and unnecessarily antagonize the peasants.

Most of the lowland Lao population experienced a sharp drop in living standards after 1975 simply as a result of the withdrawal of foreign aid, but further downward pressure was felt in relatively overpopulated areas. Some of this was progressively relieved as thousands of refugees were sent back to the Plain of Jars in Xieng Khouang. With the cessation of hostilities the internal frontier widened and offered possibilities for land-short peasants. But for many, new and more attractive frontiers opened up in America, Australia, and France, so they crossed the Mekong as refugees, along with many Thai Issan who returned home in order to become "Lao refugees." These very large movements (close to 10 percent of Laos's pre-1975 population has left the country) further decreased landlessness and "inegalitarian" distributions of land.

The facts of post-1975 Laos fly in the face of orthodox leftist demands for land reform. For example, Khan and Lee write, "It is surprising . . . that the emergence of the Marxist government was not followed, nor was the organization of the cooperatives preceded, by land reform. Before embarking on the task of building socialist institutions in agriculture one would have expected the LPDR to have put an end to some of the overt features of unequal land ownership, viz. absentee ownership, tenancy, sharecropping and wage-labor. In reality these institutions have been allowed to continue to exist. . . . This is almost certainly proving to be a major obstacle in the way of socialist transformation." The authors go on to argue that an egalitarian land reform program would create "a genuine grassroots demand for cooperation" and suggest that unless such a reform is carried out the "large private owners" will take over the cooperatives if they enter them or subvert them from without if they do not.[3] Another author, Hans Luther, argues that because the Lao government has not adopted this strategy it will soon see "rising social stratification and a growing income gap . . . among the different groups of the population."[4] There is no good empirical evidence for any of these claims, and Lao peasant society has remained remarkably undifferentiated.

Livestock

Other authors have suggested that exclusive attention to land area (leaving aside different land uses) can be a misleading index of stratification in the countryside. Athar Hussain and Keith Tribe have claimed that land statistics occupy a favored place in discussions of stratification because they are usually all that are registered, especially in historical records. "One reason is obviously that while property in land in most countries occupies a privileged status and is thus registered and documented, the same is not true for agricultural implements, livestock and other things which as well as land have an important bearing on the characteristics of the farm."[5] These means of production are important to an analysis of social relations in the countryside. Hussain and Tribe cite a study from Russia in the early 1920s which claimed that between one-half and two-thirds of all peasant holdings did not possess a full inventory of equipment, which they therefore had to lease.[6] Their example fails to demonstrate, however, that the peasants' shortage of implements and livestock was a long-term tendency toward peasant social differentiation rather than a direct result of the disruptions of the civil war.

The keeping of livestock and draft animals is a particularly problematic feature of the peasants' economy because, as Chayanov observed, "livestock is one of the most mobile of the peasant farm elements that comprise its fixed capital, for it can easily be sold on the market and without great loss in price."[7] Although livestock is a popular way of storing wealth among peasants, its viability is determined by availability of fodder and grazing areas. It may, for example, be more economically rational to sink surpluses into gold or silver. Given the relatively low and seasonal use of draft animals, expensive fodder may make their upkeep more costly than hiring them seasonally, even at a high price. This, comments Chayanov, leads to paradoxical situations in which "a semi-proletarianized family hired a rich peasant" to do the plowing on their farm.[8] Other combinations are possible, but the example illustrates the potential complexity of social relations among the peasantry.

Reactions to the new regime may have slightly modified tendencies to invest surpluses in land. Because landownership is subject to limitations of size, is subject to tax, is easily collectivized, and is not mobile or easily liquidated if under threat of expropriation some peasant economic activity was redirected toward livestock raising, which is possible in Laos because reasonable amounts of grazing land (compared with neighboring Thailand) still exist. Nevertheless, there is little evidence to suggest that livestock holding became a new source of inequality or differentiation in Lao villages. Figures for both buffalo and cattle ownership among 140 households on the Vientiane Plain (table 4.4) do not suggest serious maldistribution of livestock within villages, although significant disparities are visible between villages, differences that are easily explained by the more favorable

TABLE 4.4. Buffalo and Cattle Ownership

Variable	Year	Category 1[a]	Category 2[b]	Category 3[c]	Total
Number of households		15	84	41	140
Number with	1983	15	76	40	131
buffalo	1985	14	76	39	129
Buffalo per	1983	2.3	3.6	4.8	3.8
household	1985	3.8	3.9	5.5	4.4
Number with	1983	3	55	33	91
cattle	1985	8	55	32	95
Cattle per	1983	2.7	5.8	7.0	6.2
household	1985	2.4	6.0	5.2	5.4

[a]Category 1 households rely on upland rice and have little or no marketable surplus.
[b]Category 2, lowland, rainfed rice producing a small surplus.
[c]Category 3, lowland, rainfed rice producing a marketable surplus.

production environment in category 3 villages. Distribution of draft animals is remarkably even, and only a tiny fraction of households—10 out of 140—have no buffaloes. Fewer households—some 45 out of 140—own cattle, and their distribution suggests that they are indeed used as repositories of wealth by farmers producing a marketable rice surplus. The opportunity costs of this function appear to have shifted slightly as households in the more densely settled category 3 villages responded to forage shortages by owning fewer cattle, while farmers in category 1 villages, closer to upland grazing, increased their cattle holdings.

Cattle trading is an important activity for Lao peasants—even for those with insufficient land in densely settled areas. It is important in muang Hatsayfong because the main abattoir serving Vientiane is located there. Until January 1985 the abattoir was run by the state-controlled Society of Foodstuffs, which bought animals to be sold as meat in the state shop system. The society accounted for only about 10 percent of the output at the abattoir, the rest being taken up by private traders and middlemen occupying different positions in the marketing network. This network illegally traded into Thailand as much as 15 percent of the cattle and buffalo that came onto the Vientiane provincial market. In December 1982 the government attempted to bring the network under its control by stopping private trading and creating two cooperatives. One was primarily responsible for bovine trade, the other for pigs. At the center of these cooperatives were the merchants who previously had engaged in animal trade full time but who were now required to invest their funds in the cooperatives. The Vientiane Provincial Government Trading Society set the farm gate price for these cooperatives and the consumer price for meat. The cooperatives were disbanded in 1984, and each district was asked to set up its own cooperatives with responsibility for trading within its district, although there is considerable flexibility in trading across districts.

Cattle trading is an important activity among farmers of the muang because of the presence of the abattoir, and the turnover of animals had to be high because there was little land in the area that could be used to graze permanent herds. The beasts were either traded into the area to be sold for meat or first used to plow fields and then sold for meat. Peasants at ban Don Dou who live around the abattoir have arrangements with state/private merchant enterprises to graze animals waiting to be killed. One peasant said this job was done by his little boy, who at that moment had four buffalo in his care. The man and his son were expected to feed the animals hay, and for their services were paid a fixed rate per day per animal. Cattle and buffalo trading was also one of the main activities engaged in during slack periods by Thao Boun, the director of ban Thana cooperative in 1983. Families wishing to trade had to register with the muang for 50 kip, he said, and they could then sell their meat in the markets in Vientiane after having them killed. He claimed he traded 30–45 cattle or buffalo per month, each animal costing between 15,000 and 25,000 kip. His costs per animal were a 650-kip turnover tax and a 10-kip health check. Of approximately 750,000-kip turnover per month in slack periods he claims he netted between 3,000 and 4,000 kip per month, or around 1 percent profit on total turnover. This was a healthy supplement to his income from the cooperative.

Access to buffalo traded into the muang, combined with the relative shortage of grazing area, explains the relatively low levels of buffalo and cattle ownership in the district. Thus only 36 percent of households owned buffalo (an average 2.8 head per household) and only 22 percent of households owned cattle (an average of 3 head per household). Thus neither buffalo nor cattle were an important source of social differentiation in this area. Privately owned tractors were nonexistent.

A Rural Proletariat

The resettling of internal refugees and the departure of Lao refugees and northern Thai depleted the pool of available wage labor; in addition, communist suspicions of those using wage laborers weakened tendencies that encouraged the growth of rural or, indeed, urban capitalists.

Yet a considerable number of immigrants from Thailand remained in Laos. Some had married into families there, others had no land to return to in Thailand because land pressure had made them emigrate in the first place. Most people in the area know ban Don Dou in tasseng Bo-O as an immigrants' village because many people from Issan and Xieng Khouang live there. There are other people from Issan scattered through the other villages of the muang, and often they are landless. One of the most down-and-out characters I encountered happened to be a man who had emigrated from Issan in the late 1960s and subsequently worked for USAID in Laos. He had lost his job in 1975 and since then had scrounged work in and around Vientiane in order to make a living. On four of the five occasions I met him he was drunk; on the fourth he had a bloodied nose from a drunken brawl. The next time I saw him he was cleaned up, sober, and sweeping the floor of the tasseng office, having been brought in for corrective work as a result of the fight. Such incidents are rare. And, compared with other Asian countries, Laos has few destitute people.

Migration was a critical variable in Chayanov's scheme of peasant differentiation because it took pressure off the land and allowed the process of demographic differentiation to operate in a "purer" form. The return of internal refugees, the return of Thai laborers to Thailand, and the departure of many Lao as a result of the worsening economic conditions in the country after 1975 all contributed to the reassertion of the demographic process.

The Occupational Structure

What was the occupational structure of those who remained in Laos and close to Vientiane? The occupational distribution in villages farthest from Vientiane and other urban centers in Laos shows an overwhelming preponderance of peasants (80–90 percent) and a rudimentary division of labor as one would expect in a still predominantly natural economy. In villages closer to urban centers the occupational structure is more complex. Taillard's survey of ban Hat Kansa in Hatsayfong district shows only 40 percent of the households engaged in farming, the rest being employed in occupations generated by petty commodity production, commerce, and the urban economy and the state. Surveys undertaken since 1975 indicate a growth in the proportion of people engaged in farming, compared with Hat Kansa before 1975, which is probably a consequence of the contraction of the urban economy (fig. 4.2 and table 4.5).

The influence of the urban economy on the occupational structure of these villages, as compared with those situated farther from the capital, is marked. Significantly, the survey by Mukherjee and Jose found that less than 1 percent of the economically active people in the district claimed to be out of work and seeking employment. In other words, unemployment was close to zero.

Few people were exclusively rural wage laborers. Tasseng officials in Bo-O estimated that only fifteen families out of 1,147 in the tasseng could be considered full-time rural wage laborers, that is, 1.3 percent. Yet there was a lot of wage labor undertaken in the area, and many people were dependent on several activities to earn a living because the influx of relatives and "immigrants" into the area had led to a parcelization of land. Weaving and gardening provided many people with a mainstay; without them, they would have been compelled to leave the area. People with small

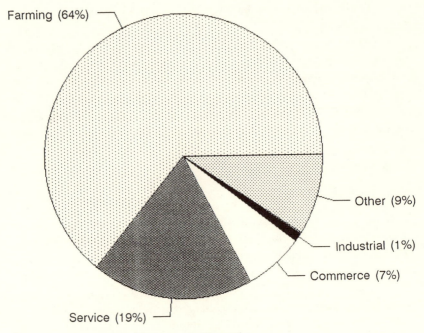

Farming (64%)

Other (9%)

Industrial (1%)

Commerce (7%)

Service (19%)

Figure 4.2 Occupational Structure in Hatsayfong

plots engage in wage labor for others after they have finished work on their own paddy fields, but the work is intermittent and whether they do this kind of work or engage in petty trading instead largely depends on circumstances and opportunities. Wage laborers also move in and out of petty trading, according to the availability of work.

Asked to comment on how conditions had changed for wage laborers under the new regime, local officials—at least the more politically attuned of them—answered that the main difference was that people who hired laborers had to work in the fields alongside them and could not perform a purely supervisory role. The latter was considered typical of "capitalism." Although this notion of capitalism is too restrictive, it does indicate the obstacles to gentleman farming in Laos after 1975. Theoretically, laborers were to be paid in kind rather than in cash, that is, directly out of the proceeds of the harvest. This stipulation was part of the government's endeavor to stimulate "collective" forms of productive organization in which people "shared out" the efforts of their labor, but, if anything, it

TABLE 4.5. Sectoral Distribution of the Labor Force

Sector	Estimated Proportion (%)		
	Male	Female	Total
Agriculture	55.6	69.5	62.2
Fisheries	0.8	—	0.4
Forestry	0.4	—	0.2
Manufacturing	0.8	4.7	2.6
Electricity and water	0.4	—	0.2
Construction	0.4	0.8	0.6
Trade	2.6	15.7	8.8
Transport, storage, and communication	14.3	5.1	10.0
Professional, technical, and civil service	23.6	4.2	14.5
Other	1.1	—	0.5
All sectors	100	100	100

Source: Chandan Mukherjee and A. V. Jose, *Report of a Survey of Rural Households in the Hat Xai Fong District in Vientiane Province of the Lao People's Democratic Republic* (Bangkok: ILO-ARTEP, October 1982), 17.

encouraged barter aspects of the natural economy. In fact, labor is paid both in cash and in kind.

Cash Income

Income levels are one indicator of social differentiation, although they are only a partial one because they do not take into account the level of self-sufficiency of peasant households. The following average income statistics gathered in Hatsayfong and Saysatane districts in Vientiane province in 1979 (table 4.6) are of only limited value because they are not correlated with family size or sources of income, and we are given no indication of the occupational status of the different households. We do know from the occupational distribution given in figure 4.2 that only about 60 percent of them could be full-time farmers. These figures do not show a drastic polarization of wealth in the community, and distribution is biased toward the middle range.

A survey of two hundred households in Hatsayfong district (1982)

TABLE 4.6. Income Distribution in Two Villages

Kip/Month	Number of Families		Percent of Families		
	Muang Hatsayfong	Muang Saysatane	Muang Hatsayfong	Muang Saysatane	Average
0–25,000	47	49	35	28	31
25–30,000	70	115	53	65	60
50,000 +	15	12	12	7	9

Source: *Vientiane Plain Rural Electrification Project* (Final Report to the Asian Development Bank, May 1980).

[a]These figures are for Liberation Kip (KL), brought into operation in the lowland areas in mid-1976. A currency swap to New Kip took place in December 1979. The official exchange rate for KL was revised to 400 per US dollar in May 1978. The open market price was usually fluctuating. Thus the real value of the kip on the open market was lower than the official figure indicates, and although the official value of 50,000KL would have been $125.00 US, its real value would have been significantly less.

discovered an average annual income of 16,000 kip. Households engaged predominantly in trade (16.3 percent) reported the highest incomes, averaging 37,000 kip, of which 88 percent was accounted for by trading income, with wages and salaries being the next most significant source. Farmers who were "members of cooperatives" (51.5 percent of households) reported the next highest average income, 14,654 kip.[9] Significantly, although income from the "cooperative" was the single major source for these households, it accounted for only 40 percent of total household income, with trade and other enterprises accounting for 21 percent, wages and salaries 16 percent, and sales of homegrown agricultural products 17 percent. Wage and salary earner households (19.8 percent) received on average 10,781 kip, and 89 percent of this was accounted for by salaries, with petty trade, sales of garden produce, and rent accounting for the rest. "Self-cultivators" (12.4 percent of households) earned on average 5,496 kip, of which the sale of agricultural produce amounted to 46 percent, rent from land or houses 33 percent, and wages and salaries only 10 percent.

There are significant income differentials in the district, but these do not seem to be a direct consequence of differential access to land and means of production. Trading households, for example, earn only 2 percent of their income from rent or the hiring out of animals. For those households engaged primarily in agricultural activities the differences between "members of cooperatives" and "self-cultivators" are not a result of the latter engaging in wage labor, for example. On the contrary, wages form a small part of their income, with rent comprising a much higher proportion. This suggests that elderly, semiretired farmers, along with female-headed households, make up a significant proportion of these households.

Clearly, households in the area engage in a range of economic activities to make ends meet. In most lowland villages, women, helped by their children and sometimes their husband, keep tiny roadside stalls in which they sell cigarettes, sweets, perhaps *Khao Poon* (a rice vermicelli), and miscellaneous items purchased in neighboring towns or provincial centers. Most families keep some chickens or pigs and tend vegetable or fruit gardens of various sizes. All lowland peasants, landed or otherwise, have diverse sources of livelihood, and their work activity each day is spread over several different, but vital, tasks. Households close to the capital whose primary activity is agriculture, for example, rely on trade and wages and salaries to account for 30 percent of their cash earnings. But these activities were seasonal for most households (table 4.7).

A *"Proletarian"* Village

The "immigrant" village of Don Dou is the "proletarian" village of tasseng Bo-O. It is recently settled compared with the long-established villages of

TABLE 4.7. Nonagricultural Economic Activities

Activities All Households	Proportion of Households Engaged in Activity	Proportion Reporting Seasonal	Average Number Persons Engaged	Average Annual Income (kip)
Processing and manufacture	8.4	52.9	1.7	6,008
Trade	13.4	44.4	1.4	18,876
Transport	9.9	10.0	1.4	10,205
Services	2.5	20.0	1.2	7,570

Source: Chandan Mukherjee and A. V. Jose, *Report of a Survey of Rural Households in the Hat Xai Fong District in Vientiane Province, Lao People's Democratic Republic,* (Bangkok: ILO-ARTEP, March 1982), 28.

ban Thana, ban Bo-O, and ban Nok, which hug the Mekong River. Dtoo Khai was the first person to settle at the present site of Don Dou, in the late 1950s. Then, he recalled, the forest there still contained deer, and Chaynamo military camp was still a monkey forest. A few years later four to six other families moved onto the uncleared land. Chaloen, a former RLG policeman, was the head of one of these families, and he moved there in 1963. Both founding members agreed that it was the establishment of the military camp nearby, a result of the escalating civil war, that rapidly brought change to their "settler" environment. Soldiers from the camp began to clear the trees and build houses for their families. They were followed by refugees from the strife, especially people from Xieng Khouang. Don Dou's population grew, and by the end of the 1960s it began to be recognized as a village in its own right. The Buddhist vat reflects the poverty of the village, for if it were wealthy it would have a *sim*, or temple. In this respect it remains a subvillage of ban Thana. Few households in the village possess sufficient land because the paddy fields were already occupied by peasants in the older, established villages of the tasseng. Don Dou has low status as a village because land is the key to status in the rural society. Only twenty-two of the villages's eighty-seven families are predominantly peasant families; the rest work in Vientiane or in the abattoir established in Don Dou in the late 1960s or are itinerant laborers and traders in the rural or urban areas or soldiers.

One would expect that Don Dou, as a poor village, would show some support for the government's collectivization program, as it promised to give landless or land-short peasants secure access to land. Don Dou cooperative was initially formed by mainly landless peasants, not landed private peasants who had "flocked" to join the cooperative. In my initial interview with Thit Ngai, the director of the cooperative in Don Dou, I was assured that all peasants in the village were in the cooperative, but this was soon shown to be an opening gambit to demonstrate total support for government policy in the village. At this first encounter Ngai assured me that no one had ever left the cooperative—this was not true either but, again, was probably designed to demonstrate the "revolutionary" credentials of the cooperative.[10]

Three of the four cooperatives I surveyed in muang Hatsayfong were composed mainly of landless or land-short peasants. For example, in dry season 1983 the ban Thana cooperative had seventeen families, only three of whom had land. Most landowning peasants left the cooperatives after

1980, but according to Thao Boun, the director of ban Thana cooperative in 1983, landless peasants remained in the cooperatives because the alternative for them was wage labor. In ban Nok there were two cooperatives, one for landed peasants and one for peasants short of land.

A Poor Villager

Real poverty and marginality are not unknown in Lao villages, as the family of Loong Tha in ban Nok demonstrates. He and his family had moved into the village as recently as 1980 from a village fifteen kilometers northwest of Vientiane. He and his wife said they had moved from their old village because they did not have enough male workers in the family and the wife had only one sister in her maternal village. They moved to ban Nok because Loong Tha had relatives there who were better off. However, the move had not proven successful. His relatives had allowed them to work on their land only occasionally because, his wife claimed, the relatives did not like associating with poor people like themselves.

Although others in the village put Loong Tha and his family in the rural wage laborer category, he had in fact worked as an assistant at the main hospital in Vientiane for thirty-eight years. He was in semiretirement because of illness, a factor that had led to his move to ban Nok so he could be nearer the hospital. It was his family's poverty, not his occupational status, that had caused other peasants to single him out. His lack of land along with his semiretired status placed him in the poorest stratum of the village. There were ten members in the family, but only the wife and two daughters were able to work. Two teenage sons worked for a rice miller in the village in return for food and board. These boys sometimes dropped in to eat and more rarely to help the family in the fields. In this example—and in these processes—we can begin to see the disintegration of a poor peasant family through a mechanism common to Laos and Thailand. Writing of Thailand, where forms of debt bondage have been common, Lucien Hanks observed, "The departing ones recognize their peripheral position under a given roof, since the most dispensable person had to be chosen from among many, yet leaving for a better opportunity in another area also signifies a parent's concern for a child's well-being. A Bang-Chan rice grower, telling of his childhood, upbraided his parents for refusing to give him into the care of a powerful government official who wanted to adopt him. The storyteller

81

commented, 'My parents could not have loved me very much.' "[11] The disintegration of the poorest families in villages was one mechanism, Chayanov argued, that reinforced demographic rather than social differentiation.

It was really Loong Tha's wife and daughters who were the "rural proletarians." Yet on closer inspection they were seen to be sometimes tenant farmers. In the wet season of 1981 the wife had rented land from Loong Tha's elder sister, but without the normal concessions for relatives—which was undoubtedly why the wife felt the husband's relatives had treated them badly. Nang Thong, the elder sister, supplied buffalo, plow, and seed and split the crop 50/50—the same percentage that was in force before 1975. In the dry season of 1981–82 they worked as casual laborers for the landowning cooperative in ban Nok and were paid in rice. During the wet season of 1982 they worked as wage laborers not only for the same cooperative but for anyone who would give them work. During the 1983 dry season they had teamed up with a "collective" at ban Don Kha Xay. Overall their returns had been just adequate, and Loong Tha still received a monthly allowance of thirty kilograms of rice from the hospital. The family earned some cash income from one of their three buffalo. Two were females which they did not wish to work because they hoped to use them for breeding. Occasionally they earned cash income from selling Khao Poon at *bouns* (weddings or religious festivals). For an outlay of 12 kip on a kilo of rice they made 40–50-kip profit, but it was a very irregular source of income. The family does not borrow money, and Loong Tha claimed they used little cash. Asked why the family had not joined the landless cooperative in ban Nok Loong Tha gave a reply that reflected even the poor peasants' ambivalence toward this form of agricultural organization. He wanted to be a cooperative member and to work elsewhere as well, he said. The cooperative, however, had insisted that if his family joined they would have to commit themselves entirely or not at all. (It should be noted that he was speaking for his wife and daughters, who would in fact have been the real cooperative workers had they joined; his wife nodded her assent.) In other words, the cooperative structure was perceived by this household as too inflexible. The example of Loong Tha shows how difficult it is to crisply delineate a proletarian stratum or class in an overwhelmingly peasant economy. The poorest members of rural society engage in a great variety of activities that constantly change in response to opportunities— according to the season, market situation, or perhaps even time of day.

The importance of gathering and hunting activities in settled peasant societies (especially to poor peasants) should not be overlooked. Naturally the contribution of these activities declines rapidly in areas long settled and subject to population pressure and where game has been forced out—as has happened in this tasseng over the past twenty to thirty years. A study of Tha Deua, located some thirty to forty kilometers from Vientiane, observed the following: "In all the villages, except for ban Khouey and ban Simano, the farmers interviewed said that they no longer go hunting because game is so rare. In ban Khouey and ban Simano, hunting is done collectively. The villagers go into the neighboring forests in groups of 30–50. In these two villages deer, wild boar, roebucks, and hares are killed. Afterwards the game is shared between the hunters and is eaten by them. But it is no longer a common phenomenon."[12] Birds are a common source of game, and before transplanting children scour the fields with woven baskets for small shrimps and crabs. Fishing, either in the Mekong or in irrigation channels, is a vital source of food. After the fields are prepared in the dry season, for example, men will often spend a large part of each day laboriously rowing back and forth in the swift-flowing river casting their net. The women at ban Nok spend many hours fishing from the banks of the river with large square nets suspended from poles.

In the remote villages of Laos, such as those of the Black Tai in the mountain valleys of Houa Phan province, game hunting remains a vital economic activity. Wild deer is especially prized. Gathering, a task that most often falls to women, is also an important economic activity among these peasants. A study of the precise nature of peasant gathering in Laos is being compiled by Carol Ireson, who described her observations of groups of women moving slowly through the forest "grazing," or gathering foods and resources crucial to their family's welfare.[13] In fact, the economy of many Lao villages resembles that of "tribal" horticultural societies.

Weaving and Petty Commodity Production

Weaving is an indispensable income-producing activity in the villages of ban Thana and Bo-O. Few women in Don Dou wove because, as the women there explained, they had simply never learned. In ban Thana, on the other hand, it was a major economic activity for women. Weaving had been declining rapidly in the late 1950s as a result of import competition. The decline accelerated in the 1960s, and weaving almost disappeared around Vientiane. This situation changed radically after the communist takeover. Restrictions on imports and government control of foreign trade revived the weaving cottage industry to the point that as published in a study in 1980, 75 percent of households surveyed in Vientiane province were engaged in some weaving—this compared with the diametrically opposite observation of Kaufman in the late 1950s.[14] Weaving was further stimulated by the government's initial ideological nationalism, which frowned on Western dress for women, especially trousers, and encouraged them instead to wear the traditional, modest shin-length *sin* woven out of cotton or silk. One of the most immediate and visible contrasts between Laos and Thailand since 1975 has been the traditionalism of Lao women's dress and hairstyles and the modernity of Thai styles. Since the introduction of new economic policies after 1987, which has caused a rapid growth of trade with Thailand and a certain cultural relaxation, this contrast has blurred.

Weaving is an exclusively female occupation, and customarily a very young girl learns it from her mother. The girl learns how to prepare the spindles and the dyes and then how to spin cotton and later perhaps silk. Traditionally, weaving was a purely domestic occupation, but much of the weaving practiced in ban Thana and Bo-O resembles the "putting out" system of the early stage of manufacture prior to the industrial revolution in Europe. For example, Dao, the wife of the accountant at ban Thana cooperative, owned five hand looms and employed five young women to work for her. Her task was dyeing and pattern design, marketing, and supervision. Her raw material, both cotton and silk, came from a Thai trader operating out of Nong Khai (his business was made possible by liberalization of trade after December 1979). He supplied a Lao dealer at Vientiane's "Morning Market," who then distributed the raw material to looms in outlying villages, collected woven garments, and paid for them.

The lucrativeness of weaving can be gauged by the following figures. Payments are given in Thai *baht* as well as Lao kip because the weavers themselves calculate their earnings in both currencies. They arrange some payment in baht because this allows them to trade goods in from Thailand. Dao said she made 2,000–3,000 baht (8,820–13,230 kip) per month in 1982–83, with the upper range calculated on the assumption that her workshop produced only silk sins. For example, a silk sin retailed for 220 baht, making a set of twenty worth 4,400 baht. The trader gives her 25 percent of their retail value, or 1,100 baht. Out of this she pays the women who work for her 500 baht per set, leaving the balance of 600 baht for herself. Each girl or woman can make four to seven sins a week, though the average is four. Thus the workers make about 500 baht every five weeks when weaving silk sins. Assuming that five sets of sins are made every five weeks, this would net 3,000 baht for Dao as owner of the workshop. However, they also weave cotton sins, which go mainly to the local market and retail at 300 kip (68 baht). These can be done more quickly, and Dao nets approximately 1,700 baht, or 7,749 kip, per month. The workshop produces both types of sin in response to external demand; therefore, Dao's income varies between 2,000 and 3,000 baht per month. Weaving is probably the most significant form of petty commodity production in the area and is far more important than what goes on in agriculture. It was in this type of manufacture—that in which "one capitalist simultaneously employs in one workshop a number of craftsmen who all do the same work, or the same kind of work"[15]—that Marx saw the beginning of a distinctly capitalist division of labor. The division of labor in Dao's workshop, however, is very rudimentary, and her position approximately that of master craftswoman rather than capitalist entrepreneur. Work discipline is a far cry from that in the factory system, and hours and output are negotiable and flexible.

Sheltered from import competition and unchallenged by local technological innovations, the workshops in the muang experience no strong economic forces pushing them beyond the stage of manufacture. However, if these forces developed in Laos, petty producers wishing to move beyond cottage industry would probably be compelled to enter into some kind of arrangement, perhaps joint production, with the state or to form a cooperative. It is clear that even in an activity in which we can identify "spontaneous" tendencies toward capitalist production, the current political structure in Laos inhibits it or, more benignly, channels it.

Dao's profits were largely consumed or sunk into precious metals or jewelry, and she trades in cattle and buffalo. In early 1983 she had five buffalo (tended by her husband and children) that she hired out to other farmers, including the cooperative of ban Thana. She is well off, but as yet there is little that is immediately recognizable as capitalist accumulation. Most significantly, the workshop closes down during the planting and harvesting seasons, when the women are required to work in the fields. The priority of rice cultivation over commercially oriented weaving shows how even this operation is geared to the economic activity of the whole household.[16]

Domestic weaving plays an important role in maintaining smallholding peasants. For example, in dry season 1983 one peasant woman, Malithong, formerly a member of ban Thana cooperative, was cultivating a private plot of 2,760 square meters. This area, she claimed, covered her needs and saved her from having to buy rice on the open market. The plot yielded 770 kg in the 1981–82 dry season and 560 kg in the wet season. Malithong being a widow with five children to support, this total averaged 221 kg per person for the year, considerably below the target of 350 kg per person set by the government. Yet the plot came close to covering household needs, and weaving covered any shortfall and provided cash income. Malithong, like Dao, had an arrangement with a trader from Vientiane. She claimed she could make one set of sins every twenty-five days and said she received 1,200 baht for them, slightly more than Dao. Her seventeen- and fourteen-year-old daughters helped in their spare time, but her permanent helper was a twenty-three-year-old daughter, who she said had been badly retarded by an attack of *falciparum* malaria yet was able to perform repetitive tasks like preparing spindles.

In more isolated communities in Laos the importance of domestic weaving has never faltered. Among the Black Tai, for example, cotton is grown, harvested, spun, woven, and dyed by each family. This supplies not only most of the wardrobe of these people, but also material for the woven partitions in the house and for bedding. Although most households now possess at least some articles of manufactured clothing from either Thailand or Vietnam, they are remarkably self-sufficient.

Ceremonial Redistribution

Before 1975 surpluses among Buddhist Lao were often directed into maintaining the vat, and ceremonial expenses and expenditures on festivals are a well-established means of redistributing wealth in Lao villages. By contributing to the vat, the donor acquires religious merit and social prestige. Bouns, which are forms of ceremonial consumption, also earn prestige for the host. Christian Taillard comments on the importance of these celebrations:

> The dynamic of the boun overcomes antagonisms and contributes to the *piep* (good-will) of social life. The individual who accumulates more material goods than others, even at their expense, will then have them redistributed among the community through the vat. This levels individual wealth and maintains a socio-economic equilibrium between the various households. By transposing social competition from

a material plane to a spiritual plane, the vat establishes a new logic of prestige: the more this is striven for the more wealth is redistributed and the more solidarity is reinforced. Thus a dynamic of redistribution is established whereby competition is no longer a problem but in fact reinforces village solidarity.[17]

The boun continues to fulfill this role in communist Laos.

One *boun khong bouat* in ban Thana was a good example of the ceremonial liquidation of wealth. This is a boun for the induction of a monk into the *sangha,* the organization of the Buddhist priesthood. It was given by an elderly widow in memory of her husband, and her youthful son was becoming a monk to acquire merit for her. The boun lasted two days. The first day was taken up with the preparation of the food and gifts to be presented to the Sangha at the vat the following day, the shaving of the youth's head, well-wishing, and praying. The men prepare the *Phasat,* a religious offering made of palm and beeswax, to which money is appended, while women prepare the food and villagers help in the general preparations. The bulk of the expense falls on the person hosting the boun, but relatives are also called on to make contributions. This particular boun khong bouat cost 280,000 kip (US$2,800). Matched against the annual earnings of the very highest income earners in the village, this amounts to approximately five years' cash income expended on one festival. The minimum expended is 30,000 kip, and there are around thirty boun khong bouat in the tasseng per year, in addition to other festival outlays. This alone shows that considerable wealth continues to be "unproductively" consumed in contemporary Laos, despite early government calls for thrift.[18]

Wealth is also outlaid on the upkeep of the vats or the building of new ones. For example, on the far side of ban Nok a craftsman and his assistant were employed full-time constructing a six-meter-high Buddha adjacent to an existing vat in early 1983. A common view is that people no longer have enough money for the vat as they did before 1975 and that what they have must be spent on consumer items. The old nai ban of Don Dou, Dtoo Khai, an active parishioner, complained about this because he wished for a better vat in the village. Ngai, the head of the cooperative in Don Dou, also claimed that there had been a significant decline in the number of ceremonies related to the agricultural cycle since 1975. Asked if this was a product of government discouragement, he replied that one's empty stomach was the main reason because a boun could cost up to three or four months of a farmer's income. It appears, however, that after 1975 there was less social pressure on people to compete for prestige by throwing bouns, partly as a result of government discouragement and partly because people did not wish to draw the state's attention to any wealth they may have possessed. One could, perhaps, argue that by frowning on the "wastefulness" of religious ceremonies the government inhibited a leveling mechanism in the Lao village.

In my early interviews with him, Ngai boasted that only the cooperatives had big enough yields to throw bouns, whereas in the past it was the better-off peasants. Here the head of a cooperative was dreaming the dream of a traditional peasant because he had already claimed that the cooperative spent little on religious activities. When the cooperative shed was first completed, monks were brought in and a ceremony held to bless it. It would seem that if the "socialist" peasantry had their way, Buddhism, with its notion of individual merit-making, could be made to recognize collective merit-making, but what would become of socialist accumulation then? After all, one reason the state wishes to gather peasants into cooperatives is so that these can function as instruments for collectively accumulating capital and investing it.

In Laos several economic systems in operation interact and compete with one another: the peasant natural economy, petty commodity production, socialist and capitalist economies. The official government position is that there are five sectors in the economy: the state economy; the collective economy; the individual economy; the capitalist economy; the state-capitalist economy, representing joint state–private enterprise. Members of peasant households could find themselves in any one of these systems, or occasionally one individual may transit between them according to the seasons.

The labor requirements of rice agriculture among lowland peasants are intensive but intermittent, and hence there is considerable scope for surplus household labor to engage in petty commodity production, petty trading, or commercial gardening, among other occupations. This is true for areas that double crop and even more so for those areas able to produce only one crop a year. As Francesca Bray has written, "The organization of resources typical of 'skill-oriented' technology such as intensive rice-farming dovetails very neatly with petty commodity production, which requires very little capital to set up a family enterprise, and absorbs surplus labor without depriving the farm of workers at times of peak demand. It can be expanded, diversified or contracted to meet market demands, but the combination with the rice-farm guarantees the family's existence."[19] The initial policies of the Lao government depressed all of these vital supplementary activities of the peasant economy, and only in recent years have they been allowed to flourish again.

The initial clampdown on petty commerce especially affected the land-short and landless peasants in the densely settled areas of Laos around Vientiane and other provincial centers. Diverse economic activities are fundamental to the viability of small plots and to peasant hopes of earning income with which they can either acquire land or buy more. The contraction of this part of the rural economy caused many poor peasants to quit the country as refugees. It also meant, as we shall see in the following chapter, that initially many poor peasants looked to the collectivization program to provide them with secure access to adequate land and income.

There is little evidence to suggest that capitalist development in the countryside fared any better after the communist takeover than before it. The impact of the revolution on the countryside strengthened the natural economy and the forces underlying demographic differentiation of the peasantry. The few technological innovations introduced into the rural areas, such as irrigation, increased the viability of small farms and therefore their ability to support a denser population. Irrigation also allowed the application of fertilizer and the utilization of high-yielding varieties of rice, such as the glutinous *San Pathong* in the wet season and various non-glutinous varieties in the dry season. For some farmers, including the cooperatives, this lifted yields from 1–1.5 tons per hectare to 3–4 tons in good seasons. Increased overall yields also made small holdings more viable for subsistence needs, and such intensification of production favored tendencies toward demographic rather than social differentiation.

Stratification continues to exist but tendencies toward its becoming fixed in class forms specific to capitalism have become more remote. Members of households engaged in bewildering combinations of occupations, and as government policy liberalized even wider opportunities opened up. The search for possible tendencies toward capitalist development in the countryside has thus revealed a reinvigorated Lao peasant society. I now turn to the new government's attempts to encourage the formation of "socialist" social relations in the rural areas.

5

"The System of Civilized Cooperators is the System of Socialism"

 The new communist government, as we have seen, unwittingly strengthened many features of the traditional peasant economy. It has simultaneously promoted new social relations of production, the agricultural cooperative, and a new social class, the "collective peasantry," with the aim of creating Lenin's "system of civilized cooperators."[1] The Provisional Regulations of Cooperatives stated, "An agricultural cooperative is a socialist collective economic organization set up by laboring farmers of various nationalities of their own free will under the leadership of the LPRP and with the advice and assistance of the state" (SWB, 24 June 1978).

As I outlined in chapter 3, the Lao government was guided by a commandist model of the economy when it began its drive to introduce large-scale collectivist agriculture. In almost all respects this was impossible in Laos, and therefore the government had to modify its general economic strategy and policies in favor of a market-oriented socialism. It took some time, however, to erase the imprint of the earlier model from official descriptions of the cooperatives. This chapter discusses the formation and progressive demise of several cooperatives. Three distinct phases can be isolated: the first, foundation of the cooperatives during the campaign of 1978–79; the second, exodus from the cooperatives following the suspension of the campaign in mid-1979; the third, government weakening of its institutional support for producer cooperatives, beginning around 1983–

84, followed by the reformulation of the whole cooperative strategy in 1988.

Cooperative Aims

Legal property relations in the LPDR remained unclear for twelve years. In its early years the government was deliberately vague about the legal status of private property in land. To some extent this was a subterfuge because the government did not wish to panic peasants into thinking that their land would be summarily confiscated, yet it was planning collectivization. Only in 1988 did Kaysone give a clear indication of the legal status of land: "Under our new system, the entire land is the common property of the entire society with the state as the representative. . . . The state recognizes the legal rights of farmers' families to use the land they possess for cultivation purposes" (*SWB*, 25 February 1988). This de facto recognition of the private peasantry by the state nevertheless attempts to circumscribe accumulation of land by asserting that the state has final legal title.

The Provisional Regulations of Cooperatives of 1978 set out the following conditions for cooperative membership:

> After being accepted as a member of a cooperative, cooperative members must hand over their cultivated and farm lands and primary means of production to the cooperative to be used in carrying out production. . . . With regard to cultivated and farm land which is given to the cooperative by cooperative members, if cooperative members agree to give such land to the cooperatives free, then it is not necessary for the cooperatives to pay anything; but if the cooperative members ask for payment for their land, the congress of cooperative members must agree on terms. However the amount of money that shall be paid to the cooperative members for their land must not exceed 7% to 15% of the value of crops that can be harvested from the land at the time it is handed over to the cooperative. [*SWB*, 24 June 1978]

Because adherence to the cooperative is voluntary and "members may resign . . . in order to return to private production or move to other areas," the commitment of land is not permanent. Individual peasants retain proprietary rights over land contributed to the cooperative and draw rent from it over and above their remuneration for work as a normal cooperative member. Members can also receive rent for other means of production, such as buffalo. Thus cooperative property is only temporarily "group property" and may change its composition from year to year or even from season to season. The cooperative has no legal claim to the land contributed, and it exercises control over it only for as long as the member wishes to stay. Resignations must be approved by the congress of cooperative members, which could perhaps delay a resignation but formally cannot refuse a request to resign. Social pressure could probably be brought to bear on the individual peasant to stay, but the cooperative's ability to do this depends on the general balance of social forces and opinion in the village.

The original provisional regulations were vague about whether cooperative members had to contribute all of their land, including private gardens, if they joined. Gardens seemed to be implied in the statement "The cooperative may distribute part of the land to the families of cooperative members to plant fruit trees, vegetables, other crops or for livestock breeding in their individual families." While the intent of this was perhaps for the cooperative to give gardens to members without them, it could also be interpreted as the cooperative taking charge of all landholdings, including gardens, and then redistributing them to individual families. The ambiguity is not removed by point 5 in the regulations, which says the members have a right "to maintain the family's secondary economic activities according to the suggestion of the cooperative." Given the commandist ideas prevalent at the time of the collectivization drive in mid-1978 cadres were probably inclined to interpret these ambiguities in the most "revolutionary" way to include gardens, and no doubt this accounts for scattered reports of peasants destroying gardens and orchards in response to pressures to join cooperatives. Not until the Congress of Cooperatives of April 1979 was the situation clarified. Kaysone told delegates that "the secondary economy in the families of cooperatives members . . . forms part of the economy of the cooperatives: it supplements the cooperative economy."[2] Peasants, he said, should be encouraged to cultivate their private gardens.

At the congress Kaysone outlined the property relations of the cooperatives. He told his audience (somewhat optimistically, as we have seen in chapter 3) that in the countryside the peasants "have already abandoned their individual way of earning a living and have switched to the collective way of life by means of setting up cooperatives, and have adopted the principle of collective ownership as a basis for production by first of all

putting their land, cattle and agricultural tools under a collective ownership system." He went on to explain the "two fundamental forms of
ownership" in the "collective economy": *"mass ownership,* which is expressed through agricultural and forestry settlements, and *collective
ownership,* which is expressed through agricultural cooperatives. The true
nature of these two forms of ownership is socialist." "Mass ownership"
means state farms. There were approximately fifty state farms in Laos in
1988 in which all means of production are the property of the state and the
workers are employed like other state workers, although in some cases
income has been dependent on the state farm's productivity. (Several state
farms are transformed reeducation camps staffed by former members of the
Royal Lao Army.) These farms are marginal to the rural economy in Laos
and do not represent significant transformations of the social and economic landscape in the countryside.

A booklet published for the managers of cooperatives in November
1979 offers some clarification, and a later document gives further clues
about the government's thinking on the nature of cooperatives. "Some
Ideas Concerning the Provisional Regulations of Cooperatives" states that
the "agricultural cooperative is the basic unit of the communistic economy,"[3] and all means of production of the peasant should become cooper-
atively owned property. It says, "in some newly established cooperatives
rent is still paid to the owners of rice fields or cattle in return for their use.
The cooperative must persuade these people to reduce their rent by means
of reeducation, discussion, and negotiation, thereby making it into a cooperative step by step. Belonging to a cooperative without transforming the
means of production into cooperative ownership means that a true cooperative does not exist in fact; it remains simply at the level of exchange of
labor." Further, "if the means of production have not been transferred to
cooperative ownership . . . [a] cooperative cannot be set up according to
socialist principles." Farther on, under the heading "What are the aims and
purpose of the cooperative?" the booklet says the aim of policy is to change
private ownership into cooperative ownership. "To eradicate the genesis of
oppressor classes and class oppression in the country so that the way to
capitalism is virtually blocked." The Lao government obviously looked
forward to peasant members of cooperatives relinquishing their property
rights over land to the cooperative. The peasants would be brought to this
by reeducation and persuasion; but "moral persuasion" is insufficient
motivation for peasants to give up title to their land. Only where cooperatives were formed out of necessity by internal refugees, whose land, vil-

lages, and agricultural equipment were destroyed by the war, did anything like "collective ownership" occur. No doubt this is why Kaysone and other LPRP officials often held up the cooperatives of Xieng Khouang, Houaphan, Phong Saly, and Oudomsay for emulation during the collectivization campaign. Otherwise, according to the stringent definition of a cooperative given above, cooperatives among the lowland peasants along the Mekong have only ever been at the level of exchanging labor and sometimes sharing the yield.

"Stages" of Cooperation

The government's collectivization strategy aimed at encouraging peasants to progress from simple forms of cooperation to complex ones (chapter 3). The following are the ideal forms of the various stages, but they are rarely found empirically and their definitions are vague. The "simplest" form is the solidarity unit for exchanging labor (*Nuay Samakhii Laek Bpian Haeng Ngaan*). This was said to be a new kind of exchange of labor compared with the traditional forms of exchange, that is, it is nonreciprocal. It entails work on houses, road building, irrigation canals, and the like. In many respects it resembles traditional festive labor that was mobilized for identical activities with payment in food and drink. Second, there is the solidarity production unit (*Nuay Samakhi Peun Phun*), in which labor was supposed to be exchanged among peasants of the unit on a nonreciprocal basis. Regardless of the size of the paddy fields, the unit moves through the field of each member either sowing or harvesting in a large group. Work points are not allotted, and there is no collective sharing of the yield. Rather, the yield is appropriated privately, and therefore the income within the unit tends to vary according to the size of one's plot. Third, is the unit for collective production, (*Nuay Phalit Luam Mu*), in which the yield is supposed to be appropriated collectively and distributed either equally or according to a mark point system.

Among both farmers and officials there is considerable confusion and difference of opinion about what exactly constitutes a particular kind of unit. Interpretations often vary as to whether a mark point system for measuring work was used or not; even on this point there is no consensus. Such vagueness is indicative of the confusion that occurred on the ground during the collectivization drive and accompanies continued attempts to promote collective forms of production. It is not surprising that the distinctions were unclear because generally all three of these forms were commonly referred to as collectives, expressed by militants and peasants alike as *het naa luam mu,* meaning basically to work together. Various linguistic conflations and confusions often allow peasants to do just what they want to do while saying they are working collectively. One peasant described his cooperative to me in 1986 as an "ordinary cooperative" *(sahakorn tamadaa),* by which he meant traditional peasant cooperation.

There are two forms of agricultural cooperative *(Sahakorn kaset).* One, the "highest" form, has fully collective ownership. In the other labor is pooled along with means of production, but the latter remains the private property of the member peasants. On the basis of empirical observation a third kind of cooperative could be added: one in which the members rent most of their land as a collective tenant. In cooperatives members have been paid according to two mark points systems: one according to the number of days worked *(Kanaen Wan Ngaan)* and the other a piece rate system *(Kanaen Haeng Ngaan).*

The main difference between the lower level cooperatives and the higher level collectives (speaking ideally) is their formal organization and their obligations as outlined in the provisional regulations *(SWB,* 24 June 1978). The regulations state that cooperatives must accumulate between 5 and 7 percent of the total harvest, 60 to 70 percent of which can be used for purchasing additional means of production and the rest for welfare work or "other public services." The cooperatives also have a "duty" to sell agriculture produce to the state. These formal conditions should be met before the local administration will recognize a group as a proper cooperative, making them eligible for favorable tax rates and priority in purchasing capital equipment and other inputs from the state. These regulations do not apply to the "collectives".

As will be seen more clearly in the following chapter, the "collectives" do not represent any fundamental change in the social relations of production in the countryside. The organization of production is organized along marginally modified traditional lines, while a form of vertical integration for the purposes of buying or selling goods and technical transformations in irrigation has encouraged some new ways of cooperation.

The cooperatives, on the other hand, do attempt to introduce new social relations of production into the rural areas. Empirically, each cooperative looked at in muang Hatsayfong varied in its social composition, and none of them conformed to the government's strictures concerning "real" socialist ownership. The following three sections discuss the individual cooperatives over phases one and two (roughly 1978–84) of the collectivization policy.

Don Dou Cooperative

Don Dou was considered a model cooperative. In a speech in Savannakhet in March 1982 Kaysone held up Don Dou as a model for wavering cadres:

> It is obvious that a number of our cadres have developed a sense of hesitancy and have lost faith in and failed to implement resolutely the Party's policy in setting up agricultural cooperatives. Several of them have argued that the policy . . . is not suitable to the current reality in our country and that the setting up of cooperatives will result in a decrease in production and a decline in living conditions. Regarding this matter I invite you to visit Phong Saly, Oudomsay, Xieng Khouang and Sam Neua [Houaphan] Provinces. Those provinces have basically completed the setting up of agricultural cooperatives. . . . The agricultural cooperative of ban Don Dou village in Hatsayfong district of Vientiane Province, which was set up only three years ago, has achieved excellent production. All visitors to this cooperative wholeheartedly hail its success. [*SWB*, 17 April 1982]

Local bards, such as Thanongsak Vongsakda, were moved to trumpet the cooperative's achievements in poems like the following, from the party paper *Sieng Pasason* (25 June 1983):

Voices from Don Dou Cooperative

The annual rice planting season has arrived, you know!
It won't do if we are to ignore it and show no concern.
The rice seeds will cry out for their owners to sow.
The rains are showering down—such a happy sight.

One shouldn't sit and wait for the sky to inundate.
One shouldn't have to wait, lest the rain seeps through the earth.
With dikes and handmills—folk inventions of bygone eras
Together with innovative technologies, we ought to get more water
into the fields. That's right isn't it?

Oh look! Those sown seeds are sprouting green leaves.
They are awaiting someone to uproot and replant them in prepared
    plots

The first sods have been turned and the final plowing is busily under
  way.
It's really up to you now to proceed.

Come, come, brothers and sisters of cooperatives everywhere
Private farmers included, from north to south.
Let's unite in purpose to rapidly sow and grow,
Grow more rice, we'll compete—and fill all silos.
We, here at this place "Don Dou" Cooperative,
Are ever-prepared to learn and draw lessons from others.
We voluntarily declare an open challenge to all
To strive to harvest in excess of our target.

Our nation will advance,
In accordance with the Party's resolutions,
If we are victorious in our agricultural vocation.
Therefore with a sense of urgency,
to this task we should concentrate our energy.
Fear not if it doesn't rain
We will, indeed, gain in the building of our country.[4]

Don Dou, however, differs significantly from the cooperatives in the mountain provinces mentioned in the same breath by Kaysone.

Don Dou cooperative grew out of a unit for collective production
formed during the collectivization drive in 1978. It was made up of twenty-
two families (eighty-nine people) and it farmed eight hectares in that wet
season. The majority of these families were landless peasants. Following
this initial season they decided that the unit did not offer sufficient return
for their work and it was, they claimed, still "imbued with the exploitation
of labor." Moves were set in train by the leadership of the group to form an
agricultural cooperative. Although some families immediately fell away,
the cooperative was recognized by the muang administration on 16 January 1979. The exact number of families who were members at the beginning is unclear. The first unambiguous figure available is for the dry season
1980–81, when there were fifteen families. At this time the cooperative
had eight hectares of paddy fields, six draft animals, six plows, and six
harrows.

Land in the cooperative was owned by three farmers: Dtoo Pheng
(5.3ha, family 2 in table 5.1), Kham Khiene (2ha, family 8), and Dtoo Khai
(2ha, family 15). The number of buffalo owned by members fluctuated

97

because of the trading in animals noted earlier. Only one family (family 15) held both means of production over four seasons (see table). Dtoo Khai was an old person, and he and his family (wife and grandchild) were completely dependent for their income on rent from the cooperative. The cooperative accountant, Vong, explained that he had been able to become a cooperative member as a "special favor" because his family possessed no labor to work the land. Just who was doing whom the favor is a matter of interpretation because the cooperative had insufficient land. To secure their status in the cooperative Dtoo Khai and his wife did menial tasks; he, for instance, cut cane slivers used to bind the rice seedlings into bundles for transplanting.

Dtoo Pheng also owned land and buffalo, although he discarded the latter when the cooperative started using a tractor. He was one of the cooperative's, indeed, the muang's, more intriguing figures. A veteran of the Lao nationalist and communist movement, he joined the Lao Issara (Free Lao) in 1945, then the NLHS and is a member of the NLSS. He is a communist party member, the only one I came across at any level in these cooperatives, and he was second director of Don Dou. (There had been another communist party member at Don Dou, an old woman who had since become a nun.) Dtoo Pheng was born in ban Thana, where he has a two-story house and where his land is registered. During the initial collectivization drive Dtoo Pheng had worked with a "collective" group in ban Thana but had subsequently been drawn into (probably directed politically into) helping set up the cooperative among the mostly landless peasants of Don Dou, whom the party presumably saw as natural allies in the cooperative movement. Only he and his wife were registered as members of the cooperative; she was an invalid, and he was deeply involved in official duties at both the muang and the cooperative levels; he helped administer the latter. Thus he relied on rent for support.

As can be seen in table 5.1, Dtoo Pheng did well out of the cooperative, in fact better than many of its members. In 1982, for example, he gained 3.5 tons of paddy for one active worker compared with an average of half that much per active laborer for other families. This difference is largely accounted for by rent.[5]

Why did this "rich peasant" join the cooperative? He, naturally, explains it as part of his ideological commitment, and there is probably a great deal of truth in this. But there are other reasons why he would join a cooperative. First, he was one of the larger individual landowners in the area and must surely have feared that some of his land could be redistributed in any land reform. The new regime's rule of thumb, though not

TABLE 5.1. Seasonal Breakdown of Family Composition and Payment in Don Dou Cooperative, 1980–82

			Dry Season 1980–81				
Family	Total Members	Number of Women	Rice for Mark Points (kg)	Bonus	Rent of Land	Rent of Buffalo	Total (kg)
1	5	2	2,706	150		450.36	3,307.5
2	1	—	1,080	—		476.8	1,557
3	3	2	2,308	200		—	2,508
4	2	1	2,867	150		—	3,017
5	1	—	1,707	50		—	1,757
6	2	1	1,572	600		—	2,172
7	4	3	1,606	—		475	2,081
8	5	3	2,840	250		—	3,090
9	4	3	2,704	150		—	2,854
10	2	2	1,253	50		—	1,303
11	2	2	1,312	—		—	1,312
12	3	2	2,041	50		—	2,091
13	1	1	944	50		—	994
14	2	2	1,197	100		—	2,197
15	1	—	—	150		349	499

			Wet Season 1981				
Family	Total Members	Number of Women	Rice for Mark Points (kg)	Bonus	Rent of Land	Rent of Buffalo	Total (kg)
1	5	2	2,527	20	—	224	2,743
2	1		773	10	1,450	224	2,457
3	3	2	1,655	50	—	—	1,705
4	3	2	1,802	20	—	—	1,825
5	2	1	1,012	40	—	—	1,052
6	1		709	40	—	—	749
7	3	2	1,328	60	—	232	1,620
8	5	2	1,478	40	600	274	2,392
9	4	3	2,174	20	—	—	2,194
10	3	2	1,711	10	—	—	1,221
11	2	2	648	—	—	—	648
12	2	2	1,089	10	—	—	1,099
13	1	1	396	10	—	—	406
14	2	1	509	20	—	—	529
15	1	—	232	30	1,000	225	1,487
16	2	2	446	—	—	—	446

(*continued*)

TABLE 5.1. (*Continued*)

			Dry Season 1981–82				
Family	Total Members	Number of Women	Rice for Mark Points (kg)	Bonus	Rent of Land	Rent of Buffalo	Total (kg)
1	4	2	3,739	126		—	3,865
2	1	—	1,639	64		—	1,702
3	3	2	3,197	315		—	3,512
4	3	2	3,372	126		—	3,498
5	2	1	2,279	252		—	2,531
6	3	1	3,252	252		—	3,504
7	2	1	3,485	378		—	3,864
8	withdrew after wet season—1981						
9	3	2	3,299	126		—	3,425
10	3	2	1,168	63		—	1,231
11	1	1	1,107			—	1,107
12	2	2	1,288	63		—	1,351
13	1	1	1,000	63		—	1,063
14	1	1	654	63		—	717
15	1			189		667	856
16	left to join husband						
17	2	1	1,705	189		—	1,894
Tractor			820			—	820
Tractor			1,046			—	1,046

			Wet Season 1982				
Family	Total Members	Number of Women	Rice for Mark Points (kg)	Bonus	Rent of Land	Rent of Buffalo	Total (kg)
1	4	1	2,346	134	—	—	2,480
2	1	—	678	67	1,050	—	1,795
3	3	2	1,562	335	—	—	1,897
4	3	2	1,404	67	—	—	1,571
5	2	1	625	268	—	—	893
6	2	1	717	268	—	—	985
7	2	1	1,040	335	—	331	1,706

(*continued*)

TABLE 5.1. (*Continued*)

			Wet Season 1982				
Family	Total Members	Number of Women	Rice for Mark Points (kg)	Bonus	Rent of Land	Rent of Buffalo	Total (kg)
8	—	—	—	—	—	—	—
9	3	2	1,877	134	—	—	2,011
10	1	1	127	67	—	—	194
11	2	2	773	—	—	—	773
12	1	1	666	—	—	—	666
13	1	1	590	—	—	68	658
14			Died				
15	1	—	—	201	630	448	1,279
16	—	—	—	—	—	—	—
17			Expelled				
18	2	1	532	134	—	—	532
19	3	2	1,816	67	—	—	1,950
20	2	2	1,131		—	—	1,198
Tractor			1,135				1,135
Tractor			782				792

rigorously applied, was that land in excess of what one's household could work should be sold or redistributed somehow. The aim of this was to discourage the use of wage labor by "idle capitalist" farmers. Dtoo Pheng's status as a communist party member would not protect him from any enforced redistribution. By joining the cooperative he made the best of both worlds—he retained title to his land and was seen to be a "good communist," thereby enhancing his prestige in the new regime. The second reason for joining was that his family lacked sufficient labor to work the land. His children worked for the government. So by placing his land in the cooperative (and one singled out by the state for special attention) he ensured it was worked by a steady supply of labor in a politically legitimate way.

The cooperative not only paid rent to its own members, but in the wet season also rented land from private farmers. Until the "third phase" of cooperativization rent was payable only in the wet season, the logic being that farmers were allegedly dependent on government supplied capital works, such as irrigation, in the dry season and therefore could not use the land or rent if not for government assistance. Taxes were waived in the dry season as an incentive for the peasants to grow two crops. Don Dou cooperative generally rented between five and seven hectares from outside the cooperative, and in both seasons worked around fifteen hectares. While rent paid to those inside the cooperative was 10–12 percent of the yield on their land, private farmers demanded the legal maximum of 15 percent.

During peak season the cooperative hired some casual labor, eight being the maximum number of workers hired in any one season. It also hired out its tractor with a driver to some private peasants for plowing. This practice had begun spontaneously when one of Dtoo Pheng's relatives was assisted and had expanded to a number of other peasants. Ngai, the cooperative's head, initially appeared uneasy about inquiries on this matter for it was happening outside the boundaries foreseen by the cooperative's founders and government policy. Access to machinery was considered to be a key incentive for private peasants to join the cooperatives. If they could get access to machinery without joining, then the incentive was gone. The cooperative was obviously feeling its way on this question in 1983, but once I indicated that I felt that the hiring out of the tractor was a rational way to use excess tractor capacity Ngai quickly said that they were in fact considering ways of expanding its hire in the wet season, as they now had steel-frame wheels and a good set of disc plows. They would try to make a small profit, but, he assured me at the time, it would be according to "state principles and prices." The practice of hiring out the tractor soon flourished as government policy on such matters moderated.

The organization of the cooperative was formally democratic. Theoretically peasants are elected to a position on the management committee regardless of ownership of means of production. In practice at Don Dou it would appear that Dtoo Pheng holds the position of second director by virtue of his landholding contribution (here tradition intersects with the cooperatives' modern, "impersonal" principles) as well as his party membership, literacy, and age. Otherwise contributions of means of production confer no special supervisory privileges.

Despite the significant presence of private ownership of means of production the cooperative group as a whole began to accumulate indivisible capital, and the earnings from the hiring out of the tractor went to the cooperative, not to any particular individual within it. In 1979 the cooperative acquired a threshing machine and two manual insecticide sprayers; in

1980 a tractor and a disc plow, a small diesel water pump, a weighing machine, and materials for building a permanent cooperative building, including a collective paddy rice storehouse. In 1981 a cement floor was laid for the building, and a mobile sprinkler system for gardens was acquired in addition to a paddy milling machine, an electric dynamo, a small forge, and a small tractor and trailer. In 1982 a rice threshing machine, another pump, a water well, a toilet, and the electrification of the cooperative building were added, all purchased from or acquired through the state (a significant, indeterminable portion was rechanneled foreign aid). The land on which the cooperative shed stands was purchased by the state. This capital is cooperative property and amounts to much more than any individual peasant farmer could hope to possess. The cooperative went into debt to the state for some of this equipment, and the level of debt was beyond what could be contemplated by a private Lao peasant. Accumulation of this sort is one of the major rationalizations for collectivization; however, here we begin to broach the issue of economies of scale, and this must be left to a later chapter.

"Mutual benefit" for cooperative members is one of the rationalizations for cooperatives. At Don Dou they had planned allowances for pregnant women to have one month off either side of the birth as well as for those hospitalized, those in self-defense units, those who fell ill during work periods (a maximum of three days), and those attending seminars to improve their knowledge, agronomic or political; in addition, small contributions were made for marriages and for the funeral expenses of members, and some subsidies were granted for children and the aged. The cooperative thus attempted to provide some of the support normally provided by the family in hard times. In fact, all of this was on paper and remained an aspiration rather than a reality.

The cooperative partially represented new social relations of production in the countryside. They were not, however, pristine forms of "mass ownership" or "collective ownership," but a mixture of the latter plus private ownership. The government clearly hoped that Don Dou would evolve into a higher "socialist" form. Its hopes were based on optimistic assumptions because Don Dou was always vulnerable to the defection of peasants with land. It was expected that the accumulation of collective capital would provide an overriding incentive to members to stay in the cooperative, and there was a possibility that it would become an industrial node in the countryside, earning the bulk of its income through plowing, threshing, and milling. But even this cooperative faltered.

Ban Thana Cooperative

Ban Thana cooperative was billed in early 1980 as one of the better-managed cooperatives in Laos. Seventy-one families had joined when it was first established in the 1978 wet season. By early 1983 sixteen families were left. Khan and Lee collected some statistics on ban Thana cooperative (table 5.2). At that time membership or participation in the cooperative fluctuated between seasons because irrigation was still available only to a portion of the members' area in the dry season, and therefore a number of families became seasonally "redundant." According to my information, the figure of sixty-six households in the cooperative in the 1980 dry season is inaccurate. Nouhak Phoumsavan toured the muang in late 1979, following the promulgation of the Seventh Resolution, stressing the voluntary nature of cooperatives. As a result, only forty-three families remained in the cooperative at the beginning of 1980, and many of these were landless. (Khan and Lee estimated that 68 percent of their sixty-six households were landless.) From then on a process of attrition set in, and by dry season 1982 only twenty-seven families remained; this figure fell to nineteen in the wet season of 1982 and to sixteen by the following dry season. The fluctuations no longer reflected the lack of irrigation: it was simply that the cooperative was disintegrating.

All the peasants who left owned land. By the wet season of 1982 the cooperative was paying rent to four members of the cooperative (each of whom held land below one hectare), and it was paying rent to two outside landholders—one with 3.2ha and another 1.6ha.[6] The total land cultivated that season was 8ha, less than half of which was held by cooperative members, and by the following season yet another cooperative landholder had left. In dry season 1983 they were cultivating 12ha. As can be seen from table 5.3, rent accounted for one-third to one-half of the income of those owning land who were in the cooperative in the wet season of 1982. Unfortunately there is no breakdown of income for those who owned buffalo. For the dry season of 1983 eleven members earned rent from buffalo (table 5.3), and the rent contributed considerably to their income from the cooperative. For seven households rent accounted for 25–30 percent of their income and 100 percent in the case of one household (Dao's husband, the cooperative accountant, Alom—family 18). The ownership of some means of production added significantly to the earnings of some members of ban Thana cooperative, as it did in Don Dou.

The cooperative work force was thirty-one in the dry season of 1983,

TABLE 5.2. Basic Data about the Ban Thana Cooperative

	1979 Dry Season	1979 Rainy Season	1980 Dry Season
Number of member households	55	71	66
Total number of households in village	183	183	183
Percentage of village households in the cooperative	30	39	36
Land cultivated by the cooperative (ha)	16	70	35
Cultivated area per worker (ha)	0.12	0.16	0.18
Rented land for which payment is made (ha)	—	35	—
Labor force	132	429	191
Paddy output (ton)	41	88.7	—
Yield of paddy (ton/ha)	2.56	1.27	—
Payment for rented land (tons of paddy)	—	1.4	—
Payment per ha of rented land (tons of paddy)	—	0.04	—
Total mark points earned by all workers	54,000	150,000	—
Average number of days worked per worker	30.7	26.2	—
Payment per mark point (kg of paddy)	0.7	0.5	—
Average earning per worker per day (kg of paddy)	8.4	6.0	—
Output distributed to all workers (tons of paddy)	37.8	75.0	—
Total collective earning per worker (kg of paddy)	257.9	157.2	—
Distributed output as percentage of gross output	92.2	84.6	—
Estimated labor days[a]	4,050	11,250	—
Estimated labor payment as percentage of gross output	83.0	76.1	—
Labor days per hectare	253	161	—
Output per day of labor (kg of paddy)	10.1	7.9	—

Source: A. R. Khan and E. Lee, Employment and Development in Laos (Bangkok: ILO/ARTEP, 1980), 50.

[a]It is assumed that 20 percent of work points were distributed for plowing for land preparation, a process in which human and animal labor earn equal points (12 each for 60 × 60 metres of land). Thus, 10 percent of the work points would be allocated to the owners of animals. The remainder is divided by 12 to obtain workdays in standard units of 12 points each.

TABLE 5.3. Ban Thana Cooperative

		Wet Season 1982			
Family	Mark Points Plowing/Sowing	Mark Points Harvesting	Total Points	Rice Payment (kg)	Paddy for Rent (kg)
1	896	731	1,627	813	350
2	658	333	991	495	—
3	839	577	1,416	708	—
4	683	278	961	480	—
5	883	523	1,406	703	—
6	381	1,098	1,479	739	—
7	981	896	1,877	938	—
8	981	883	1,864	932	—
9	298	626	924	462	—
10	562	974	1,536	768	350
11	295	485	780	390	—
12	284	546	830	415	420
13	389	428	817	408	210
14	189	455	644	322	—
15	121	254	375	187	—
16	215	349	564	282	—
17	375	706	1,081	540	—
18	109	737	846	423	—
19	205	374	579	289	—

Rent paid to outsiders: 1,400 kg. for 3.2 ha.
700 kg. for 1.6 ha.

				Dry Season 1983			
Family	Persons in Family[a]	Labor Mark Points	Buffalo Mark Points	Other	Sowing Mark Points	Instrument Depreciation	Total Points
1	7	535	474	178	285	68	1,540
2	Left cooperative						
3	5	501	515	94	554	60	1,724
4	10	479	436	10	579	68	1,572
5	12	638	151	123	500	32	1,444
6	9	346	335	174	466	58	1,379
7	13	272	272	105	342	56	1,047

(*continued*)

TABLE 5.3. (*Continued*)

Family		Mark Points Plowing/Sowing		Mark Points Harvesting	Total Points	Rice Payment (kg)	Paddy for Rent (kg)
			Dry Season 1983				
9	6	344	192	127	399	—	1,062
10	7	304	260	67	—	50	681
11	8	—	—	58	775	—	833
12	Left cooperative						
13	9	376	339	89	224	59	1,087
14	5	—	—	32	385	—	417
15	Left cooperative						
16	7	—	—	48	399	—	447
17	6	—	—	117	655	—	772
18	6	—	423	—	—	67	490
19	8	—	—	46	429	—	475

[a]Persons in family does not equal active members of cooperative.

but the management committee said they hired thirty-three extra "casual laborers" during peak periods. Nineteen of these were children below cooperative membership age (sixteen years) who came mainly from the families of the members. The mark points of these children were simply added to those of their parents or relatives, and labor hired from outside the cooperative was often engaged along kinship lines because the mark points of these workers were also subsumed under those of the relatives inside the cooperative. It was peasant family labor in another guise; actual wage labor was minimal.

Not surprisingly, ban Thana cooperative was seriously disrupted by the mass defection of members, and some corruption in the management (something I shall discuss later) compounded the problems. Consequently, its records were sketchy, its formal organization weak, and its members increasingly demoralized.

In contrast to Don Dou cooperative, ban Thana had collectively accumulated only a cooperative shed, which stood deserted and unused. The cooperative had no machinery at all, which was a source of bitter disappointment to its members. When the collectivization program was launched in the muang in 1978 a Pathet Lao soldier from "outside," along with the ban committee, told a village meeting that if peasants joined the cooperative they would have machinery like cooperatives in advanced socialist countries. They would have planes to spread fertilizer and insecticide and tractors, and if there was ever any trouble with the machinery the state would always help to fix it. But, said the management committee, they had received nothing. Many peasants stayed in the cooperative after Nouhak's tour in late 1979 because they expected machines to be delivered. As the years passed and the machines failed to materialize, these peasants peeled away from the cooperative.

The head of ban Thana cooperative in 1983, Thao Boun, explained that many of the peasants joined during the initial campaign because they felt pressured to do so. At that time military personnel were more visible at various administrative levels in the area, and there was great concern about security along the Mekong River. In this atmosphere many of the peasants thought that if they did not join the cooperative they would be sent to a reeducation camp. Thao Boun said that many private peasants at that time feared that the "people without work," that is, the landless peasants, would take their land and rice. This fear was indirectly confirmed by their experience in the cooperative during its first season, when, they complained, there were "too many mouths to feed." Members of the Don Dou cooperative also said that there had been a lingering fear among the private peasants that the landless would expropriate their land. In the ban Nok cooperatives the tension between landed and landless peasants can be seen most clearly, and it profoundly influenced the development of cooperatives there.

Ban Nok Cooperatives

Precisely because there were conflicts of interest in ban Nok it was hard to get unbiased information about what had occurred there. One of my most voluble informants, Maha Houa, the head of one of the cooperatives, was not only dynamic and intelligent but also cunning and eccentric, which only added to my difficulties.

A cooperative was established in the wet season of 1979 with fifty-five member households. Before then it was a "collective" over the dry season of 1978–79. After the 1979 wet season and after Nouhak's visit, twenty-eight landowners left the cooperative, leaving some sixteen peasants with land and ten landless families still in the cooperative. This group lasted only through the dry season and split before the beginning of the 1980 wet season. Ban Nok 2 cooperative was established the following year (wet season 1981) after a period of malaise among the land-short and landless peasants, while ban Nok 1 was made up mostly of landed peasants.

There is some broad agreement between the two groups concerning the reasons for the split. Those in ban Nok 1 reckoned that there were too many landless people and that the high labor/land ratio meant there was not enough to eat for all the families in the cooperative. The landless peasants agree that the main complaint of the others was that the landless peasants were receiving too much of the yield; but, not surprisingly, they offer a somewhat different explanation for this. They argue that the landed peasants did not have enough labor in their families and therefore did not contribute enough full-time labor to the cooperative's work. They claimed it was mainly casual labor done by schoolchildren or people with government jobs. Some informants exaggerated, saying that the landed farmers contributed only one full-time laborer per family. Furthermore, they complained, these workers did not turn up on time, and because the landowners had not worked before—that is, before 1975—their children did not know how to work. The landless families, on the other hand, contributed three to four workers as well as casual workers. Therefore, they argued, they deserved the payment they received. In the old regime, they went on, landowners could hire wage labor when they needed it or engage tenant farmers with whom they would split the yield 50/50. When the cooperative system was established the yield was distributed according to labor and said rent for land could be no more than 15 percent. As a result the landless peasants had enough to eat, but the landowners had less than before. Wealth had been redistributed.

Much in this analysis is self-serving and draws in an undigested way on government rhetoric about idle landowners before 1975. It does, however, bring into focus the latent tensions between landed and landless peasants in the village and demonstrates a clear conflict of interest within the cooperative. For the landless peasants the cooperative was a means of achieving social mobility, and it offered the possibility of a more secure existence through access to land. For them, joining the cooperative was "truly voluntary" (*samak jai thae*), while many of the landed peasants, they said, joined because they were scared and remained in the cooperative only until the direction of the government's policies became clear. Other peasants in ban Nok stayed in a cooperative because they perceived that it might hold advantages for them—however, they were not interested in redistributing their wealth to the landless.

At the cooperative meeting at which the landless were expelled the latter did not put up any resistance to the move. It was pointless, they said, because they were outvoted. The landless did not even argue against the move because they accepted the landowners' right to do as they please with their land; and in traditional peasant society landownership is a prerequisite to "citizenship" within a village. One sensed the landless would have acted in exactly the same way had they been owners of land, and they knew it. The decision had to be accepted by the muang administration because it was a majority decision by the cooperative members.

While this situation had not been anticipated by the government when it launched the collectivization campaign, it had nevertheless recognized its possibility in the supplement to the provisional regulations it released some two years later. It noted, "In some localities poor persons without ricefields and without buffaloes have not been accepted into the cooperative. This is not right."[7] Can this be characterized as a conflict of class interests? I think not, even though the tension arises out of differential access to means of production. At ban Nok we do have one section of peasants who own means of production asserting their group interests against another section of landless peasants. However, the actions of the better-off peasants do not propel the landless into a condition of dependence on them, although they may use these poor peasants as wage laborers at seasonal peaks. The landed peasants are not dependent on a pool of free wage labor as a precondition of production. Landlessness in the area is a result not so much of the transformation of the social relations of production in peasant society as of demographic pressure. What the peasants with land are doing is refusing to allow the cooperative to become a mechanism for redistributing income in the village at their expense. Their assertion of group interests is based not on a thirst for profit but on their desire to secure a good livelihood for their family.

The interesting point about ban Nok 1 cooperative compared with, for example, ban Thana is that the private peasants in the former cooperative reacted to the redistributive implications of the cooperative not by leaving it but by ejecting those they saw as a burden. Why did they adopt this strategy? Some of the reasons are the same as for those private landholders who stayed on for a while in ban Thana—access to irrigation, lower taxes, fertilizer and insecticides at preferential rates, and the hope of acquiring machinery. Yet these incentives to stay had worn thin at ban Thana, so when one searches for the factor unique to ban Nok 1 to explain why landed peasants stayed in the cooperative one is left with the personality of the general manager of the cooperative, Maha Houa.

It should be said that there was considerable controversy in the tasseng about ban Nok 1's cooperative status, outsiders arguing it was only a cover for private farmers to get concessions. My first interview with Maha Houa in fact came only a few days before a meeting at the tasseng offices of the managements of all the cooperatives in the tasseng. At this meeting ban Nok 1 was criticized because it was alleged that it really distributed yield along private lines rather than according to the work points system that distinguished "real" cooperatives. Maha Houa, his assistant, Khamsay, and accountant Nang Phay were obviously aware of the impending criticism and were extremely circumspect at our first meeting because they openly feared that I had been sent to search out information that could be used against them. Thus when I asked if I could peruse any records the cooperative kept I was treated to a long, involved story about how these were being typed up in Vientiane because Maha Houa had decided that a proper record of the cooperative be produced for posterity. Subsequent requests, made following the tasseng meeting, never succeeded in securing these records.

Nevertheless, the way Maha Houa talked about the elusive records and the need to produce them as a booklet for posterity was my first inkling of his eccentricity. To explain at least a little of this I need to talk about the man himself. Two things are important to bear in mind about Maha Houa. The first is that he is a well-off peasant as the owner of close to seven hectares, and the prefix Maha indicates that he had acquired considerable stature in the Buddhist sangha. Second, in the old regime he had worked for some time as a low-level official in the Ministry of Justice, which means he is relatively better educated than most. He is an active, intelligent, strong-willed man in his sixties. He commented with some irony that he had been jailed twice under the old regime, accused of being procommunist. Then, because of his job in the Ministry of Justice, the new regime accused him of being reactionary and sent him off to a reeducation camp in the far northern province of Phong Saly for three years. These years understandably left a profound mark on Maha Houa's way of thinking and acting (though I must say if there was any bitterness it was well hidden). In Phong Saly the inmates of the camp had built their dwellings and grown their food collectively and were lectured on the virtues of socialism and collectivism. What had most struck Maha Houa about these lectures was the communists' emphasis on large-scale mechanized farming and the application of science to agriculture, rather than notions of social justice, reputed to be bound up with these developments. In this regard he has the imagination of a technical enthusiast, and upon his return home he threw himself into the activities arranged by the farmers' association connected with the experimental agricultural station in the muang.

His experience in Phong Saly had taught him to be politically wary and ensure he stayed on the right side of the communists. If this meant being in a cooperative he would be in one. Thus a peculiar mixture of technical enthusiasm and pragmatism guided Maha Houa's activity in the cooperative. It fended off political criticism and secured his land. He also knew very well that the cooperatives were the best means of gaining access to the modern inputs he coveted.

Maha Houa was elected to the managing committee of the cooperative soon after his return from Phong Saly in 1979. He says that some people in the muang administration opposed his election, claiming that he held reactionary opinions and therefore should not be allowed to hold a responsible post. But they were unsuccessful, and Maha Houa was elected unanimously by the members of the cooperative. Maha Houa commanded influence in the cooperative because he was a significant landholder, and he also held prestige as a result of his achieved stature in the sangha. His background as an official was thought to qualify him as an able protector of the interests of the cooperative vis-à-vis the administration. That is, he was elected because in addition to his strong personality, he possessed traditionally valued qualities. After the cooperative split in 1980 he became its managing director because the various defections and expulsions from the cooperative had shifted its kinship composition in his favor.

The cooperative included 23ha in its domain in 1982, 10ha of which was in a consolidated block, the rest being scattered widely among the plots belonging to private peasants. Such dispersal of land in itself sets up practical obstacles to the functioning of the cooperative: long distances for cooperative work groups to travel with equipment and seedlings or for the harvest and difficulties of coordination and supervision of labor. Only the families in the big block worked collectively, while those on the dispersed plots worked in smaller groups. Maha Houa initially insisted that the work of the cooperative be done through a contract system while distribution of fertilizer and yield be done centrally. Their devising of these contradictory systems of accounting, however, appears to be an elaborate subterfuge on the part of Maha Houa and his management committee (something I shall return to in chapter 7). The degree to which the subterfuge is conscious is very difficult to assess because they clearly see the cooperative through the eyes of relatively well-off peasants who regard it as a means of bettering themselves. Their ideological understanding of the role of cooperatives in the new government's strategy is naive to say the least. For example, at one point Maha Houa complained about how little assistance his cooperative had received from the government. He then drew an unfavorable comparison with the Thai government's promotion of cooperatives. He had watched on television how the Thai government clears land and resettles farmers on it, a process he understood as a Thai attempt to demonstrate that not only communists were capable of establishing cooperatives. The television had shown the Thai king, who he remarked was a good leader, and his family out inspecting cooperatives. To which he added the observation that the old Lao king had been a good gardener, implying that he too would have approved of cooperatives. Thus did Maha Houa give a traditional gloss to his participation in the cooperative, one that contained no obvious socialist ideological references.

Ban Nok 1 would probably be best described as a form of marketing cooperative that buys inputs on a collective basis from the state at lower prices, collectively pays tax at a lower rate, and sells some of its produce to the state collectively. Its headquarters were Maha Houa's large, unfinished concrete house, where some rice is collectively stored in case of emergency needs on the part of any one of its members; therefore the cooperative does fulfill some mutual help functions. But given the close family ties operating in this cooperative it also looks strikingly similar to the largesse held by a rich peasant that is distributed by him to those in his entourage who are in need.

The main drive behind Maha Houa's enthusiasm for the cooperative, which he managed to communicate to the other peasants remaining in it, was that it promised access to machinery and scientific farming. His enthusiasm had led to a hastily conceived attempt to begin triple cropping by growing two crops over dry season 1981–82, and for this they needed a tractor because it could plow the fields more quickly than a buffalo. The management of the cooperative secured the services of a tractor from the Machinery Department of the Ministry of Agriculture by offering to sell to the state one hundred tons of paddy by the end of the dry season. The tractor cost 20,000 kip to hire. However, they planted the crop too early and it was affected by cold weather. Thus they received a return of only forty-two tons off 30ha rather than Maha Houa's hoped-for figure of more than one hundred tons. This led many of the farmers in the cooperative who had used the tractor to want to renege on their deal with the state. After much arguing it was decided that they would sell only sixteen tons to the state, with the managing committee arguing that they could not totally back out of their commitment or they would never be able to hire a tractor again. As Maha Houa explained, "The new regime is like a turning wheel. If you do something for it you will get something good in return." This explanation did not placate a number of families, who left the cooperative completely.

Expelled peasants claimed that the number of members on the books in ban Nok 1 was inflated in order to bolster their application to the muang level for a tractor and a milling machine. Characteristically Maha Houa had requested the most sophisticated and expensive milling machine. He scoffed at the rudimentary one used at Don Dou. He alleged that his requests for machinery were being blocked at the tasseng and muang levels by people who distrusted him because he was well off. He recognized that the reasons for the obstruction were related to accusations (coming particularly from ban Nok 2) that ban Nok 1 was not a real cooperative, but, he responded, the administration officials listen only to "some people" when they carry out their investigations. They do not "come out into the field and see the real situation." Fired with indignation, Maha Houa began to speak with the confidence, indeed arrogance, of a rich peasant speaking his mind about poor peasants. The members of the other cooperatives were jealous of landowners and therefore they made "false" reports to the tasseng. "It does not mean that we are rich, but all the same there is jealousy between superior and inferior, people who are richer and people who are poorer." He implied that Don Dou cooperative should not have received so much assistance from the state because it was made up of poorer peasants, especially as his cooperative worked so much better. He accused the Ministry of Agriculture of favoritism toward Don Dou and said that more assistance should have come to his cooperative because it had land but no machinery. "We still have to follow the buffalo's back and yet we do not even owe the state 100th of a kip!"

Maha Houa's attitude has won him enemies in the village and in the tasseng, yet he remained socially more powerful than the landless, even under the new regime. His enthusiasm about science and technology placed him in the category of "progressive farmer" in the eyes of the administration. His political skill at deflecting criticism is shown by the clever way he points to the fact that most of the officials in the ban, tasseng, and muang committees are not in the cooperatives, and he argues that this is one of the main reasons private peasants are reluctant to join cooperatives. Maha Houa also drew a skillful contrast between the officials in muang

Hatsayfong and those in the north of Laos whom he observed while in reeducation. There, he said, collectivization had been successful because officials who preached collectivization also practiced it.[8] In this way Maha Houa deftly placed himself in a relatively unimpeachable position if the officials attempted to reproach either him or his cooperative. The tensions that existed between ban Nok 1 and ban Nok 2–including those caused by Maha Houa's attitude of superiority—were not a product of class differences, however, but arose out of the values and ranking system of traditional Lao peasant society.

New Pressures on the Cooperatives

Attempts to form cooperatives during phases one and two of the Lao government's drive for agrarian change were far from successful in creating new social relations of production in the countryside. Don Dou was the only cooperative that had accumulated any substantial collective capital which prefigured new social relations, but even this was a precarious achievement. Ban Thana cooperative had collapsed by the end of the second phase, as had ban Nok 2 cooperative. Ban Nok 1 was held together by the mercurial Maha Houa, but it embodied no substantial change in peasant social organization. The shallowness of the roots struck by the cooperatives was demonstrated in the next phase.

A new muang policy on dry season farming adopted in 1983 entailed a clear shift in favor of private peasant production. Previous policy, the application of which had been becoming less stringent since the 1980–81 dry season anyway, was that cooperatives had priority over the use of irrigated paddy land in the dry season, and private farmers could only farm land left over after cooperative needs had been satisfied. As explained earlier, because irrigation was allegedly dependent on state inputs for its operation land rents could not be demanded openly by private farmers during the dry season, and owners had no rights over this land if they were not going to use it themselves. The cooperatives had first claim on unworked irrigated land in the dry season. This policy was changed by the muang administration in the dry season 1982–83. Cooperatives were no longer given priority and had to compete with private peasants for land just as in the wet season.

The reason for the new policy, Dtoo Pheng explained, was that the private peasants had carried the whole of the extension of the canal system on their own backs in the absence of promised government assistance.

Therefore, he said, administration officials had been disarmed and could not enforce government policy by asserting that the peasants would be without water if it was not for the state. The state's claim was further weakened by the fact that the irrigation system was not state administered. It was run by the local peasant community, and this soon led to them asserting their "moral rights" over the system.

The policy was also a product of the gradual but general weakening of the cooperative movement after 1980. As private peasants withdrew en masse from both ban Thana and ban Nok cooperatives, the area farmed by them shrank dramatically, leaving an increasingly large number of peasants farming privately during the dry season anyway, a fact only exaggerated as the irrigated area expanded. It became obvious that one did not have to be in the cooperative to secure dry season irrigation, and for peasants who remained in the cooperative only so they could engage in dry season cultivation membership became redundant. By late 1982 private peasants were in a position to argue for a change of policy, and the muang was compelled to agree.

The new policy led to the open charging of rent during the dry season whether one was in the cooperative or not. Ban Nok 1 of course was not affected by this, as Maha Houa, the ever-proud landowner, was quick to point out, and he predicted the policy would see the disappearance of the landless cooperatives. Thao Boun and his associates at ban Thana cooperative were more disappointed about this shift in policy than about the fact that they had never received machinery. It meant there was less and less reason for them to remain in the original cooperative.

Over 1983–84 a pretense that the original ban Thana cooperative was still in existence was maintained so that members could gain access to fertilizer at preferential rates and to lower taxes; and, as Thao Boun expressed it, there was still some faint hope that the state would channel other assistance their way. The actual organization of production had reverted to family-based farming, with the cooperative being no more than an outer shell—or a skeleton cooperative (*sahakorn hoop haang*), as one peasant put it. The peasants were paying 500–600kg of paddy rent per hectare, which was approximately one-third to one-half the crop, that is, rents similar to those that existed before 1975 and comparable with those in neighboring Thailand. By 1985 the cooperative had collapsed completely, and the peasants who owned land farmed it through labor-exchange groups, as did the landless who could find land to rent. By 1987 Thao

Boun, for example, was cultivating 1.5ha of his own land in a labor-exchange group of tenants and owners.

Ban Nok 2 collapsed almost immediately after the implementation of muang policy in 1983. Some members managed to acquire land over the next two years, and they, along with other landed peasants, restarted the cooperative in late 1985. The fifty-one families in this cooperative were really organized into labor-exchange groups. The rice they claimed to pool as a cooperative (50kg/ha) was what they had committed to sell to the state in exchange for fertilizer. Compared with the models outlined earlier in the chapter it too was a skeleton cooperative.

Ban Nok 1 was unaffected by the change in policy, and in mid-1983 Maha Houa's cooperative finally acquired a tractor. By 1984 they had a plow and were using improved varieties of rice. Even Don Dou was adversely affected by the shift in policy toward the private peasants. The cooperative found it difficult to rent enough land, but because it had a tractor it attempted to reclaim some swampland two kilometers away from the village, parts of which were first planted in the dry season of 1984. A further blow came in 1984 when Dtoo Pheng retired from the cooperative and took most of his land with him. He subsequently rented 4.6ha to three peasants in a ban Thana labor-exchange group. Less than a hectare of his land remained in the cooperative. This defection was offset somewhat by marriages between Don Dou residents and the surrounding villages, which brought land into the cooperative, at least on paper. In fact Don Dou itself increasingly resembled a skeleton cooperative whose basic units of production were kin groups.

Compared with other cooperatives in the area, Don Dou had accumulated collective capital by 1983: a Kubota and Massey Ferguson tractor, plows, and threshing machines, all of which had come through the Ministry of Agriculture. On paper this had been valued at 575,830 kip, plus 49,185kg of paddy, of which the cooperative had paid off by 1983 15,000 kip and 20,500kg of paddy. Yet at the beginning of 1987, 450,000 kip was still outstanding. By this time there were few expectations that this money would be repaid, not least because Don Dou, as a previously favored cooperative, had received rechanneled foreign aid as equipment. The attempt to establish Don Dou as a model cooperative had faltered in 1984, as it lost direct access to the central Ministry of Agriculture and was transferred to the responsibility of the provincial Ministry of Agriculture. This soon deprived the cooperative of privileged access to spare parts, and by

1987 some of the equipment had become unusable and the cooperative shed had taken on a deserted air. This loss of privileged status led almost immediately to the falling away of four of the cooperative's long-standing members, including Dtoo Pheng. Several core kin groups (I shall return to this in the following chapters) continued to use the collective capital, but this use corresponded more to the organizational forms of the traditional Lao peasantry than to the modern, rational, and instrumental form of organization the cooperatives were planned to be. By 1987 twelve of the original seventeen families in Don Dou in 1982 had either retired, left the cooperative to farm privately, or become refugees (the case for two families). In fact, there was little left of Don Dou cooperative.

Trading Cooperatives

Since 1983–84 trading cooperatives have been promoted by the state in accordance with the LPRP's growing appreciation of the role of trade in surmounting the natural economy and building a "socialist commodity economy." Here too "model" cooperatives emerged to be trumpeted by the party leadership. Dan Sang cooperative, just north of Vientiane, is one example. It was used to pioneer some of the new policies on cooperatives to be discussed below.[9]

Until the new policies began to take hold more widely, visitors to Dan Sang, located some thirty kilometers out of the capital, were likely to be surprised by the range of consumer goods available in the various roadside buildings. The cooperative began in 1984, when twelve people took out shares, each worth 1,000 kip. In 1985 the trading cooperative incorporated an agricultural cooperative of 35ha and reissued shares worth 200 kip each. By late 1986 it had issued 27,000 shares (worth approximately US$13,500) and had 178 shareholders. The largest shareholder had 400 shares, while the average was 152 shares. Of its turnover 20 percent was used for costs and reinvestment, 12 percent set aside for social welfare, 8 percent for bonuses, and 60 percent as distributions to shareholders.

The cooperative's activities divided into trading and agriculture, the former being its major activity. It drew up contracts with the state for deliveries of rice and contracts with the farmers for the exchange of goods. In 1986, for example, of the commodities it procured from the state trading organization approximately one-third was directly bartered with the farmers in the cooperative, really those organized into solidarity units for exchanging labor and for buying inputs and selling their produce. The rest of the trading cooperative's goods were retailed through its shops. As a result, shareholders in 1986 netted, on average, approximately US$140.00 return on their shares.[10]

One of the most notable changes in Lao villages since 1984 has been the flourishing of trading cooperatives. Some are small, slightly dilapidated shops in local markets, while others occupy more substantial buildings and are more obviously sophisticated operations. In contrast to the production cooperatives, they have had a spontaneous appeal and have drawn people's energies away from the agricultural cooperatives. The villages of muang Hatsayfong are no exception.

Former members of the collapsed ban Thana agricultural cooperative went immediately into a trading cooperative in 1984 with links to the production groups (the *juu phalit*) that succeeded the agricultural cooperative. In late 1986 it had 136 members, to whom it had sold 2,077 shares each worth 120 kip. Its largest shareholders held between 50 and 100 shares. The cooperative distributed profits to its shareholders every three months, and every three months membership turned over slightly, with some withdrawing their cash while others joined. Of the proceeds 28 percent was used to cover the wages of those who administered the cooperatives' operations and for investment, 5 percent was reserved for a welfare fund, and the rest distributed to shareholders. It ran a small shop and provided some raw material for the weavers in the village, although it had made no inroads into trading the finished products. One of its main activities was to buy rice from the farmers and to exchange it with the state for fertilizer and insecticides at a preferential rate. Members of agricultural production groups can be members of the trading cooperative, but it is not mandatory. A similar organization established in ban Nok had several officials who were former members of the landless cooperative, but it served all production groups in the village. Don Dou village also sported its own small trading cooperative.

A Strategic Compromise

An apparently tactical retreat on the question of agricultural cooperatives has become a strategic compromise with the private peasantry. After several years of malaise in the area of cooperatives, the LPRP began to adopt, along with its new economic policies, a much clearer evolutionary approach to agrarian change in the countryside, part of which we examined in chapter 3. A crucial statement on agrarian development came in early 1988 when Kaysone addressed the SPA.

In his speech Kaysone made an important theoretical shift away from the orthodox Marxist emphasis on the primacy of production relations and the imperative to transform these relations, at least in agricultural production. He reiterated the importance of trade in breaking the hold of the natural economy on peasant production:

> Certain persons may voice the concern that our regard that trade work is a primary link is akin to paying less attention to production and abandoning the decisive role of production. We hold that under the conditions of the natural economy in our country, if we wish to translate the objectives of the production development plans into reality we must utilize trading. . . . In the past, a considerable number of our people entertained the idea that transformation of the natural economy could only be done by establishing many more agricultural cooperatives. . . . Some said that the broadening of trading and exchanges of goods and motivation of production development in each family would pave the way for farmers to follow the capitalist path. . . . Production relations must conform to the characteristics and the speed of development of the production forces. [*SWB*, 25 February 1988]

Kaysone now lays primary stress on mobilizing the resources of the peasant family economy to transcend the natural economy, to lift production and thereby enter into economic relations with the state. Trading cooperatives are considered to be the primary link with the individual peasants. Kaysone spelled out in detail a new set of definitions of collective forms of production all regarded as compatible with socialism and all conceptualized in an evolutionary scheme traced in terms of a particular organization's distance from the natural economy.

The first form is the trading cooperative: "farmers' collective trading associations which link up with the state." They are to provide the farmers with a "two-way service"—supplying them with commodities they need and distributing the products the farmers have for sale. The second form is "production solidarity units which link with the trading cooperatives." These are labor-exchange units that also buy and sell as a group from the trading cooperatives. Kaysone clearly envisages a form of vertical integration not unlike that of agribusinesses between these two levels of organization. "Through the production solidarity units trading cooperatives are to put forth their buying and selling plan and to sign buying and selling contracts with the farmers. They are also authorized to give suggestions to the farmers on how to carry out production." Furthermore, the solidarity units are to be encouraged to invest in various forms of collective capital formation—irrigation, road building, land improvement, welfare—that are to "serve as common material conditions for everyone to advance to building production cooperatives in the next stage."

Agricultural cooperatives remain the aim of policy, but the LPRP's conception of them emphasizes joint benefits more than earlier descriptions. They are "joint ventures" and "collective commodity production business units." "Families of cooperative members who put their farmland and capital in the cooperatives for use in jointly carrying out production business are entitled to receive compensation for the lands and to receive profit, more or less depending on the amount of their capital. This is the key issue which will encourage farmers to turn voluntarily to the collective way of earning a living." The cooperative is to use contracts with the families of the members of the cooperative. Production over and above the amount contracted for (the latter includes taxes, collective expenses, and accumulation) can be sold by families on the open market. "The cooperatives are to take responsibility for various points that each family cannot manage separately, such as the irrigation systems, insecticides, and so forth." The role of the cooperatives in this plan calls for them to break with the natural economy by developing a more elaborate division of labor in cultivation, livestock breeding, and processing.

Cooperatives did not experience great successes in muang Hatsayfong, and none conformed to Kaysone's definition of a full-fledged socialist cooperative. Only Don Dou accumulated any collectively owned capital and even so failed to survive. The failure of the government to furnish other cooperatives with machinery was a major reason for private peasants quitting with whatever they took into the cooperatives originally. Had they accumulated some collective capital they might have had second thoughts about leaving it behind.

The supply of scientific and technical inputs raises productivity and as a consequence the carrying capacity of the land. Without them, cooperatives made up of landless and landed peasants in a densely populated area became a mechanism for redistributing income at the expense of the peasants with land. The latter rejected this in one of two ways: by leaving the cooperative or by ejecting the landless. This action set them on a potential collision course with the government, which could have tried to force private peasants back into the cooperatives and forced ban Nok 1 to accept landless members. But the social and political costs of such an approach were obviously rejected as too high, and the government had to contemplate alternatives to mass forced collectivization.

The private peasants' rejection of the redistributive role of the cooperatives was an act of rational self-interest, not a symptom of class conflict. The cooperatives had little to offer them and their families. A major failing of other collectivization programs has been that the redistribution of a fixed rather than expanding cake has led to peasant demoralization and to a further diminution of production. Latent and manifest tensions between richer and poorer members of the village exist in all known peasant societies, but they are the expressions of small town snobbishness or jealousy, not the confident superiority of social class. Wealth relativities are neither high, nor securely anchored. Thus land partitioning or misfortune can easily lead to this generation's rich peasant family being next generation's poor family. The attitudes expressed by Maha Houa, for example, derive from traditional Lao peasant social values, and these continue to influence the functioning of the cooperatives in a number of ways. One cannot say, as Potter did of the Thai village, for example, that "the landed classes run the village pretty much as they see fit."[11]

Landless peasants were often the backbone of the initial drive to form cooperatives in muang Hatsayfong. However, this soon presented the state with several policy dilemmas. The gathering of landowning and landless peasants into the cooperatives ruined the incentives of the former, thereby undermining the government's goal of increased productivity. When the peasants with resources abandoned the cooperatives, the remaining peasants became dependent on state inputs to remain viable. Rather than becoming engines of productive growth, the cooperatives were in danger of becoming a form of social security, much in the way poor peasant cooperatives did in the Soviet Union in the 1920s.[12] Don Dou was the most substantial foothold the new social relations had established in the area, but this had been achieved only as a result of the privileged attention it received as a model cooperative. The government slowly realized that subsidized models were no model at all. After 1983, Don Dou lost its model status as government policy on cooperatives began to shift. In most of the rest of Laos, where villagers have access to land and few cooperatives ever received any inputs, the situation was much simpler and clearer: cooperatives quickly and easily dissolved back into peasant society.

Hmong woman in Xieng Khouang harvesting opium.

Young boy with his bird trap.

Yao woman in Houaphan; note the French piastre on her turban.

Black Tai woman in Houaphan.

Black Tai woman carding cotton.

Lao weaver.

Men prepare the *phasat* for a *boun* to induct a young monk into the *sangha*.

A cooperative threshing team.

Carting hay from the threshing floor.

Lao bride serves drinks to guests.

A well-established peasant house.

Transplanting rice.

Two Black Tai men winnow rice.

Lao farmers argue over water rights.

Repairing a small dam (*faay*).

6

Peasant Economy and Society versus Collective Economy

Having asserted that peasants are spontaneous capitalists, communist governments and many left-leaning Third World governments have also, paradoxically, celebrated the alleged inherently "cooperative" nature of peasant society. The Lao government, for example, tried to draw legitimacy for its attempts to collectivize agriculture by asserting that its aims were in harmony with traditional peasant practice. At the Congress of Cooperatives in 1979, General Secretary Kaysone Phomvihane claimed that "the new [collective] relationship constitutes a continuation and development of the tradition of mutual solidarity and assistance among our people. . . . Everyone knows that individual happiness is linked to collective happiness."[1] This view is propagated among militants and by officials at the village level.

One could argue, perhaps, that the objective of government policy was to accentuate the allegedly "socialistic" tendencies of peasant society at the expense of its imputed capitalist tendencies. However, the argument pursued in the following pages is that peasants are no more spontaneously disposed toward socialism than they are toward capitalism. Peasant economy and society have their own irreducible logic and rationality. Attempts to collectivize *production* in the absence of compensating mechanisms, such as the provision of modern technology, cut across the substantive rationality of the peasant economy and thereby engender peasant resistance to it.

The following chapter will focus on the sociological implications of collectivization in the absence of technology, where efforts to reorganize peasant production have no obvious economic rationality and disrupt the traditional peasant way of doing things to no obvious advantage to the peasant. Collectivization interferes with traditional peasant rights and codes of action and upsets the "moral economy" found in the interior of family farms and kinship and neighborhood groups.

The Peasant Family

The basic unit of Lao peasant economy and society, like that of most peasant societies elsewhere, is the small farm (on average around 1 to 1.5 ha of rice fields), which operates as a production/consumption unit and is worked primarily by labor belonging to a specific domestic group. If one takes a snapshot view—a view adopted by many anthropologists and sociologists of Lao and Thai society—peasant families in Laos live in what appear to be nucleated families, but in fact an examination of the domestic cycle of the Lao peasant family reveals a domestic group best described as a "multihousehold compound."[2] The creation of multihousehold compounds follows preferred rules of inheritance and domicile. The crucial feature of this system is a preferred matrilocal residence for daughters and a general rule of female ultimogeniture for the house of the mother and father. That is, the youngest daughter and her husband *usually* inherit the family home. A typical domestic cycle of a Lao peasant family entails the eldest daughter and her husband living in the family house, along with her brothers and sisters. She and her husband work on the land of her mother and father and also attempt to rent other land or engage in some wage labor in order to eventually acquire their own productive property. When the next eldest daughter marries, she and her husband come to live in the family home, while the eldest daughter and her husband build their own house, with the assistance of their kin and neighbors (often the same thing), in the courtyard of the family home or as nearby as possible. This process is repeated until the last married daughter, having cared for her parents in old age, inherits the family home; the inheritance of the family home is more or less compensation for the care of the parents. Meanwhile, the sons have married and gone to live with the families of their wives, either in the same village or in another village.

An in-marrying male, however, becomes the household head. He, therefore, has authority over any in-marrying husband of his daughters, the consequences of which are that the males in the household tend to be affinally related, in contrast to the women. Unlike relations between father and son, which are normally warm, the relations between father-in-law and son-in-law are problematic, though in the areas of Laos I have studied the problem does not amount to a virtual taboo on communication between them, as is reported to be the case in northern Thailand, where the daughter directly mediates between the two.[3] (Thus in the cornucopia of Lao folk wisdom and jokes there are many stories about the relations between father-in-law and son-in-law; on the other hand, there are few about mothers-in-law and daughters-in-law, a relationship that is more problematic.) The practice of matrilocality, combined with male authority vested in the husband, has been called by one anthropologist working in northern Thailand, Sulamith Heinz-Potter, a "female centered system" to distinguish it from matriliny.[4]

The daughters and their husbands labor under the father's tutelage and augment the productive potential of the peasant farm, which at this point in the domestic cycle is at its zenith. The daughters and sons-in-law who are not going to inherit the homestead attempt to save enough money to build a separate house and to buy land and thereby, especially for the husband's sake, gain independence from the control of the father. Naturally, there is always some pressure for the early distribution of the inheritance. But this is kept in check by the fact that the multihousehold compound at its productive height is also best placed to secure more land and wealth, which will be divided up later. It is therefore in the interests of everyone, generally, to prolong this phase of the cycle and delay demands for its distribution. One could say the arrangement represents a genuinely dialectical incentive structure because the group's corporate structure is maintained in the interests of the constituent units into which it will ultimately dissolve.

Inheritance of productive property—paddy fields, gardens, buffalo, and cattle—is bilateral, and children generally are considered to have rights to equal shares. The division of property occurs either during the parents' dotage or immediately following their death. The general rules of residence tend to favor the accumulation of family land by daughters because sons are more likely to go to live in other villages and therefore, because they are not in a position to work the land, may sell their land to one of their sisters. Of course, it is also possible they will sell to a brother who has married within the village.

Naturally, there are exceptions to these general rules. For example, population pressure, death, demographic imbalance such as siblings of only one sex, illness, and so on will all lead to variations and exceptions to common practice. But the rule tends to assert itself in the long run. Let me offer some examples.

The following household compound is a good illustration of the mixing and matching of social rules (figs. 6.1, 6.2). Taking house number 1 and X as the original houses of two intertwined families, one gets the following histories: household number 1 was held by a younger daughter of a family in which her older brother and sister were the holders of households 7 and 8. The eldest daughter of household number 1 looked after the mother until she died; the older daughter subsequently died, whereupon the house devolved to her brother. During the mother's illness the next two youngest children were adopted by a childless neighbor in house X, while the very youngest, who was a simpleton, was looked after by the now-eldest brother. The daughter who was adopted has subsequently inherited house X (originally the house of the mother of the adoptive mother), while the adopted younger brother now occupies house 3. The occupant of house 5 is the son of the stepbrother of the adoptive mother, but is the stepson of the stepbrothers' stepsister, who had no children.

Empirical examples like this should give one a healthy skepticism of

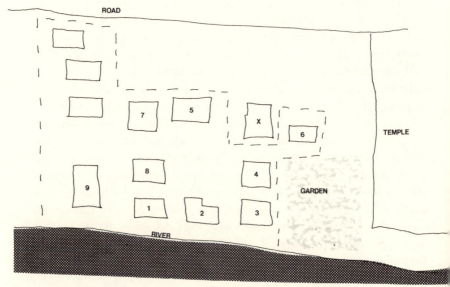

Note: The dotted line indicates the boundary of a village administrative unit, the <u>khum</u> or <u>nuay</u>.

Figure 6.1 Compound Layout

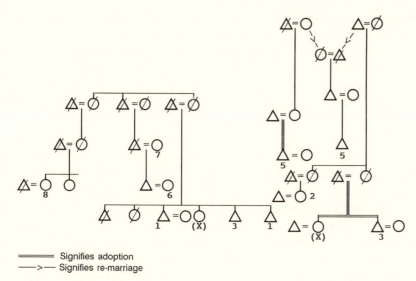

Signifies adoption
Signifies re-marriage

Figure 6.2 Kinship in Compound

rules, but there is a basic pattern of matrilocal inheritance. Five of the eight occupants of the houses inherited them through their mothers; the pattern is not smooth because of factors such as death, disablement, and childlessness. Only the wife of household 1 comes from an adjacent village, while the other three have come from distant villages. Women generally shift from their own village when their husband's prospects are better than their own. War in the recent history of Laos has also disrupted the pattern.

As for the inheritance of land, my inquiries in the tasseng, or district, showed an almost perfect pattern of bilateral inheritance. In ban Thana twenty-eight of the landholders were women and twenty-eight were men; in ban Bo-O twenty-three were women and twenty-eight men; in ban Nok there were thirty-four women landholders and thirty-one men in 1982. Such perfect bilaterality indicates that fewer men in this area migrate to their wife's village, and this fact is due primarily, I would suggest, to the area's proximity to Vientiane. After all, Vientiane and its environs are a target of immigrants from the hinterlands. Already in the early 1960s this pattern seemed to be emerging, according to a brief note in George Condominas's survey of the Vientiane plain that says males are "increasingly receiving inheritances comparable to those of their sisters."[5] Proximity to Vientiane offers opportunities for occasional wage labor or the practice of part-time farming and places less pressure on males to move, especially to a situation in which their wife's inheritance prospects may not be much better than their own. Consequently, they are more likely to remain in their maternal village and to activate claims to land there. As we have seen, the collapse of the urban economy in Vientiane immediately after the communist takeover at the end of 1975 appeared to intensify pressure on people's desire for access to land and on tendencies toward female inheritance.[6]

There may be a slight male bias in the above general statistics with regard to claimed land ownership because there is a tendency for male heads of households, when surveyed, to refer to the land they work as "their" land; closer investigation of various farmer groups, however, suggested a different picture, as revealed in the following typical example: in one group of twenty-one families, nine worked land inherited by the wife, six land inherited by both the husband and wife, and six land inherited only by the husband.[7] Thus certain rights are inscribed in the pattern of kinship in the Lao community and certain forms of action prescribed. How are these affected by collectivization?

Authority in Production

One key to understanding the economic and social dynamics of the peasant farm is recognition that the head of the domestic group is also head of the family's economic enterprise. Kinship therefore structures the organization of production, and the moral authority of the head of the family is reinforced by his position as controller and perhaps owner of the means of production. This combination of production and consumption in the peasant family or domestic group structures the economic, social, cultural, and biological functions of its members. It decisively influences not only their standing in the family group itself, but also their role and status in village life. As I have already said, the eldest married male in the Lao domestic group exercises authority within it. He controls most basic production decisions and activities of the domestic group and is its recognized spokesman in the village and the outside world. Therefore the status of the head of any domestic group is likely to be challenged by any collectivization program or attempt to form producers' cooperatives.

Theoretically, production cooperative members join as individuals, and this alone calls into question the peasant family's function as a production unit. Ideally, the production units of cooperatives, work groups or brigades, are not constituted around kinship connections but according to rational, functional criteria; impersonal rules rather than personal ones. Implementation of this system of modern rationality can challenge the household head's double role as head of the family and head of production. He no longer allocates production tasks to others but, on the contrary, has them allotted to him by the head of the cooperative or the leader of the work group. In the domestic production group the eldest male is also the "master farmer," who passes his knowledge on to those under him, and his wisdom in farming matters is deferred to. In a cooperative he is at best equal with other master farmers and placed in a situation of potentially invidious comparison with them; and as the cooperative begins to rely on, or regularly call in, experts from outside, this farming knowledge is potentially further devalued.

A cooperative's theoretical commitment to democratic organization— one member, one vote—on all important decisions of the cooperative also diminishes an elder's power. Not only younger men but women have votes of the same theoretical weight as those of their familial superiors. A further consideration is that the basis of parental authority in the peasant family is parental control over inheritance. Any transition to "ownership in common" naturally weakens this form of social control by peasant elders in a fundamental way.

The communal organization of work within the domestic group and the absence of economic reckoning within it favors domestic solidarity, and moreover, the head of the domestic group can take credit for the general results of production. Attempts to use a system of strict accounting in the cooperatives clearly advertises the relative contributions of each member of the family and therefore can loosen or undermine the bonds of dependency and the sources of authority within the peasant family.

Lao Peasant Women and Cooperatives

The foregoing issues are particularly salient in peasant systems with deeply entrenched patriarchal structures, like those in China and Vietnam. Because the status of women has traditionally been very low in these societies a number of feminist writers have suggested that collectivization actually improved conditions for women in the countryside. In a sense they argue that women had a vested interest in collectivization even if they did not clearly recognize it. Discussing collectivization in northern Vietnam in the 1950s, Christine Pelzer-White has argued, "Traditional forms of marriage which were disguised forms of labor recruitment had continued after land reform as the practice of finding strong young women to work as unpaid family labor by marrying her to a son below working age. Not surprisingly, young women caught in such marriages often become activists in the campaign to form cooperatives, as membership in a newly formed cooperative gave them independent access to employment. Moreover, husbands tended to be more reluctant to join cooperatives than their wives, because of the threat to their 'independent' status as household head managing a family farm."[8] Similar general arguments have been made for China, and while they point to a serious tension at the heart of Vietnamese and Chinese family patterns that could give rise to female activism, it would be a mistake to overestimate the extent of women's participation in collectivization.

The mobilization of women in both Vietnam and China first occurred during the land reform campaigns of the early 1950s. In contrast to women in China, women in Vietnam did possess some rights to land within the traditional structure, though the real extent and significance of this still require research.[9] But perhaps it was the relatively uncontroversial nature of women's demands for access to land that made this a less divisive issue during the Vietnamese land reform campaign and meant that more women were elevated to positions of leadership than in China. However, the subsequent criticisms of errors committed during the land reform campaign soon saw women lose these newly won positions of authority.[10] By gaining access to land, women in China and in Vietnam were expected to secure some economic independence. But there were many complications, not least of which was the powerful patrilineal and patrilocal kinship structures: "Customs of village exogamous marriage, which meant that women were likely to be married outside their village, . . . made it . . . difficult for young women to make meaningful use of their land rights."[11] Most often a woman's land was simply considered part of patrilineal property, and even women who did secure independent title to land soon saw it lost during collectivization.

It is true that collectivization also removed formal title to land from patrilineages and therefore was expected to weaken patriarchal control in rural society. Unexpectedly, it had the opposite effect, as John Lewis observed: "When the communists encouraged the pooling of land for use under the centralized management of the co-op head they inadvertently recreated the critical ingredient of lineage and village power, the collective land holdings. . . . Party leaders enforced obligations to the village and consciously reestablished many defunct village activities and functions such as the village meeting and the collective control of family and village life."[12] Restrictions on internal movement further reinforced tendencies for men to remain in their birthplace surrounded by kin and for the transfer of women "outsiders" between geographically anchored patrilineages. "Indeed in the absence of hiring labor," Elizabeth Croll writes, "the recruitment of women through marriage had become one of the major means of expanding the labor resources of the household."[13] The training of young women in economic and political skills was "a poor form of investment for local communities," as they were destined to move to their husband's village, and there their attempts to gain positions of responsibility were restricted because they were surrounded by strangers.

While the situation of women is best documented for China, there is little reason to doubt that similar processes were at work in Vietnam. Thus although collectivization opened up some opportunities for women to gain positions of responsibility that would have been unavailable in the traditional structure, it was not the avenue of emancipation it was initially expected to be.

In Laos the situation of women differs in a number of crucial respects from that of women in the Vietnamese and Chinese family structure. The female-centered nature of the Lao domestic group is structurally quite different from the male-dominated ones in the countryside of its northern and eastern neighbors, and this gives Lao women comparatively more power and influence in the family. In Laos, women have some power by virtue of their possession of land and the general practice of matrilocal residence. Their ability to dispossess their husbands through divorce tempers male tyrannical tendencies, and the fact that the husband often moves into a situation where he is surrounded by a network of his wife's relatives and friends attenuates his social and political command over her. Lao women also have a much greater say in their choice of spouse than do either Chinese or Vietnamese women. Arranged marriages among the Lao peasants are rare, although, of course, the parents wield considerable informal influence over the choice of a partner.

Seen in this light, Martin Stuart-Fox's assertion that "the loose social structure of the Lao village made it likely that people would be less amenable to collective action and the regimentation of cooperative methods of farming than in the case of the Vietnamese with their deeply ingrained Confucian social values" seems oversimplified.[14] In fact, "Confucian" men in China and Vietnam resisted collectivization, and women in revolt against Confucianism were likely to support it. Resistance to collectivization in Laos has not come from the so-called loose nature of the social structure or even from the allegedly "easygoing Lao national character" of journalistic commentary, but from the nature of the peasant economy and society and the structural position of women and men in that society.

True, as in almost all peasant societies, in Laos women are considered socially inferior to men, and this is codified in, for example, Buddhist ideology, which claims that women are on a lower level of being than men. Peasant women are expected to defer to their husbands and fathers in most areas of social life, except those that are the specific preserve of women, such as spirit cults. One author gives an example of the behavior of the *ideal* Lao woman: "Every night before going to bed, Lao women prostrate themselves at the feet of their husbands to ask pardon for all the bad things they have done during the day. They cannot lie on the same pillow as their husbands, who have a pillow placed higher. . . . During a meal they may only begin to eat when their husbands have reached the third mouthful."[15] It must be emphasized that this is pure ideology, and I know of no examples where this practice has actually been observed. As ideology, however, it underlines the subordinate status of women.

A clear division exists between the public and private spheres for men and women. Men generally speak for the household and are elected or seconded to positions of authority within village social and political organizations. Women by and large are confined to the private, domestic sphere, except for the important economic activity of trading. On the basis of these cultural facts, it may seem that cooperatives could hold some advantages for Lao women. But this is not so. The formation of cooperatives would entail women handing over control of their most important social asset, land, to a group that any one woman could have only a minor influence over and that is most likely to be dominated by male officeholders. Cooperatives would cause women to surrender some of their autonomy. Thus in Laos, spontaneous peasant resistance to collectivization arising from the heart of the peasant social structure comes from both men *and* women because both stand to lose some of their former social prerogatives by joining a cooperative. The only person structurally situated to potentially gain from such a reorganization is the landless son-in-law who is still under the tutelage of his father-in-law. But he desires to become the future head of the family farm, not a member of a producers' cooperative. By contrast, the structurally weak position of women in China and Vietnam did not promise a future in which their current status would be significantly changed, and consequently a number of them were attracted by the new possibilities *promised* by collectivization.

Socialist revolutions have generally called for and sparked desires for female emancipation, and in rigidly patriarchal systems such a program has sometimes led to serious conflict. In a sobering overview, Maxine Molyneux writes, "Evidence from Soviet central Asia in the 1920s and China after 1949 shows that many thousands of women committed suicide or were murdered by their families for claiming their new rights; many more paid a heavy price in prolonged personal suffering for attempting to defy their families and elders."[16] Women in Laos are not confronted by such tremendous obstacles, but their road to emancipation does not obviously lead through the cooperatives.

In summary, while the formally democratic organization of the cooperative potentially challenges male authority, it does not automatically favor women because the cultural reality of Lao society means that women as a group and individually would most likely hand over their social power to male cooperative officials. Therefore neither males nor females were spontaneously attracted to the cooperatives.

The Labor/Consumer Balance

Domestic groups form the basis of the Lao peasant economy, and peasant resistance to collectivization arises out of the logic of this economy. As a producer/consumer unit, the Lao domestic group, like those in other peasant economies, is preoccupied by what Chayanov called the labor/consumer balance. That is, the family is concerned to have a sufficient work force to meet the needs of its economically active members as well as of its dependents (young and old). This balance shifts throughout the developmental cycle of the domestic group. The period of greatest prosperity for the peasant farm is that when the domestic group contains the lowest percentage of dependents (elderly people and small children), which generally coincides with the marriage of the eldest daughter and the addition of her husband's labor. It is a time when the latter have no children of their own, the younger children are of some help in the field, and when one or both of the grandparents are dead. Consider figure 6.3. Tracing the family at three intervals over a period of ten years, from point A to point B to point C (and assuming the contribution of the daughter's younger unmarried

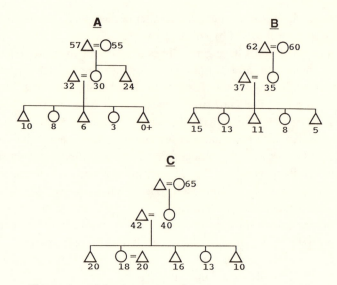

Figure 6.3 Illustration of the domestic cycle

brother at point A, the semiretirement of the parents at point B, and the departure of the brother for his wife's household), we get a progression of the labor/dependent ratio of, say, 5.5 : 3.5 to 6 : 2 to 8 : 1.[17] At each "stage" the productive potential of the domestic group increases. Calculation of this balance is employed by peasants as a yardstick to judge the cooperatives, as revealed by all the private peasants I interviewed about either their reasons for not joining a cooperative or their reasons for leaving.

Peasants consistently complained that their households did not have enough active members to enable them to earn sufficient labor points (or mark points) in the cooperative to cover their subsistence needs. However, this is often only the peasants' *subjective* perception of the situation inside the cooperatives and is not necessarily based on factual knowledge or actual experience. So, for example, peasants in a labor-exchange group I surveyed repeated the peasants' general critique of the cooperatives. Hedging his bets, one member said he would be interested in joining a cooperative if he had a more favorable labor/consumer balance in his family. This is family 1 in table 6.1, but as we can see if we compare his family with the labor/consumer balance in the families of the cooperative in table 6.2, it

TABLE 6.1. Labor-Exchange Group

Family	Work Force	Of Which	Casual[a]	Children	Aged
1	4	1 teacher	3	—	—
2	5	1 abbatoir	2	—	—
		1 teacher			
		1 full-time weaver			
3	4	1 truck driver	2	—	—
4	2		2	2	—
5	2		—	3	—
6	2		—	2	2
7	2.5		—	3	0.5
8	1		—	6	—
9	2		—	3	—
		60%		40%	

[a]Casual refers to school-age children who work part time.

has a more favorable balance than most families in the cooperative. In fact, if we compare the general labor/consumer balance for the cooperative over three years with that of the labor-exchange group, we see that the exchange group has a more favorable balance than the cooperative. Indeed, over the three years, even with a turnover of families, the labor/consumer balance for the cooperative worsened, as five people who had been in the work force in 1981 became dependent old people by 1983.

The peasants are claiming that one needs a high labor-to-consumer ratio to make ends meet in the cooperatives. In reality, as the tables indicate, the peasants outside the cooperatives often have a higher labor/consumer ratio compared to the cooperatives. On the other hand (here we encounter the circular logic directed at the cooperatives by peasants), the fact that cooperatives can be shown to have a higher percentage of consumers than the exchange groups confirmed private peasants' fears that if they joined the cooperative they would have to support more dependents through cooperative mechanisms of redistribution. While I have already enumerated several sociological barriers to spontaneous peasant enthusiasm for cooperatives, these are reinforced here by a critique that springs from the economic logic of the individual peasant farm.

TABLE 6.2. Work Force/Dependent Relationship in Don Dou, 1981 and 1983

Family	Work Force		Casual (10–15 yrs)		Children (0–9 yrs)		Age	
	'81	'83	'81	'83	'81	'83	'81	'83
1	3	1	1	1	1	1	—	2
2	1	—	—	—	—	—	2	2
3	3	3	—	—	5	5	—	—
4	2	3	2	—	1	1	—	1
5	1	2	—	—	2	4	—	—
6	1	1	2	2	4	1	—	2
7	3	2	—	1	6	5	—	—
8	4	—	1	—	4	--	—	—
9	3	2	2	—	1	—	—	—
10	1	—	—	—	—	—	—	—
11	1	2	—	—	—	—	—	—
12	1	—	—	—	—	—	—	—
13	1	3	1	—	—	—	—	—
14[a]	2		—		2		—	
15	2	—	—	—	1	1	2	2
16	1	—	1	—	—	—	—	—
		57%				43%		
17		2		—		2		—
18		3		—		2		1
19		2		—		1		—
		48%				52%		

[a]Family 14 left the cooperative in 1982.

Children

Another objection that springs from this peasant farm logic is the claim that in the cooperatives farmers cannot collect work points for children below sixteen years of age (this being the official qualifying age for cooperative membership), whereas private farmers are able to reap the benefits of this pool of labor.[18] The peasants' criticisms of cooperatives, therefore, show how acutely aware they are of the importance of child labor to the viability of their farms, although their comments on the actual functioning of the cooperatives are not entirely accurate. But as the head Don Dou cooperative, Ngai, explained, the labor points of children up to the age of sixteen go under their parents' names "so as not to violate the cooperative's principles." This, of course, is more possible (or less problematic) under a family contract system in collectivized agriculture, as was introduced in China and Vietnam after 1979 and proposed latterly in Laos. But in fact this system has application only in an already-collectivized agriculture in the process of devolution. For peasants like those in Laos, the decision is whether to take their family into a cooperative in the first place, and in this context even the family responsibility system is simply a more complicated form of family farming. So why bother with the complication? On the other hand, for peasants in Laos who have already been in and out of a cooperative in which such matters as child labor were not taken into account, namely, during the initial attempts at collectivization, this remains their hard and fast memory of the disadvantages of the cooperative, regardless of later talk about contracts.

In addition, the state's greater insistence on children's attendance at school has cut into child labor time available to the peasant farmer, and therefore he sees his pool of labor under challenge from two directions— the state education system and the cooperative. The time demands of education can place strains on the peasant farm's economic performance at the optimum moment in its domestic cycle, namely, at the point most of the children are capable of productive work. Depending on the level of education they aspire to, students, far from contributing to the well-being of the family, require its support. Therefore, from the point of view of the peasant farmer, the advantages so looked forward to at the peak of the domestic cycle are under threat.

Consider, for example, the inroads schooling has made on the worker/dependent ratio in the multihousehold compound group we considered earlier (table 6.3). True, school holidays are scheduled to coincide with periods of peak labor demands, and children still engage in considerable economic activity before and after school. However, this labor is no longer at the beck and call of the head of the household.

At the other end of the scale, elderly farmers expressed the fear that they would be penalized in the cooperative system because they would not be able to work as fast as the younger workers and therefore would not earn as much. This is a legitimate concern, as is anxiety about the vagaries of cooperative welfare when one is too old to work. Old farmers still in charge of their own land and family do not express the same worries.

TABLE 6.3. Age Composition of Compound

Household	Age	Male	Female	In School
No. 1	52	+		
	50		+	
	44	+		
	24	+		
	20	+		+
	17	+		+
	14		+	+
	11	+		+
No. 2	78	+		
	55		+	
	17		+	+
No. 3	48	+		
	42		+	
	13	+		+
	5		+	
	3		+	
	2	+		
No. 4	53	+		
	44		+	
	20		+	+
	17	+		+
	14	+		+
	9	+		+
	6	+		+
	4		+	
Nos. 5 & 6[a]	60		+	
	39	+		
	38		+	
	17	+		+
	15	+		+
	12	+		+
	12		+	+
	10		+	+
	7	+		+
	3		+	
	60		+	
	42	+		
	40		+	

(*continued*)

TABLE 6.3. (*Continued*)

Household	Age	Male	Female	In School
No. 7	19	+		+
	16	+		+
	14	+		+
	9		+	+
	33	+		
	28		+	
	20	+		+
No. 8	18		+	
	7		+	+
	5	+		
	3	+		
	2		+	
	83		+	
	58	+		
	55		+	
	35	+		
	33		+	
No. 9	23	+		
	19	+		+
	10		+	+
	8	+		+
	6		+	+
	3	+		
	55		+	
	28	+		
	27		+	
No. X	21	+		
	19		+	
	5		+	
	3	+		
	2		+	

ªHouses 5 and 6 are considered one household.

Traditional Labor-Exchange Groups

Concern with stabilizing and securing their seasonal labor demands throughout the developmental cycle of their domestic groups is a major preoccupation of Lao peasant farmers. At certain points in the cycle they require labor from outside the domestic group from those whose cycle is at a different phase and can spare the labor; this can be reciprocated at a later stage. Thus labor-exchange groups are formed to iron out the fluctuations in the domestic cycle and to respond to the seasonal demands of agriculture. These are forms of traditional peasant cooperation, and presumably they are the ones General Secretary Kaysone had in mind when he spoke of the "traditions of mutual solidarity and assistance among the Lao people."

Not surprisingly labor tends to be mobilized along already existing lines of kinship. Bilateral kin who happen to have neighboring rice fields are ideal labor-exchange partners, and, of course, for practical reasons, neighbors in the field who are not kin are also ideal partners. But, given the importance of the idiom of kinship, attempts will often be made to establish some distant or quasi-familial link. As one farmer quipped when I was inquiring about kinship relations in his labor-exchange group, if you pushed it far enough then everyone in the village was related. Statements like this, however, should not allow outsiders to be seduced into thinking that kinship is treated lightly or is a vague arrangement, as some "loose structure" theorists would seem to want to argue. For example, George Condominas suggests that Lao villagers are kin "more or less distant with the majority of members of the collectivity,"[19] that is, the village. This, he says, is reflected in the villagers' tendency to use kinship terms when talking to outsiders about members of their village. For example, young men and women are likely to refer to any elder male as "uncle." What Condominas confuses, however, is the fact that the general pattern of social interaction in the village is governed by old/young relationships, with age determining the degree of respect. The transposition of kinship terms into the social sphere serves to reinforce social rank and social obedience at all levels and has little to do with a strictly sociological concept of kinship. It is easy to see, when considering these transpositions, how populist ideas of village cooperation can take root among communist and Third World nationalist elites.

Populists are also misled by the moral virtue that is placed on helping one another out within Lao peasant ideology, an ideology that is in part generated by the necessity of labor exchanges at crucial times of the year. Monks preach the virtues of mutual help and selflessness in the temples, parents impress them on their children, and communist governments sanction and promote them. But the world of folk sayings also contains a range of complementary imperatives concerning the merit of hard work: "Support the hard worker, chase away the talkative"; "Don't make friends with someone who is lazy." These encourage a hawk-eye among those who engage in exchange labor, and ill-feeling and gossip about those who do not fulfill, or are felt not to have fulfilled, their obligations.

The exchange of labor is a nonmonetized exchange, and therefore the general problem of calculation arises. This leads us into general considerations of the nature of reciprocity among the Lao peasants. In a fully monetized economy the general model of exchange is one of strict reciprocity (though even in a full-fledged capitalist system this remains an ideal model).[20] That is, one returns exactly what one is given. Monetary calculation, of course, makes this easy to manage. The material conditions of a peasant economy often make such calculation dysfunctional.

Within the domestic group what Marshal Sahlins has referred to as generalized reciprocity and what Alvin Gouldner refers to as "rough equivalence" is the rule. As Gouldner argues, rough reciprocity "induces a certain amount of ambiguity as to whether indebtedness has been repaid and, over time, generates uncertainty about who is in whose debt."[21] As noted many times, the importance of this type of exchange is that it bonds social groups and forestalls hostility. Now, again as a general rule, the farther one travels from the core of the domestic group, the more exchanges move toward a situation of strict reciprocity. Thus, for example, rent for buffalo or paddy fields will often be determined by the affinity of the renter to the rentor, the terms becoming more strictly reciprocal—or more approximating the going market rate—the less related by kinship or friendship the two parties to the exchange are. Similarly with loans of rice. A neighboring farmer with whom one wishes to have continuous exchanges of labor falls within a similar spectrum as kin. In this case, rough reciprocity serves the purposes of bonding several farmers over time and thereby securing a stable labor pool from season to season. Bonds formed in the field may, of course, be strengthened if the associates are household neighbors or friends, and may be further reinforced if they encourage their children to marry one another. These are possible, but not necessary, outcomes. Strict reciprocity, on the other hand, involves no indebtedness and therefore no future commitment to work together.[22]

Farmers thus make strategic decisions when they enter into labor exchanges, and who one exchanges with varies over time and according to where one is situated in the system of village stratification. Perhaps this can best be illustrated by surveying the economic activities of the multihousehold compound considered earlier. The members of the individual households are involved in various labor-exchange groups that crisscross the paddy fields. The households in these groups are members of what I will call irrigation collectives (and sometimes buying and marketing groups), and these have approximately fourteen farmers in them. Irrigation collectives, naturally, are made up of farmers who have adjacent fields. These collectives usually are a pool of potential labor exchangers, but core groups of kin reside, as it were, within them. Thus households 1, 2, 6 and 8 are a core group in one collective, while households 2, 3, 5, (X) are at the core of another irrigation collective. (Household 2 overlaps because it holds land in both groups.) Other bilateral kin are also members of these collectives, and hence core cooperators, as are permanent neighbors. Added to which there are arrangements whereby household 3, for example, assists his brother in household 1 but is not considered part of his brother's irrigation collective because he has no land in that group.

I will focus on household 3 because it is a relatively poor family in terms of land.[23] The area that the household head owned was not sufficient to live on, so his family labored on his brother's land, on his land and that of others within his own irrigation collective, and occasionally on rented land. He also received income in kind from farmers for overseeing irrigation in the district. Put simply, he and his family work extremely hard to earn a living.

The way he explains his activity gives us an important insight into the way a peasant farmer in his position makes strategic decisions. Bounpheng, the head of household 3, works on a small amount of his own land in a labor-exchange group with relatives and neighbors and exchanges labor with his elder brother. In discussing these relationships, he (like others) prefers the language of helping (*suay leua*) rather than the language of reciprocity (*dtorp thaen*), which has the much clearer implication of paying back. In these relationships, he said, there may be some delays or poor coordination in exchanging labor in which either he or others will not be ready at exactly the right time to, for example, help transplant the rice seedlings; or the labor may be offered late or not at all. But, he explained, these miscoordinations are manageable because the groups always work together, and therefore there is always the possibility of future help (repayment). Indeed, if labor comes late or not at all in the current year it allows an individual the luxury of magnanimity, which can be traded on socially until the next season—but rarely longer.

From this slender but relatively secure base Bounpheng could rent out land in another village around two kilometers away. He was able to do this in the dry season in this irrigated area because some landowners who had harvested enough rice in the wet season would concentrate either on their gardens or on trading or perhaps even some wage labor in Vientiane during the dry season. Hence land-short peasants like Bounpheng or peasants in a similar predicament in nearby areas where there is no irrigation, or indeed some government workers and their wives are able to cultivate land in the dry season. Irrigation collectives and labor-exchange groups of usually unrelated people spring up over the dry season and take a range of forms— from groups of friends to groups of office workers to families like Bounpheng's working in conjunction with some other friends from the village who find themselves in a similar situation. The dry season also provides an opportunity for sons-in-law and their wives to rent land and accumulate some earnings in their attempts to buy land.

The instability of these groups from dry season to season has a number of consequences: first, strict reciprocity tends to be the rule in exchanges of labor between seasonal field neighbors; one day's work is returned by one day's work or by a payment of the going daily rate. The second is that, on the one hand, the breadth of the group tends to be smaller because of the accounting problems that arise in a situation of strict reciprocity; therefore, the amount of land a particular farm family can cultivate is limited. On the other hand, people try to engage in as much semiwage labor as they can. But opportunities are restricted because people who are unfamiliar with irrigation systems and the use of high yielding varieties of rice are reluctant to take the risk of hiring labor to help them cultivate a larger area in case their harvest is poor, owing, for example, to bad water management or insufficient use of fertilizer and pesticides. Third, partly because of inexperience, but also because the farmers in the dry season irrigation collectives have no necessary long-term bonds, there is a tendency for regular disputes to occur over water management. Farmers who want water ignore the general irrigation plan and block some canals and open others in order to direct water into their own fields. Floods and heated arguments often result. The absence of long-term bonds, therefore, induces a degree of anarchy.

Bounpheng did not speak of paying rent to his landowner; rather, he said he "shared" his crop with him because the person who owned the land had helped him by "loaning" him the land. No doubt this way of speaking about rent partly arises out of the ambivalence that is abroad under the new regime about land rental and its suggestion of landlordism. But it is also in Bounpheng's interest to speak in this way. It downplays the contractual side of the relationship while simultaneously trying to elevate it to a friendship, the aim being to secure some obligation on the part of the landowner to rent the land to him again the following dry season. It is important to realize, however, that this way of seeing things arises out of the contingencies of the peasant economy. It is in no one's interest to insist on clarification, and in this way peasant culture continuously reproduces the language of reciprocity and mutual assistance while safeguarding the interests of those involved in exchange arrangements.

Peasants who own land and who therefore have relatively stable relationships often prefer to use as little wage labor as possible, first, because, where wages are paid in cash, this reduces their cash requirements, and second, because wage labor is not an enduring relationship, and this contravenes the aim of traditional labor exchange within the peasant economy, which is to secure long-term access to labor. These issues are pressing in most areas of Laos that, unlike the rest of Southeast Asia, are relatively underpopulated. Where the use of wage labor is less constrained by considerations of long-term stability, the risks run by dry season intermittent cultivators restrict the breadth of wage labor relations.

The opportunity to rent land is a welcome one for domestic groups at the peak of their economically productive cycle, but it can be an unstable arrangement, as kin of landowners are always potentially able to displace nonkin. This places those peasants who have insufficient land in an insecure position. Therefore, they work hard and hope that at the peak of their family's productive cycle they will be able to accumulate enough wealth to buy land. But a single death can ruin the plan: Bounpheng's sixteen-year-old son was gored to death by his water buffalo in 1986; this death was offset only, perhaps, by that of his four-year-old, unproductive daughter. Labor exchange among landed peasants also has the purpose or effect of obligating farmers who have excess land at one point in their domestic cycle to rent it to others who are in need because they are reaching their period of peak demand, or even of obliging land-surplus peasants in the group to sell to peasants with land shortages. So sometimes labor-exchange obligations can lead to access to land.

Landownership, even if only of a small parcel, gives peasants the opportunity, however slender, to engage in relatively stable exchange relations with kin and others within the peasant community and therefore the potential to improve one's lot. Landlessness, on the other hand, gives one little basis on which to construct ongoing ties, and therefore the landless have low status in village society. No one is in their debt, while they are likely to be indebted to others.

Peasants use several accounting variables when exchanging labor: adult male labor, adult female labor, child labor by boys or girls, which is coupled with specific tasks, such as transplanting, weeding, plowing, harvesting, threshing, winnowing, and so on. Pure reciprocity, for example, returns one day's adult male labor with the same, or a day's transplanting work with the same, etc. An obvious implication of using several variables is that insistence on strict reciprocity means the keeping of accounts that can quickly become cumbersome, and this can restrict the range or breadth of possible labor-exchange transactions, at least without disputes. Hence a natural ceiling is placed on the size of the groups. Conversely, it makes rough reciprocity within defined smaller groups more attractive and manageable. One also finds what might be called "mixed" labor-exchange groups, in which some people are involved in a roughly reciprocal arrangement, while others work on the basis of strict reciprocity, and still others as day laborers.

The sexual division of labor in agriculture complicates calculations of reciprocity not only because one has what is generally considered women's work and men's work, but also because women's work is often accorded less value than men's. For example, men usually do the plowing and repairing of dikes and channels, while women transplant rice seedlings or weed. There are no absolute barriers to sexual interchanges of work, and I have observed women plowing. But generally even women who were farmers in their own right (either because their husband had died or they were divorced) hired males to do their plowing while they went and worked for others or in some cases used the time for weaving for commercial exchange, the returns of which would be used to pay the man. On the other hand, one often sees men transplanting and weeding. One consequence of male labor being more highly valued than female labor is that it is substitutable for female labor, but usually not vice versa. The idea of sending your wife or daughter over to the neighbors to offer help with the plowing is unthinkable. But a husband could stand in for his wife or a brother for his sister in transplanting, for example. Therefore, sexual balances—and age distributions—within families play an important role in the farmer's calculations of the range of obligations that can be entertained. Or, among more defined groups, these incommensurabilities add another element, perhaps even an attraction, to the practice of rough reciprocity. Interestingly, in the cooperatives the sexual division of labor and valuation of male versus female labor have been reproduced. Activities that are predominantly female tasks, such as transplanting, are given fewer work points than, say, tractor plowing, a male occupation.

The initial collectivization drive in 1978–79 cut across the logic of traditional peasant cooperation in Laos. It attempted to encourage the formation of large labor-exchange groups or cooperatives regardless of traditional lines of solidarity. In a sense, and in true populist style, it asked the peasants to work together as one big, happy family. But these attempts threw together people who felt no natural affinity for or commitment to working together, and it led to feelings of injustice as the group worked individual peasant land, regardless of size. As one peasant woman explained, in the early stages remuneration was based simply on turning up, "showing your face," and she claimed there were no fixed hours. Some people would turn up late and others would work lazily and sloppily. They worked in big groups on a single plot rather than splitting up into smaller groups and working on specified plots. In the end, she claimed, everyone received the same amount of payment, and this meant that lazy people got the same amount as hard workers, which was terribly demoralizing and led to poor workmanship. As another woman exclaimed with some passion, she would never join such a cooperative again even if her husband did. "They allowed lazy people to live off us!" In a family, the first woman said, working together was easier because it ensured that everyone turned up to work at the same time and took care in their work.

Labor-exchange groups among the peasantry in Laos are designed to both stabilize and potentially enhance the peasant farm's productive capacity. It is a system in which rough reciprocity is designed in such a way that everyone comes out ahead. It is not a zero-sum game, as many writers seem to imagine. But although we talk of rough reciprocity, labor exchange is a delicately tuned social mechanism, with checks and balances. Indebtedness cannot be allowed to get too far out of hand or else rough reciprocity will be transformed into bonds of dependency whereby the contracting parties are no longer considered equals. The delicateness of the relationship is one of the reasons it requires careful social regulation, and in peasant society kinship is most readily to hand to fulfill this task. A collectivization campaign that simply attempts—or has no alternative in the absence of technology but to attempt—the collectivization of labor disrupts all these checks and balances. Moreover, the banding together of landed farm families with different land endowments and the landless can lead only to the redistribution of wealth downward, in this case the sharing of poverty, and to the destruction of one of the mechanisms by which peasants attempt to get ahead. The incentive structure built into the peasant economy, which among other things rewards skillful farmers, is therefore stifled. What is a non-zero-sum game at one level of labor organization, the peasant farm, is transformed into a zero-sum situation at another level, the cooperative. It is a good example of diseconomies of scale in labor organization.

Furthermore, while more or less asking the peasants to work as one big family in the cooperative, the labor point system itself (which I shall examine in the next chapter) along with the formation of labor teams according to the rules of modern formal rationality undermines the rationale of rough reciprocity, which bonds laborers within the traditional groups. The cooperative system, through its method of calculation, encourages an attitude of strict reciprocity, that is, the kind that creates no bonds, and this probably explains why cooperatives of this sort collapse so spectacularly when they do.[24] Generally, only outside coercion can hold them together in the absence of innovations or technology that can transcend the logic of traditional labor cooperation.

It has often been asserted that the widespread existence of traditional forms of cooperation in peasant agriculture helps account for the apparent relative ease with which the Chinese and Vietnamese communist parties were able to carry through collectivization programs in the late 1950s. Thus John Wong, for example, claims that the Chinese communists "built on some fairly strong elements of collectivism which had long existed in the traditional background of Chinese agriculture."[25] Similar assertions have been made for Vietnam.[26] These claims are true only to the extent that communist cadres in both cases attempted, in the early years of their respective revolutions, to formalize preexisting labor-exchange arrangements and to facilitate new exchange arrangements, especially following land reform. Beyond this step a qualitatively different form of organization was involved.

The much-vaunted lack of overt peasant resistance to collectivization— or lack of overt state coercion—in both China and Vietnam has overlooked the widespread rural violence that accompanied the land reform campaigns which immediately preceded collectivization. During the land reform millions of opponents—landlords and "rich peasants"—were killed, and rural society cowed by the often uncontrollable violence sparked by the state-endorsed assault on the old structures of village society.[27] Terror was an essential component of these campaigns. As Edwin Moise writes of the land reform campaign in northern Vietnam, "The main point of the executions lay in their psychological effect. . . . It seems likely that to have the proper effect on the whole population the Party wanted to have a few executions, but not too many, in each area." But in both countries the party unleashed an unexpected wave of spontaneous violence and recriminations. The consequences were that the "land-reform errors had sown hatred and fear in the villages; neither the victims nor the perpetrators could quickly forget the past and learn to work together again." The violence and persecutions engulfed both ordinary peasants and rural party activists alike, causing deep demoralization, and even attempts at "rectification" by the state often failed to restore confidence. Many feared that "with another change in policy they might be attacked again."[28] Paybacks and retribution continued on a local level for years afterward, and it is hard to understand how the long-term impact of this upheaval in the villages could be overlooked by analysts of collectivization. After these events it would have been a brave cadre or peasant to have spoken out against the formation of cooperatives. Once collectivization had been carried out, the only alternatives available were those already approved by the party. Thus state coercion, real or threatened, has been an integral part of mass collectivization programs, alongside which the influence of preexisting forms of peasant cooperation pales into insignificance.

Perhaps one of the major ironies concerning communist beliefs in the continuity between what they see as traditional peasant communalism and socialist cooperatives is that the organizations they encourage in fact dissolve the bonds of traditional cooperation in favor of a form of individualism. It is an irony that sociologists Weber and Durkheim would certainly understand and appreciate. It is doubly ironic inasmuch as communists and their opponents see alleged peasant individualism as a major obstacle to collectivization.

On a broader canvas, one of the fundamental ideological weaknesses in the Lao communist government's commitment to cooperatives is populism. This may sound peculiar given the usual Marxist-Leninist emphasis on class conflict. However, the necessary nationalism that accompanies state-building disposes all new states in the developing world toward populism, an ideology that tends to emphasize the allegedly solidaristic nature of their societies. As Peter Worsley wrote in his excellent book *The Third World* back in the early 1960s, "The populist asserts that there are no divisions in the community, or if they are discernable, they are 'non-antagonistic'. Thus class divisions can be dismissed as external ('imperialist') intrusions, alien to the society. Ethnic differences can equally be dismissed as consequences of 'divide and rule' or as vestigial, disappearing legacies of the past ('tribalism' or 'feudalism'). . . . All these divisions, it is held, will soon disappear, leaving a united society."[29] Thus populism is not well equipped to recognize local and indigenous roots of opposition to any of the state's nationalist projects. As an ideology that articulates the logic of state power, it is not predisposed to seeking out, for example, the peculiar dynamics of peasant economy and society.

The Lao communists have invoked traditions of "mutual solidarity and assistance among [the Lao] people" but discovered that these do not translate directly into production cooperatives. Peasants in Laos are prepared to adopt new forms of cooperation in irrigation, for example, or consumer and marketing cooperatives. The Marxist-Leninist emphasis on the primacy of relations of production in the development of social life has meant that communists have often underrated the importance of other forms of cooperation—ones that the peasants are receptive to precisely because they do not impinge on production relations within the peasant economy.

7

Cooperation in the

Cooperatives

Labor organization and management is a major problem in agricultural production cooperatives, especially in labor-intensive, underdeveloped agriculture. Thus a Vietnamese study on agricultural management wrote, "In northern Vietnam, agricultural cooperation has preceded mechanization, rendering *the organization of work a matter of primordial importance.*"[1] The Lao government justified its planned collectivization program by claiming that it would allow the application of science and technology to agriculture and that this would lead to a growth in agricultural productivity. However, in the intervening absence of these vital inputs they too looked to labor reorganization to augment productivity. As Kaysone told the Congress of Cooperatives in 1979, "Without sufficient machinery and equipment . . . only by reorganizing labor" is it possible to raise production efficiency.[2] Cooperatives attempt to displace a familial organization of labor with a "rational," formal organization that allocates labor according to an organizational plan, and, naturally, because a cooperative operates as a larger unit than the family farm it must create a new system of labor allocation and supervision. Reorganization of labor, however, proved to be a major stumbling block in the formation of cooperatives.

"Industrial Democracy" in the Countryside

The cooperatives are formally committed to democratic principles. As one Lao government document declared, the "protection of democracy" is the

150

principle that forms the "moral and revolutionary soul of the people as self-masters in a cooperative community, in carrying out every duty of the cooperative, such as deciding on the production plan, cooperative expenditure, distribution of the product and the election of management personnel."[3] Of course, similar formal commitments to democracy were given, for example, by the Chinese communes and the Vietnamese cooperatives when in fact management and party cadres were able to wield considerable autocratic power. Consolidation of this sort of power did not occur in Laos for the same reason that the cooperatives themselves never consolidated, and that meant they were unable, therefore, to provide a local power base for managers and cadres.[4]

The rights and duties of the cooperatives were set out in the provisional regulations as follows: "The congress of cooperative members shall cast ballots to elect the board of directors of the cooperative, the size of which shall depend on the size of the cooperative." The responsibilities of this board of directors were to formulate annual production and financial plans; to "provide guidance to labor units in implementing the production plan and in applying technical methods"; to distribute income; to sign agreements on "economic obligations with the various state organs and other cooperatives"; to set up "working units specifically to handle cultivation, animal husbandry, handicrafts, irrigation projects, seedlings, fertilizer and so forth"; to "call extraordinary or ordinary sessions of the cooperative, submit reports on the cooperative's activities and the board's leadership to the higher echelons and answer questions raised by cooperative members on all activities carried out by the cooperative"; to supervise and control all activities of the cooperative. "The head of a cooperative shall supervise and control the daily work of his or her cooperative."[5] The "foremen" in the work units established by the cooperative are elected by the people working in the unit, while management has the power to appoint members with specialist knowledge to specific tasks, although these can be challenged through members' meetings. Not one of these formal rules, however, ever attained more than a notional correspondence to reality.

As we shall see in the next chapter, the organizational strength of the LPRP was insufficient to reach down into the majority of villages or cooperatives. The leaders of the cooperatives, the management committees, were drawn from local peasants, who usually owed their allegiance to their fellow farmers and were unused to offering it to some higher organization. With few exceptions the people elected to head the cooperatives were smallholding, male peasants. Because landlessness was not a widespread phenomenon it was not surprising that management committees should consist of landowning peasants. Only in a few areas, such as the districts adjacent to Vientiane, were demographic conditions such that there was a small but significant group of landless peasants. The new regime attempted to mobilize these people during the collectivization campaign as a spearhead for agrarian reform—as communist governments in neighboring countries had done. However, despite such tactics, these peasants were rarely able to dominate the management committees except when, after 1979, landowning peasants began to abandon producer cooperatives, leaving them increasingly in the hands of landless or land-short peasants.

An important criterion for election to the management committee was some degree of literacy, which generally tended to be possessed (if at all) by better-off peasants and males. Election was also influenced by more enduring social factors, such as age, gender, Buddhist piety, or success as a farmer—in short, qualities that determined one's respect in village society. Possession of land generally qualified one for active "citizenship" in Lao village society, and heads of households exercised those rights, not individual members. The communist government attempted to change this, yet individual members of a household would not dare vote against the household head in any public forum. Similarly, while landless peasants hold formal voting rights, they do not command sufficient respect to be spontaneously elevated to positions of leadership in villages or cooperatives, except where they are the majority in the latter.

In the cooperatives in muang Hatsayfong traditional patterns of leadership have been maintained, and these have been closely associated with small, kin-based entourages. Indeed, since the end of the campaign in 1979 kinship has increasingly come to regulate the internal workings of the outwardly formal structures of the cooperatives. For example, consider the kinship relationships among the members of ban Nok 1 cooperative (fig. 7.1): fourteen of the twenty-two listed members are related through the families of the manager and his wife (family 1). The cooperative divides itself into three work groups of farmers who work adjacent plots, although these plots are themselves situated far apart; some plots overlap into the paddy land of a neighboring village. Families 1, 2, 4, 5, 6, 7, 8, 10, 13, 17, 21 are in group one, families 9, 11, 12, 20, 22 are in group two, and families 3, 6, 14, 15, 16, 18, 19 are in group three.

At the center of each of these groups is an elder farmer with a substan-

Group 1

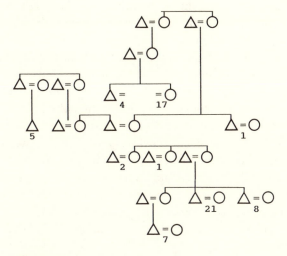

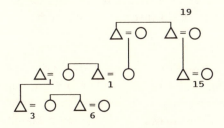

Group 2 (No kin)

Group 3

Figure 7.1 Kinship in Ban Nok 1 Cooperative

tial plot of land, accompanied by younger smallholders or those without land. In fact, the land per member family in each group is approximately 1.4ha, while holding differences in group one, for example, range from one farmer with 5ha to five others with below half a hectare, and yet another two without any land at all. Given the kinship composition of this group, however, most of the latter seven must be seen as being in an ascending phase of the domestic cycle and therefore still hoping to accumulate land. In each group the elder farmer performs for the cooperative the formal role of being in charge of production, when in reality each group is a variation on the traditional labor-exchange group. In group one, for example, families 1 and 2, who own eight hectares between them, rely on the labor supplied by families 4, 5, 6, 13, and 17, while families 7, 8, and 21, who are more closely related, tend to exchange labor among themselves as well as with peasants centered on the plots owned by families 1 and 2. Group three is centered on the household compound of families 3 and 6, whose father is in fact in charge of the group's production, although he is not listed as a formal member of the cooperative, and household 19, whose land is worked jointly by his son and by a landless member of the cooperative, family 16. The other two members of this group, who between them have 5ha, exchange labor with families 3 and 6. Group two is made up of field neighbors, among whom there are several widows and widowers. Family 12 (who is a widower) owns 2.5ha that is worked jointly by his son and daughter-in-law, while exchanging labor with households 9, 11, and 22, who have small amounts of land and disproportions in labor. They also rent land from family 20.

The key members of the cooperative committee are the manager (from family 1, male), the head of planning (from family 2, male), and the accountant (from family 3, female). Thus the key positions in the cooperative are in the hands of a core group of kin, just as the whole formal organization of the cooperative is a facade for a functioning system of traditional labor exchange.

Two core kin groups also lie at the heart of Don Dou cooperative and effectively control it (fig. 7.2). The head of family 1 was manager of the cooperative until his retirement in 1987, his son (family 2) was the accountant, while the head of their in-laws (family 7) was in charge of planning and maintenance. However, because members of this cooperative have little land (fig. 7.2 does not include Dtoo Pheng, as it is a picture of the cooperative in 1986) the work groups are not as stable as in ban Nok 1. The most stable is group one, which coalesces around the land belonging to family 2, which has 2ha, and family 4, which has 4 *rai,* and is worked along with families 3, 5, and 6. Other kin combine together according to where they can rent land and according to convenience. But, as can be observed from the figure, two-thirds of the workers left in the cooperative are women centered on household compounds. Their husbands have other jobs, and therefore the women rent land under the auspices of the cooperative and "hire" the cooperative's tractor, driven by one of the males in the cooperative, to prepare their land. Thus Don Dou exhibits characteristics that have been observed elsewhere, namely, the "feminization of agriculture" as

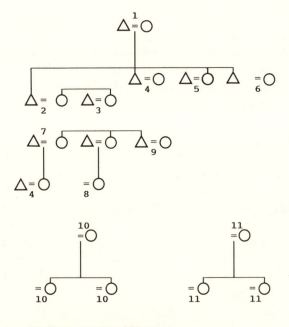

Note: Spouses are not featured if they are not
registered members of the cooperative.

Figure 7.2 Kinship in Don Dou Cooperative

nonagricultural wage-earning possibilities become available. Tractor plowing is monopolized by men and is highly rewarded, and because it can be
done quickly it releases the men to other part-time occupations, such as
petty trading or wage earning.

The Mark Point System

In the initial phase of collectivization serious attempts were made to establish a "rational" accounting system for the remuneration of labor. Mark
points or work points were used. Like the income of the peasant farmer,
that of cooperative members is decided by the size of the harvest, which of
course is subject to the same vagaries as those that affect the ordinary
peasant. However, in the peasant farm the situation is relatively simple. The
total harvest, minus perhaps rent, taxes, and debts incurred for inputs,
belongs to the household alone to be consumed by them or sold in exchange for other goods as the need arises. There is no need to allocate fixed

proportions to individual members of the household, as they all "eat out of the same pot." In the cooperative, on the other hand, the harvest belongs to the members as a unit, but it also has to be divided up and distributed to its individual members. Therefore, a satisfactory accounting and distribution system must be established. Failures and complications in distribution lie behind endless government laments about lack of management expertise in the cooperatives. As we shall see, however, more than skilled management is at stake.

The mark point system for labor is one in which yield is distributed according to the number of accumulated points on a fixed scale. For example, if the total yield is 20 tons and there are twenty workers with a total of 1,000 mark points each, then each mark point would equal one kilogram of rice and each worker would receive in payment one ton. In reality some would receive more and some less, but this is where what looks like an essentially simple system becomes complicated. Furthermore, there are decisions to be made concerning retained earnings and investment, social welfare, and so forth.

Accounting complexities in agriculture arise out of the great variety of work that needs to be performed—tilling for rice growing differs from that for other food crops; tending pigs is different from tending draft animals, and so on—and all of these have to be given some value. In Laos, however, we are concerned only with rice production. Calculations for the work point system are theoretically based on work norms. The Vietnamese study quoted above defines norms in the following way: "Work norms define the *quantity* and *quality* of work that should be done by a worker of average ability, qualifications and strength in a normal eight hours' workday, in well-defined conditions and with a correct attitude to labor. During periods of intense cultivation, the workday may last 10–12 hours (and even more) but norms are always calculated in 8-hour stints. They are average norms which a great number of workers can fulfill or overfulfill." To establish the norms, communist reorganization of agriculture has resorted to Taylorism with a vengeance, setting up experiments in an attempt to "scientifically" establish work norms on which rational calculations of labor performed can be based. Essentially these are the familiar time-and-motion studies. As the Vietnamese document goes on, "The *work process* is the sum of movements done by a worker or group of workers."[6] The cooperative management is encouraged to conduct experiments to measure movements for different jobs with a "chronometer" in order to cut out unnecessary movements and streamline the execution of them in order to raise productivity. Labor-time is the key dimension of these studies and is divided into necessary and unnecessary labor-time. Calculation is supposed to be made of the time required to carry out the principal work task and of necessary time spent on maintenance or preparation of work instruments (rest times may or may not be included in these calculations); the residual time is classified as wasted time. The task then is to cut out the waste. A dual process is set in motion: the management of the cooperative has to try not only to ascertain the *normal* amount of work required by a peasant for a particular task, but also to rationalize that labor process. According to the ideals of "scientific management" this would progressively reduce the normal time required, and hence would create a norm continuously moving toward its scientific ideal.

One has to establish norms for each separate activity in order to avoid the likelihood of peasants opting for lighter and easier work. The following are some of the variables that must be taken into account by whoever is constructing these norms in rice agriculture: for plowing one could classify the sorts of buffalo (male or female), the types of plows (wood or steel), soils (heavy or light), depth of plowing, regularity of clods, and so forth. Similar criteria would apply to harrowing. For transplanting one would have to consider the quality of the mud, the bundling of the seedlings, the level of the water in the rice fields,[7] technique and skill of the planters, number of seedlings per planted tuft, number of tufts per square meter, planting in a straight line or not, and so on. With fertilizer one would evaluate its collection and preparation in the case of natural manures, its transportation, technique used (broadcasting or digging in), and period when done. During harvesting calculations would consider the instruments used, the size of stacks, quality of the rice and the rice-fields, transportation, and various forms of threshing (mechanical or manual). There is also irrigation and maintenance of the dike system and tending of the draft animals.[8]

The idea of establishing a work norm within a specific task is a formidable one in itself, but there is the more fundamental problem of establishing a basic unit by which disparate tasks can be compared so that workers in different jobs do not feel cheated. However, the cooperatives face a basic problem: although labor is a common denominator between various work activities, the problem of determining the actual *value* of that labor persists in the absence of a labor market or a "market" internal to the cooperative that is capable of determining the distribution of rewards. In this respect the cooperative is a micromodel of the administered economy, or of the natural economy of the peasant. It is affected by external prices, but these do not determine "wages" inside the cooperative. This issue points to a fault in the very conception of agricultural production cooperatives, especially as they cannot rely on the practice of rough reciprocity, as the peasant family can.

The complexity of the mark point system is generally beyond the capabilities of the peasants and their management committees and therefore is in itself a strong disincentive to join a cooperative. The inevitable mismanagement of the system gave rise to disputes over distribution and was a major cause of peasant dissatisfaction with and defection from the cooperatives. The whole structure and situation provided many pretexts for peasants to quarrel if they were dissatisfied.

Take the example of Kham Khiene (family 8, table 5.1), who left Don Dou cooperative after the 1981 wet season following a dispute over payment in which he felt the cooperative had cheated him. At that time each worker kept a record of his own work points in a small book. A separate record was kept by the cooperative itself through the work of supervisors. Kham Khiene claims he had 5,000 points in his book while the cooperative register had only 4,000. (This claim itself is inaccurate, as can be seen from table 7.1). He even suggested that there may have been corruption, though he quickly modified this claim by adding that the management may simply have forgotten to enter his points. The management, according to Kham Khiene, offered to make up the points to him, presumably in an effort to keep him in the cooperative. He refused to be mollified and declared that he disliked the system anyway. It was all right in theory, he said, but not in practice.

According to the cooperative's accountant, the dispute was really over the fact that Kham Khiene felt his family should have received more mark points because it was bigger than family 9 in the cooperative—five persons against four—and furthermore, because family 9 had neither buffalo nor land from which they could get points. The respective figures are given in table 7.1. (The fact that family 9 was a member of one kinship core is probably what prompted Kham Khiene's allusion to corruption). Kham Khiene had applied a strictly peasant accounting logic to the situation, arguing that if one has more workers then that should automatically entitle one to a greater share of the product. The accountant said that Kham Khiene consistently refused to argue in terms of mark points.

Perhaps Kham Khiene did have a legitimate grievance, and perhaps the cooperative, in offering to make up the points to him, acknowledged the fact that it could have gotten the figures wrong. It is equally plausible that

TABLE 7.1. Comparison of Mark Points
of Two Families, Wet Season 1981

Kham Khiene's Family	Bonus	Land Rent	Mark Points	Yield
Kham Khiene			151.5	577
Wife			72.9	277
Daughter			70.5	268
Son			93.3	355
Son			92.3	351
[Buffalo]			72.1	274
Total	40	600	552.6	2,102 = 2,742
Family Nine				
Head			213.3	812
Wife			98.0	373
Daughter			140.8	570
Daughter			80.6	307
[Storekeeping]			29.1	110
Total	20		561.8	2,172 = 2,192

their offer grew out of the vulnerability of the cooperative to private peasant defections or out of their capitulation to the pervasive logic of the peasant environment surrounding the cooperative, which among other things stressed the need to avoid conflict.

In his first year out of the cooperative Kham Khiene admitted he harvested less than when he was in the cooperative (he lost access to certain inputs). But he did not regret leaving. In his eyes the advantages of being out of the cooperative outweighed the advantages of being in. Kham Khiene is a strong, forthright person, and there were other reasons for his leaving. The calculation of the work of each member of the family is, as I indicated in the previous chapter, irksome for the head of the peasant household, who likes to consider the product of his farm the result of his skills and effort alone. Not only does the points system establish unwelcome comparisons of work within the family, it also sets up invidious comparisons with the efforts of other families. Compared with the head of family 9, Kham Khiene, according to the mark point system, could be seen to have done significantly less work. This directly wounded his pride and authority, and it is certainly plausible to argue that he left to avoid future embarrassment, while covering himself by accusing the cooperative of cheating.

In ban Nok 1 similar problems were avoided by adapting the formal system to the logic of the peasant economy. While it was difficult to secure accounting data for this cooperative, I was able to do so for wet seasons 1981 and 1982 and found that different accounting units were used each season. Asked to explain the variation, Maha Houa said that as a "scientific" cooperative they were always trying to find a better way of administering the mark points system, and therefore they changed it every year. A consequence of this was that figures from season to season were not strictly comparable. One could interpret this as a subterfuge that made it impossible for authorities to check on the cooperative's internal working, but a more straightforward explanation is possible. The provisional regulations stipulated that cooperatives must have accounting books. In ban Nok 1 they had invented a system that attempted to match the formality of the mark point system to what peasants would have received as private farmers. Arguments had occurred earlier when an attempt to apply the mark point system had resulted in a peasant receiving less than he would have outside the cooperative. Thus hurried adjustments had been made, and a system devised that averted disputes. In this way an accounting structure was developed that gave the appearance of cooperative distribution when in reality little had changed. Nevertheless, compliance to outward form allowed ban Nok 1 to continue officially as a cooperative.

Besides its complexity there are mundane, amusing reasons for the system's unmanageability. A mark point book is designed to fit into a peasant's shirt pocket. However, this also makes its pages a perfect size for rolling cigarettes. When peasants in the field run out of cigarette paper they are likely to use the pages from their mark point booklet to roll their tobacco in, whereupon their record of work performed literally goes up in smoke. This in turn led to further disputes over points and work.

While there is ample room for misunderstandings and suspicions to arise between families in a cooperative, there is equal room for conflict with the management committee in charge of the accounting system. A simple example of the management's lack of clarity about what they are doing is given by the bar graph for production painted up in the Don Dou cooperative shed (fig. 7.3). The person who drew this graph had obviously acquired the idea that graphs always go up, not down. So even when the yield was less, the graph continued to rise, though, as can be seen from the figures beside the bars, there was no attempt to hide the fact that the yield

Graphs at Don Dou

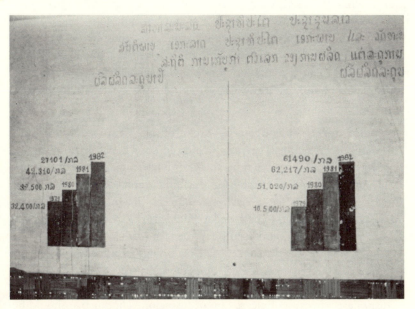

Photo of graphs in Don Dou shed showing yields per season.

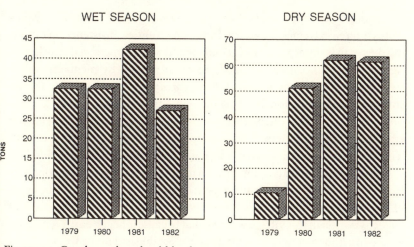

Figure 7.3 Graphs as they should be drawn.

was less. Visually the picture it gives of the cooperative's performance is quite different from its actual performance, and the redrawn graphs below the photograph show how the Don Dou graph should look. Such simple mistakes could lead to serious misunderstandings, and obviously do.

Ronald F. Dore has drawn attention to some very real problems related to the attempt to implant modern forms of management in cooperatives in rural areas, especially as to how its assumptions may clash with traditional social values:

> Modern forms of cooperative organization are based on institutionalized suspicion. They are predicated on a belief in original sin. Man, the assumption is, has an inevitable tendency to corruption. Therefore organizations must build in checks and balances such as the audit and the periodic re-election of officers. The modern cooperative does deserve, in fact, to be called a "higher form" because it requires a rather sophisticated appreciation of the idea that this institutionalized suspicion in the long run benefits all, including those against whom it is directed. Thus the treasurer welcomes the audit—even though the audit only makes sense on the assumption that the treasurer might have been dishonest—because it clears him of suspicion. That justice should be done may be in the interest of the members; that it should be seen to be done is in the interest of the elected officials.[9]

As Dore points out, however, an understanding of impersonalized processes is often extremely limited in rural communities. Insistence on following them can be interpreted by incumbent officials as a personal attack; and figures that do not tally are likely to be attributed by members not to straightforward incompetence, but to corruption. Furthermore, the institutionalized suspicion of an audit only strengthens distrust. Yet, the obvious paradox is, if these processes of institutionalized suspicion are not enforced because of injunctions concerning avoidance of conflict or criticism then the way will be opened to abuse of power and corruption.

All of these problems cropped up in muang Hatsayfong, and in one case led to violence against the management committee at "ban Pao" (the name of the village is changed here for obvious reasons). The development of collectivization in this village was unusual because it began early. A cooperative consisting of ninety-four families was established in the wet season of 1976 because for some reason a group of "activists" focused on the village. As at ban Thana, these activists promised tractors, harvesting machines, and a high income for those who joined. The cooperative lasted for one season. According to the peasants, the management never did any work and only walked around supervising others. Allegedly they were always going off to meetings or to try to get inputs but never worked in the field. Others claimed that the committee members were engaged in the black-market. When the time came to divide up the first yield many peasants felt the distribution was unfair, that members of the management committee got too much. A row broke out at a meeting of the members, with peasants threatening to attack the committee with machetes and hoes. They were restrained only by the intervention of village elders. The committee members then relinquished some of their payment. However, the ill feeling caused by this incident did not dissipate immediately, and a little while later, at a village meeting in January 1977, a still-disgruntled peasant walked into a meeting and shot dead one of the committee members, then fled to Thailand. According to my informants, the two other committee members were shot dead in separate incidents in 1977, allegedly while smuggling goods from Thailand. This is possible, but it is also likely that they were murdered by disgruntled peasants. Either way, people quickly realized that being part of management could be a dangerous job. As one man told me, it was hard to get people to do the job, considering the fate of the earlier committee.

Yet in 1978 ban Pao got swept up in the collectivization drive, and some families were prompted by "activists" to form a cooperative. This collapsed after dry season 1979, again because of disputes over distribution. In this cooperative members were given a flat daily rate of 10 points and the management 15 mark points. No points were given for casual labor or children, the peasants complained. As a result, the yield was "unfairly" distributed once again. One informant, who was on the management committee at this time, said that the general manager of the cooperative for the wet season of 1978 also got involved in smuggling and blackmarketing and ended up getting killed (by whom remained unclear). The next general manager was better, the peasants said, but still the system did not work, and the peasants remained unhappy with the distribution system. The members gave managers an extra 5 points because they had been advised to do so by the tasseng officials, but management had to work in the fields as well to get points. If they went off to a meeting they would be awarded only a 5-point allowance.[10]

The differential for the management committee was, of course, an incentive for peasants to take on the task. At ban Pao they were obviously using a simplified flat rate or "showing face" points system, which has all the defects outlined earlier. But on top of this, peasants were clearly reluctant to allow extra points for administrative work, obviously because they recognized it was fundamentally superfluous.[11] The government issued detailed instructions on payment for management and tried to offer a system that was sufficient to be an incentive for some to take on administrative responsibilities but not so great that it would cause dissatisfaction among the farmers. Significantly, they felt it necessary to spell out that the members of the committee, including the general manager, had to engage in direct productive work in the fields. The Ministry of Agriculture recommended the following: "The head and deputy head of a production unit get 30 to 50 percent of an average labor day in his unit. The allowance must be relative to the output of their own production unit. One calculates the average labor day, X, by dividing the total labor points by the total number of laborers. Then the allowance for the head of the production unit is

$$X \times \frac{(30-50)}{100}\text{"}^{12}$$

For example, if 20 laborers over one day accumulate 230 mark points (some gaining more, some less), then the average labor day would be 11.5 mark points, in which case the head of the unit would get approximately 15 mark points for one day's work. These calculations naturally rest on the ability of the cooperative to resolve the problems associated with establishing an adequate mark point system in the first place, and, as we have seen, this is no simple matter. The calculation for management is, therefore, just one more problem for peasants in a cooperative.

Guidelines for the setting up of management committees are sensitive to the problem of committees being too big for a cooperative and a burden on it. In small cooperatives the government recommended only two paid officials in committees because, it argued, their responsibilities are not great, and "because the production of such a cooperative is not diversified and its level of intensive cultivation low, the calculation of the labor day for managing officials should be only 8–10 percent of the total labor day of the cooperative. If it is more than that it will adversely affect the income of the members of the cooperative."[13] These strictures, however, overcame neither negative peasant attitudes toward administrative work nor the difficulties of the accounting system, and hence relations between management and members in the cooperatives remained problematic.

Corruption among cooperative leaders inevitably had a corrosive effect on cooperative ventures, as Dore predicts it will. The dramatic disintegration of ban Thana cooperative, for example, was the result not only of dissatisfactions with labor/consumer imbalances in the organization, but also of small-scale corruption on the part of its former manager, Outhong. He had embezzled money from the cooperative, participated rarely in fieldwork, and spent considerable time wheeling and dealing on the black market in goods the cooperative had privileged access to, such as fertilizer. Tremendous disillusionment followed Outhong's arrest. He was expelled from the cooperative and sent off for six months' "reeducation," but the punishment did not stop peasants from leaving the cooperative, for their suspicions about the venture had been confirmed.

Supervision and Organization of Work

The complexity of rice farming and the skills it requires demand either high worker motivation or close supervision. Motivation is found in private peasant agriculture because of the multistranded bonds between family members, which include an already established "natural" hierarchy. In the cooperatives, on the other hand, supervision of work is usually a vital activity, especially where the system relies on the efficient use of labor to raise productivity in the absence of scientific and technological inputs. However, it has no naturally established hierarchy of responsibility, and moreover the economic efficiency of supervision has itself come under scrutiny.

In formally constituted cooperative work groups it is assumed there are no preexisting bonds between the members of the group and no preestablished organizational hierarchy. The head of the group has to be elected or appointed, and it is this person's job not only to coordinate activities but also to guard against "free rider" problems, that is, members of a group not pulling their weight, a consequence of which, as we observed in the last chapter, is a general lowering of effort in the whole group. Time and energy are then redirected into private economic activity, at least to the extent that it is possible. If private economic activity is restricted, the result may be expressed as a "preference" for leisure and a general lowering of economic activity throughout the rural economy. To overcome or avert free-rider problems requires the allocation of labor time to supervision, which raises the proportion of unproductive to productive labor. Because of the difficulties of supervision in agriculture (compared with that in industry) it requires a comparatively greater amount of supervisory labor, and therefore the economic problem becomes one of a tradeoff between resources allocated to supervision and the increased productivity supposedly stimulated by this supervision. In the absence of technological inputs (which I will assume are indivisible for the moment) the facts are that cooperative work groups are no more productive than individual peasant households functioning in the established peasant economy, and indeed, to the degree they have to allocate labor to supervision they are less efficient.

Furthermore, given that the task of supervision falls to those who are elected to the head of the work groups, cultural factors need to be taken into account when evaluating the efficiency of supervision in cooperative groups. A purely formal organization, as we have seen, cannot be assumed in a country like Laos. Therefore, any group organization would, for example, have to attempt to avoid a situation in which young persons issue orders to elder persons. Or a work group may happen to be dominated by one family, which naturally elects its family head to supervise the group. This is a certain recipe for interfamilial tension and lowered work morale. Peasants especially disliked criticism and self-criticism sessions of their work, especially when criticism was expressed by someone outside the family group. For many, such public criticism was unbearable and was reason alone to leave the cooperative. In traditional cooperation the sanctions against bad work simply involved refusing to exchange labor with the offending household or individual the following season. The rebuke may come in the form of gossip, but it was not obviously public. In the cooperative, such sanctions do not exist, and if bad work is not criticized then there is a tendency for people to begin to work according to the standard set by the worst worker. Such avoidance of public criticism, therefore, undermines the aims of supervision and makes it unworkable.

Not surprisingly, peasants dislike having their work monitored by a "foreman." One day, while I was watching a group of around fifteen women from the cooperative at Don Dou weeding under the eye of the accountant, a person nearby commented, "The dog watches while the pigs work." These sentiments were also voiced by the peasants at ban Pao, who complained bitterly about their managers because they had not worked in the field. Supervision is resented in most work situations but is especially onerous when it leads to a decline in production rather than an increase, which is its rationale in the first place.

The interrelated problem of monitoring and motivation contributed to the evolution of the contract, or "responsibility," system in collectivized

agriculture in China and Vietnam.[14] Lao cooperatives began to follow suit
in the early 1980s, but with more radical consequences. In Don Dou, for
example, the system initially entailed contracting out to particular work
groups or family groups specific tasks, such as plowing or sowing an area
of cooperative land in return for an agreed number of mark points plus
bonuses for speed. However, the arrangement soon led to a number of
problems; for example, groups competed for land that was relatively easy
to plow and therefore more easily finished, thereby causing dissension over
allocation of land. Or the land was not worked carefully in the interests of
finishing it quickly in order to get the bonus. But in Laos, where land is not
collectively owned anyway, attempts to devolve responsibility simply
hastened the reassertion of traditional peasant household economic organization inside the cooperatives and the rapid fragmentation of the cooperatives.

Perhaps it could be argued that the preceding discussion undervalues
the role of leadership in cooperative activities. Samuel Popkin, for example,
rightly underlines the vital role leadership plays in collective action: "If a
skilled leader can convince peasants to join a larger mutual aid group, there
is a potentially substantial profit both for the peasants and the leader."[15]
Absence of good leadership, he argues, is often the reason for peasant
failures to innovate technologically or institutionally. The importance of
leadership is certainly demonstrated by the activity of Maha Houa at ban
Nok, although his leadership remained circumscribed by the peasant economy. For cooperatives other than producer cooperatives leadership of this
sort is vital, but only technological change, which requires institutional
change, can provide a rationale for an enhanced leadership role in a producers' cooperative.

Economies of Scale

Communist orthodoxy has commonly transposed a simplified industrial
model of scale and labor organization onto agriculture.[16] Although technological developments in industry often favor the construction of large-
scale units employing large numbers of workers, in agriculture they more
often favor small units.[17] Although there are few unambiguous technological advantages to be gained from large-scale farming, there do appear to be definite diseconomies of scale in the management of farm labor.
Yet communist discussions of economies of scale in Laos or Vietnam are

remarkably ignorant of Western literature on this problem, and economies of scale are discussed primarily in terms of labor organization. Kaysone told the Congress of Cooperatives in 1979, "In conditions where production tools have not been extensively modified and labor still primarily depends on hand crafted tools, the reorganization of labor to use it in an appropriate manner is a key issue in making cooperative production overall more effective than individual production." Yet, while Kaysone warned against creating "excessively large cooperatives," he offered the following, seemingly arbitrary criteria for size: "It is appropriate to set up agricultural cooperatives with the village being used as the mainstay. In using the village as the mainstay, the size of a cooperative will generally range from 30–50 families. A big village may initially set up two or three cooperatives. In the plains the size of a cooperative may range from 50–70 families or up to 100 families in some areas. If a cooperative is too small because a village is inhabited by only 15 or 20 families, there may be difficulties and the redistribution of work may not take place. There may be nothing new in production in such a village."[18] He offered no theoretical or empirical justification for these recommendations concerning the size of cooperatives.

The Department of Cooperatives of the Ministry of Agriculture in Vientiane could not supply any clearly worked out justification for these estimates either. They simply replied that the size of a cooperative was determined by the problems of managing labor. Thus they said cooperatives of over fifty families are generally too difficult to run in Lao conditions. Cooperatives of twenty to fifty families, "middle-sized cooperatives," can just be managed. Cooperatives of fewer than twenty families with an average family size of four will not have an adequate work force to permit a proper division of labor. "What is this proper division of labor?" I inquired. Answer: The required labor for each production unit was twenty-five to thirty laborers in a cooperative of fifty families. How did they know this? They did not know, these figures were purely guesses. Studies had not been carried out, and the sizes of cooperatives and work groups were little more than subjective perceptions of what seemed to be "manageable" in terms of labor. Combinations of labor and capital in optimal proportions given Lao conditions did not enter the picture.

When questioned about what the difference would be between a private peasant's productivity and a cooperative peasant's productivity if both possessed the same capital/labor ratio, the Department of Cooperatives replied that there would be no difference. The difference, they said, was essentially subjective and involved concern for the welfare of the whole village. They conceded that an individual peasant might experience a drop in his personal income if he joined the cooperative—it could be a result of problems related to management of the cooperative, but it could also be the product of a redistribution of income in the village. This argument, however, simply displaced the issue to the thorny economic problem of egalitarian objectives versus the required incentives to generate higher productivity.

During the brief resurgence of orthodoxy in late 1984 there were further estimates given of the optimal size for a cooperative in Laos: "Actual experience has indicated that a large-scale agricultural cooperative should not be set up in the initial stage. According to a guideline defined by the higher level, 15 to 30 or so families in each village should be organized into a single cooperative to cultivate rice on 30–50ha. This is the ideal size of a cooperative, suitable for the level of management at the present stage."[19] Beyond acknowledging that there are some size limitations on labor management in the cooperatives, no economic justification has ever been forthcoming for these rough estimates either. This alarming situation highlights the government's all too often ideological, as against economic, commitment to agricultural cooperatives.

What are the advantages of cooperative production over individual peasant production in the eyes of the LPRP? Kaysone has claimed, "Collective production is able to utilize labor in a more appropriate manner. It broadens production by increasing the number of crop growing seasons, by clearing new farm land, building irrigation facilities, getting rid of weeds, using fertilizer, selecting good rice strains and modifying techniques so as to advance centralized agriculture."[20] However, none of these supposed advantages enumerated by Kaysone require large-scale agricultural cooperatives for their implementation. They could all be put into effect on the basis of small-scale peasant agriculture. So, what are the economies of scale in agriculture, given that the advantages of large units have been held as dogma in most communist countries?

It should be said at the outset that extensive research has suggested, not surprisingly, that there are no a priori appropriate farm sizes.[21] The basic question concerning agricultural economic development is, In what quantity and in what proportions do scarce resources need to be combined on a farm unit in order to achieve a relatively low cost expansion of farm production? If we approach the issue of collectivization in Laos from the perspective of relative scarcities of factors of production, a number of points are highlighted: the country has a serious shortage of all modern inputs—machinery, fertilizer, pesticides, scientific expertise—and a relative abundance of land and, to a lesser degree, of labor. The factor costs of the former are very high, those of the latter very low. Hence the government quite sensibly opted for maximizing the use of labor rather than capital—but this says nothing about their optimum combination.

A factor affecting farm size in the developed capitalist countries (taking them as a paradigm of developed agriculture) has been the cheapening of capital inputs relative to labor. This has enabled less labor to work a significantly larger farm than formerly. The labor in the countryside displaced by capitalization was catered for by an expansion of industry. In this way the industrialization of agriculture was intimately bound up with the general process of industrialization. A distinction, however, needs to be made between two forms of technology: that which saves labor and that which intensifies land use. The first raises the productivity of labor, the second that of land, and in particular dynamic settings they can combine to produce simultaneous growth of land and labor productivity.

Empirical studies have indicated that yields, certainly those for rice, are higher on small farms than on large ones; or, at the very least, size has little effect. One of the most thorough studies, that conducted by Berry and Cline, argues, "It is precisely the small-farm sector that is most successful in achieving high levels of production relative to modest inputs of capital and land—through the ample use of labor. Moreover, the new technology of high-yielding varieties can be applied on small farms, since it has no threshold scale."[22] Naturally, large, well-funded units are needed for experimentation with seed varieties and new techniques. For this, however, one needs experimental state farms, not cooperatives. Laos has such state farms, and they are cooperating with international aid organizations. The real practical problem is devising the best way of delivering these improvements to the farmers. The government has asserted that producer cooperatives are the best organizational structure through which to channel improvements to farmers in the fields. It is true that the extension service in Laos is poorly trained and understaffed, but they can just as easily work through the marketing cooperative structures that have come into being since 1984.

One of the main inhibitions to ordinary private peasants adopting new techniques is the size of initial outlays for them, which, combined with the fact that Lao peasants have very small margins to play with, means that failures carry high costs. Where irrigation and double cropping have been possible (most peasants in Laos still grow only one crop per year), allowing the peasant a wider economic margin, the risks of adopting new ways have been reduced. Thus in muang Hatsayfong peasants easily adopted new rice varieties, fertilizer, and new irrigation practices. In fact, the major inhibition to their adoption of new practices has been the failure of the government to *supply* adequate inputs. Initially this was a result of conscious government obstruction, as officials restricted supplies to private farmers in an attempt to pressure them into joining cooperatives. This policy was dropped in January 1980 when the private farmers were theoretically given access to inputs such as fertilizer, insecticides, improved seed varieties, and farm credit. Only with more radical subsequent economic reform have these inputs become more easily available. A proper supply of farm inputs and consumer items is a crucial stimulus to peasant production. As noted earlier, the production ceiling in the peasant economy is determined by what the peasant considers to be "enough" to satisfy the labor/consumer balance. This perception is variable through time and is a response to newly created needs. When an item moves from being a luxury to being in sufficient supply at a reasonable price it will become a social necessity, and increased effort will be made to cover that new necessity. In the absence of adequate supplies, the need is not created and the peasant has less incentive to adopt new techniques. In this way there is an interaction between the macroeconomic decisions of the state and its trading organs and the microeconomic decisions of the peasant farmer. The important point is, however, that government assertions that certain key technological inputs, such as fertilizers, pesticides, or higher yielding rice varieties, can be properly supplied and utilized only through the medium of the cooperatives is shown to be a political assessment rather than an economic one.

Mechanization is the other avenue for increasing productivity in agriculture. Perhaps the main argument for introducing tractors, for example, into Lao agriculture is that they would facilitate more widespread double cropping—assuming, of course, that irrigation facilities have been installed—to the extent that there are labor constraints on intensification. It is argued that only cooperatives would have sufficient capital to own such tractors. But the type of tractors introduced need not be "lumpy" items. Small, hand-held tillers able to be utilized on a family farm are a viable form of mechanization. The large tractors that are in evidence in the Lao countryside come, often as aid, from the Eastern bloc and are not necessarily the most suitable type. They are designed for large-scale agriculture, and they are not the necessary or inevitable form of mechanization required for field preparation in rice agriculture. On the other hand, large tractors can be used—as they were at Don Dou cooperative, which hired out its excess capacity to surrounding private farmers. On this basis it would seem more rational to make some cooperatives into industrial nodes in the countryside that could serve private peasant households and perhaps specialize in threshing and milling machines as well. In muang Hatsayfong, for example, the most sophisticated milling machines are in the hands of small, private millers, and it is against these individuals, not the private peasants, the cooperatives could or should be competing. This, however, assumes a strategy of vertical integration of the farmers, whereas the communists, until recently, have been fixated on horizontal integration.

A fundamental constraint on the mechanization of agriculture in Laos is, of course, the scarcity of foreign exchange. In this context the rationality of mechanization becomes tenuous given that its provision entails the expenditure of scarce foreign exchange on goods that simply substitute for a resource Laos already has, labor. Possibly there will be labor constraints in Lao agriculture when multiple cropping occurs, but this has not yet happened for the majority of peasants, and hence other ways of raising productivity are more rational. Furthermore, mechanization would eat into future foreign exchange because of its demand for petroleum, though this is not necessarily true of milling or threshing machines, which could rely on Laos's abundant (if unevenly spread) supplies of electricity. A more efficient strategy in terms of available resources would import fertilizer and pesticides, both of which assist productivity increases. However, neither of these inputs is dependent on economies of scale and therefore does not require a cooperative for maximum utilization. In Laos, where sophisticated indivisible capital is in short supply, a strategy based on developing small farm productivity is economically most rational. It achieves maximum returns for minimal capital expenditure and releases the small surplus available for industrial or other developmental projects. Collectivization as a *general strategy* for modernizing agriculture—indeed, as part of a general program of industrialization in Laos—would seem to be economically inefficient.

Underemployment?

I have spoken of labor as being a relatively abundant resource in Laos, but does that mean it is underemployed in the peasant economy? Kaysone has complained that the "average farmer works only 100 days a year. At most he works 150 days a year in certain areas where it is necessary." This must be increased to at least 200 days a year, he said. "In the various socialist countries which have a highly developed economy, a worker is still required to contribute between 250 and 300 workdays a year. This has also been the practice in the Soviet Union, the United States and Japan. Only by doing so can we improve our living conditions, make our cooperatives prosperous and achieve a healthy economy."[23] Cooperatives, therefore, are conceived of as institutions for mobilizing idle or underutilized labor and for skimming off *potential* surpluses in agriculture in the manner suggested by Paul Baran (see chapter 1 above).[24] Marsh Marshall's study of China shows that cooperatives were successful at mobilizing "underutilized" labor in the countryside and at stimulating accumulation and capital construction, especially irrigation systems. However, he also notes that "the establishment of co-operatives in rural China was associated with a substantial decline in the rate of growth of total consumption."[25] Marshall is writing about the initial results of collectivization between the years 1955 and 1957, and few writers would deny that surpluses can be "squeezed" out of the peasantry in this way, at least up to a point, because after 1957 labor productivity in Chinese agriculture plateaud.[26] It would be hard to argue, however, that this process was voluntary, and one cannot ignore the human costs involved in this mobilization, namely, the squeeze on personal consumption and increased labor. A vital source of "underutilized" labor was women, whose workload escalated dramatically as they were drawn into the public cooperative sphere of the economy.[27] Besides domestic housekeeping and childcare, women were engaged in the informal economy, which persisted despite the restrictions placed on it. The importance of this so-called informal sector (really an integral part of the peasant economy, as argued in chapter 4) is ignored by assertions of labor underutilization that are made from the point of view of the official economy and the state's thirst for surpluses.

The picture of the indolent Lao peasant is overdrawn, although it is one regularly expressed by officials and is indicative of their ignorance of both the peasant economy and the range and diversity of peasant economic activity.[28] Needless to say, the assertions made by Lao officials are based on no obvious empirical research. One of the few studies of labor utilization in Laos that does take account of the diverse activities in the peasant economy is Taillard. He demonstrates that "underemployment" exists for less than five weeks in areas with ready access to markets and between five and eight weeks in areas more distant from markets.[29] That is, rather than working for 100 or at most 150 days per year, as asserted by Kaysone, peasants are occupied for at least 300 days per year. As William Klausner has pointed out in his study of the work cycle in the Thai northeast, peasants are occupied with a multitude of activities all year round. "One of the principle misconceptions about the village society of the northeast is that the villagers only work one rice crop a year and, after its completion, retire to a life of rest and ease until the next rainy season crop." In fact, he argues, "villagers work hard throughout the year"[30] on a wide range of activities, which may include making charcoal, weaving, or trading.

If peasants are in fact more indolent under communism in Laos to date, it is owing to the state's restricting access to markets and therefore the possibility of peasants engaging in diverse occupations, such as handicrafts. Peasants will expand their working hours in the rice fields through double cropping if the irrigation facilities are there and prices are sufficient to act as a inducement, that is, if the opportunity costs of reallocating labor away from other activities are sufficient. Provision of irrigation is in fact one of Kaysone's main practical suggestions for raising working days on rice cropping per year, but producers' cooperatives are not vital for achieving economies of scale in irrigation either.

Irrigation

The development of irrigation projects has been used as a lever to pressure peasants into joining producer cooperatives. It has been argued by the government that, first, because it provides the farmers with the irrigation system, they therefore have an obligation to conform to the government's policy on cooperatives; second, that the peasants should then sell their second crop to the state because it has provided them with the means to produce a second crop; and third, cooperatives are necessary to manage large-scale irrigation systems. Few people who are familiar with the complexities of irrigation systems would dispute this last point, inasmuch as some form of villagewide or supravillage cooperative organization is needed to manage an irrigation system. It does not, however, necessarily imply a full-fledged producers' cooperative. On the contrary, the promotion of irrigation projects would appear to be one instance in which the new regime could build on traditional forms of cooperation.

Writing on mutual help irrigation associations in northern Laos before 1975, Christian Taillard noted that they had three aims: "the construction and upkeep of the irrigation system, controlling the distribution of water when it proves necessary, and to arbitrate differences between members." In most villages he studied there were several dams, each corresponding to an association and to a specific section of village land. "One third of these associations had up to twenty households and the organization of irrigation corresponded to a group of kinsmen. More than half of the dams had between twenty and fifty households, which often corresponded to groups of neighboring families held together by cultivating contiguous paddy fields."[31] The association elects its chief, the *nai faay* (literally, dam chief), who is usually the most respected person in the kinship group or among neighbors. Their main common work task is the annual repairing of the dams and canals, and for this each household sends along one or two people, depending on the actual surface area they cultivate. Sometimes the upkeep of certain canals is distributed to particular families, the amount of maintenance being proportional to the area cultivated; in this case work on repairing the dam is all that is done in common.

The nai faay is charged with controlling the water flow and level. Group pressure is used to regulate attempts by members to use water at the expense of neighbors, and conflict is mediated by the nai faay. Controlling conflicts between distinct groups of water users, however, was not so easy. Taillard comments, "Here we touch on one of the limits of organization of the traditional society in the Vang Vieng basin. It is necessary to go beyond these older forms and create lines of solidarity not only between individuals of the same village but between different village groups, because the organizational limits of the society bring with it limits to its spatial organization." He concludes his article by remarking that the traditional associations could not cope with the scale of a modern irrigation scheme; however, they could still fulfill their functions at the level of secondary canals. He proposes, "These associations could become an ideal sociological framework, if the given level of Lao society is respected, for receiving outside assistance, being a ready framework for receiving credit or for commercialization. They would furnish an effective mediation between the Administration and the farmers."[32]

Precisely such an arrangement was attempted on an irrigation project constructed in muang Phiang, Sayaboury province, before 1975 and was still functioning, if somewhat raggedly, when I visited there in May 1986. According to E. Walter Coward, traditional organizations of small and large groups similar to those found by Taillard existed in the area primarily to carry out annual construction of temporary dams. Following the construction of a large dam, the role of the group headman, the nai nam (water chief) in this case, shifted from one of mobilizing labor for the annual reconstruction of a dam or repair of canals to one of overseeing water distribution. The irrigation bureaucracy, or project staff, conceptualized the area in terms of small groups, each headed by a nai nam, rather than in terms of individual farm units. Water is delivered to Group A, not to Farmer A.[33] In the current context these groups are known as collectives and are integrated into a cooperative type structure, but not of the sort initially envisaged by the LPRP.

A similar situation exists in tasseng Bo-O, whose irrigation system is serviced by one main pump that serves approximately 200ha. The nai nam, a smallholder, is appointed by the subdistrict, and he manages the area with two assistants. Their main job, besides pumping water into the main canals, is to direct water into various feeder canals and to forewarn "collective" groups that water will be directed toward the secondary canals servicing their fields. One does not have to be in the villages for too long to hear complaints about neighbors, for example, releasing excess water into another's field or stealing water from a neighbor. When this occurs it is primarily up to the "collective" to solve the conflict. The nai nam and his assistants mediate conflicts between groups; however, as noted in the previous chapter, many of the groups formed in the dry season are one-time affairs, and therefore they are often required to mediate conflicts within groups as well. The more permanent groups also form "collectives" for maintenance of the canal system, and they are levied for water as groups. This pays for the electric power for the main pump and wages for the water controllers. These collectives also buy various inputs for agriculture from the commercial cooperatives.

As mentioned in chapter 5, government policy had given cooperatives priority in working irrigated land in the dry season partly as an attempt to pressure farmers to join the cooperatives. However, in areas like muang Hatsayfong and muang Phiang the communist government is clearly not responsible for the existence of the system, and furthermore, the improvements that have been made were made largely independently of government assistance. Local farmers are responsible for the maintenance of the system. Therefore, two of the government's arguments for peasants joining cooperatives had no substance. One consequence was, as I noted at the end of chapter 5, that preferential access to land by cooperatives in the dry season collapsed in 1983. A workable structure for cooperation had been established by the water users both at a supravillage level and in the field, but it did not require a producers' cooperative as a precondition for its operation.

There are other, larger government/foreign aid-sponsored schemes on the Vientiane Plain and in Savannakhet: for example, a 1,000ha pump irrigation scheme in muang Na Say Tong adjacent to Vientiane. However, these are very new, and structures for administering the scheme were still being established in 1986, when I surveyed the area. The system, however, was evolving in a climate that reflected the government's evolutionary attitude toward cooperatives; as a result, less insistence was being placed on the formation of full-fledged cooperatives, even though the scheme was under the government's control. A situation similar to that in Bo-O was in the process of formation.

Vice-Minister of Agriculture Khamsing Sayakone had suggested to me during an interview that large-scale irrigation was inseparable from collectivization.[34] Only in this way could labor and capital be mobilized to create such schemes. The first point is clearly not true, either for Laos or elsewhere. Various types of organization and responsibility can be found in both public and private schemes throughout the Third World.[35] As for the second point, there is no question that collectivization can allow massive mobilization of labor and capital resources for irrigation development, such as in China, where, as Marsh Marshall points out, much of the irrigation infrastructure created by the communes has been vital to the success of the more recent "responsibility system."[36] However, extreme authoritarianism was a prerequisite (as it was in Pol Pot's Kampuchea).[37] I have no illusions that the LPRP would have resorted to authoritarian methods had it been able, but in reality it was not. Thus a system of irrigation development has evolved that is even less authoritarian than ones which exist in some capitalist states.[38] Indeed, in recent years the Lao government's gaze has shifted from large-scale schemes to programs aimed at upgrading traditional village irrigation systems by, for example, helping them build more permanent dam structures. This is truly building on traditions of cooperation among the Lao peasantry, whereas government insistence on producers' cooperatives as a prerequisite for irrigation development would not necessarily improve irrigation and would have to be administratively imposed. Irrigation systems are, by their very nature, "authoritarian" and not only restrict the range of choices available to any individual farmer, but also exact some level of cooperation.[39] Producers' cooperatives are, of course, compatible with irrigation systems but not necessary to them.

Given that labor was the one major resource available for the development of agriculture in Laos, the government decided that reorganization of it was the best way to achieve agricultural development, and the producers' cooperative was promoted as the institutional form most suited to the fulfillment of this aim. This approach had been adopted by other communist states as well, for example, in Vietnam and China, where they were most successful at mobilizing labor for irrigation construction and subsequent multiple cropping. These states were strong enough to enforce mobilization of peasant labor and to be able to hold down consumption in order to channel surpluses away from agriculture into development elsewhere in the economy. The Lao state was not as strong, and resistance to labor reorganization arising from the structure of the peasant economy was successful at spontaneously aborting the push toward collectivization.

Communist orthodoxy conceives of cooperatives as *corporate* units in much the same way as the family is a corporate unit. Thus the cooperatives have been seen, at least implicitly, as one big peasant family. This view sometimes slipped out unconsciously, such as in the rhetoric of activists during the collectivization campaign in muang Hatsayfong. They compared the government's attitude toward the "collectives" (that is, the labor-exchange groups) with a parent's attitude toward an adopted son. The state would help the "collectives" if it already had the material resources on hand; cooperatives, they said, were like a real son for whom the state would go out of its way to find resources if it does not have them already. However, the cooperative cannot be thought of in these terms because the cooperative itself is made up of corporate households (despite formal membership being allowed only to individuals) who are not prepared to engage in rough reciprocity in the same way as they would within a domestic group or, perhaps, a labor-exchange group.

The mark point system is an attempt to surmount this problem, but as a system it simply reproduces the dilemmas of the administered economy within the cooperatives because it is difficult to establish objective criteria for evaluating work. Mark points are a source of dissatisfaction among the members. Furthermore, this system of evaluation encourages individualism and "squaring off" within the cooperatives, rather than solidarity. In fact, individualism is mediated by the persistence of economic households within the cooperatives, and thus the squaring off occurs between households.

The formal democratic aims of the cooperatives are also swamped by the reality of kinship networks, which in fact constitute the informal real structures of the cooperatives and guide their internal politics. They personalize the seemingly formal workings of the cooperatives and form the basis for suspicions that individuals or families are using the cooperatives for their own ends. To some extent abuses of cooperative systems are inevitable in cultural contexts in which kin relations are fundamental to social organization and requests or favors asked by kin are difficult to refuse. But the issue is especially explosive in Laos because the organization of peasants into cooperatives produces no significant productivity advantages for them. Peasants whose margins are already slim quite correctly see the distribution of income and resources within the cooperatives as a zero-sum game, and consequently disputes (when they are allowed to occur) quickly take on life-and-death dimensions. Management is considered a net loss, and when it is combined with corruption or suspected corruption, as at ban Pao, the consequences can be murderous. Only when productivity is rising are such conflicts likely to be defused. In most of Laos, however, cooperatives did not result in increased productivity and too often caused a decline.

It is true that rice agriculture responds favorably to increased labor inputs, so the communist focus on labor was not entirely misguided. However, it is not work reorganization that is required to increase labor inputs, but technological inputs, such as irrigation rehabilitation or expansion, new rice varieties, fertilizers, and insecticides, all of which are possible without cooperatives and the radical reorganization of labor they involve. Tractors, especially if they are large, are usually beyond the means of any individual peasant and therefore could be owned and operated collectively. But outside of irrigated areas they have little rationale, and even then they can be collectively owned without other means of production being collectively pooled. Irrigation, of course, forces some level of cooperation on peasant farmers, but such associations can remain specialized. The degree of compulsion declines and the level of anarchy rises, however, when the necessity of maintaining long-term relationships is not present and therefore is not cemented and reinforced by other social relationships.

The communists argue that it is rational to gather all of these discrete forms of cooperation into one structure and then further streamline them. The argument has a superficial appeal. (The other implicit argument is that cooperatives are more easily integrated into the command economy and surpluses more easily "siphoned off" from them.) But collectivization strategies often not only rob the whole structure of its flexibility, but often exaggerate or even introduce new tensions into the workings of the peasant economy. And in the end, cooperation in the cooperatives runs up against the obstacle of the attempt to marry two disparate corporate bodies, the cooperative and the household.

8

"The New Countryside":

Cooperative–Village–State

 Several motivations led the Lao government to launch its collectivization program when it did. It felt economically vulnerable and saw the formation of cooperatives as a means of securing rapid agricultural growth. In 1978 it also felt politically threatened, both internationally and internally, and believed that political challenges could best be met if the independent peasants were incorporated into collective structures. The drive, therefore, had two prongs: one economic, the other political. Cooperatives were designed to incorporate both of these aims by forestalling a feared capitalist economic development in the countryside (thereby heading off an expected capitalist class challenge) and by installing socialist economic and political relations in the countryside.

The collapse of the collectivization campaign, however, and the government's growing feeling of security have not led to a jettisoning of the economic and political role envisioned for the cooperatives. The party still wishes to bring into existence a new social class, "the collective peasantry," and a new political structure along with it. In this plan the cooperatives have a central place, as Kaysone told the LPRP Congress in late 1986:

At present the great majority of the peasants in our country are organized under different forms of collective work, ranging from mutual aid teams, solidarity production groups to various types of cooperatives. It is necessary to understand that those labor collectives are not only economic but also *political organizations*. Therefore, we must try our best to consolidate and heighten the effectiveness of those organizations in mobilizing and educating the peasants, raising their political consciousness, deepening their patriotism and love of socialism, enhancing their tradition of diligent labor, solidarity, mutual love and mutual assistance, thus inspiring them to implement actively the party's and state's policies, to intensify production in order to build up a civilized style of living and the new countryside.[1]

These new institutions are projected as the main vehicles of socialism and social transformation in the villages.

It is fairly easy to see why communists have been attracted by this vision. Economically it conforms to a centralized, planned economy in which cooperatives become the lowest planning unit. But, even given shifts toward a decentralized economic system, aspects of Marxist political theory continue to pull them in this direction. Marx's idea of workers' self-government as embodied in the Paris Commune saw the commune as a "working not a parliamentary body."[2] In the *State and Revolution* Lenin explored ways of drawing Soviet citizens into close contact with the daily workings of government. These semianarchistic ideas, with their inadequate theorization of the problems of bureaucracy and the state, have provided a basis for communist political practice that aims at mobilizing citizens to participate in the polity through a range of organizations that reach down into the neighborhood. The cooperative would, therefore, seem an ideal institution through which to realize the political and economic aims of the communist state.

More ominously, cooperatives can be seen as part of communism's "totalitarianism." The latter concept has been justly criticized not only because of its propagandist usage, but more seriously because it distracted the attention of scholars from institutional and factional disputes within communist states and from the salience of informal social mechanisms in the everyday workings of institutions in communist societies.[3] However, I agree with Barrington Moore when he says the concept is meaningful to the degree that it "refers to a regime that tries, with considerable success, to control the whole range of human thought and action from a single center for the purpose of achieving a total transformation of human behavior in the direction of some allegedly higher goal."[4] In this light there is no doubt that the LPRP aimed not only to transform social institutions, but also to create the "new socialist man." Several times in his speech to the LPRP

Congress in 1986 the general secretary criticizes those (unnamed) who support "peaceful evolution" in Laos, by which he means those who believe that transformation will occur spontaneously, presumably in step with the development of the forces of production, and without party guidance. Against this, Kaysone counterposes the leading, directing role of the communist party.

Moore makes a distinction between autocratic and totalitarian regimes. Autocratic regimes, he suggests, leave the basic social structure intact, and many social activities that are not perceived as a political threat to the regime are allowed to go their own way. Various military dictatorships in the Third World may be seen in this way. Totalitarian regimes, on the other hand, *attempt* (one must say that total success is impossible) to organize all aspects of cultural and social life. The Lao state can be located somewhere between the two because it has never had the capacity to carry through more than a limited totalitarian reorganization of society, as the failure of the 1978–79 campaign clearly demonstrated.[5]

Commentators in the West have had a tendency to see economic liberalization in Laos and in other communist countries as leading to some form of political liberalization. To some extent this is accurate because there is a degree to which tolerance of private enterprise, autonomous cooperatives, and an independent peasantry does enable people to resist state directives and run counter to the state's totalitarian reflex. Liberalization does broaden the space of civil society and therefore may provide arenas for wider nonstate-sponsored social action. On the other hand, recognition of these "anarchistic" tendencies sometimes produces calls for even greater unity and discipline within communist parties in order to ensure that the long-term aims of the party are pursued.

Administration

Laos today is divided into sixteen provinces (Khoueng) and one prefecture (Khamphaeng Nakhorn) in Vientiane, having grown from thirteen in 1983. Each province is divided into approximately fifteen districts (muang), which are further divided into subdistricts (tasseng), which administer between five and ten villages (ban). These administrative divisions are broadly similar to those of the RLG, and the communist government has revived a system of cells in the village. In the early 1960s the RLG had promoted the creation of cells under a *nai sip* in charge of around ten households. George Con-

dominas thought the cells "originated . . . for purposes of political security," but in his view they could also become useful in programs of
community development.[6] The system was never successful, but the new
regime has tried to establish similar cells, *khum* or *nuay,* of approximately
ten households as well.

The provinces are the key units of administration and are run by administrative committees, and these are replicated at the district and subdistrict
level. The provincial administration has services corresponding to those of
the central ministries—Finance, Agriculture, Interior—although local
staff are directly responsible to the provincial administrative committee
rather than to the central ministry. This means there is an important degree
of administrative decentralization in Laos and considerable room for institutional friction. Paralleling this structure and often overlapping with it
is the party organization, whose job, as Kaysone says, is to ensure "the
party's all-round absolute and direct leadership over all links, from the
mapping out of lines and policies, to the organization of execution and
control."[7] However, the party's strength—with membership standing at
45,000, or 1.3 percent of the population, in the mid-1980s—is not sufficient to fulfill this aim. As one travels down the administrative hierarchy,
the direct influence of the party begins to peter out and is often nonexistent
at the village level.[8]

Yet the LPRP has developed an array of mass organizations beyond the
party designed to project its influence: the Lao People's Revolutionary
Youth, the Association of Lao Patriotic Women, the Lao Front for National
Reconstruction (formed as the successor to the NLHS in February 1979).
The party-controlled education system should also be included. The existence of these mass organizations (the communist party is an elitist party
that recruits on a restrictive basis) constitutes a critical structural difference
between, for example, the former RLG and the LPDR. They bridge the
administrative hiatus that existed at the muang level under the old regime.

Under the new regime, ban, tasseng, and muang are run by committees,
not by individuals. When asked to describe the main difference between the
new and old regimes the former head of Don Dou replied, "Before there
was only one person to deal with, but now there are committees everywhere!" These committees elect presidents (*pathan*), and thus there are
now pathan ban and pathan tasseng, a lexicon that sheds the paternalistic
connotations of *pho ban* (literally, father of the village) and *luuk ban*
(children of the village). (But there is also a more colorful description of
village leaders as elephant drivers.) Many villagers, however, continue to

use the old lexicon, at least in everyday, nonofficial speech. Members of these committees have specific areas of responsibility—youth, women, self-defense, education and culture, health—and at tasseng and muang level the committees have a person whose job it is to promote cooperatives. Each of these positions is linked vertically within the administration, and there are discrete meetings of persons charged with specific responsibilities. All the individuals in the muang responsible for cooperatives, for example, can be called together for a discussion about common problems. Such meetings may also include persons who are not technically administration officials, such as the heads of cooperatives. Meetings may also be held occasionally at more inclusive levels. In the new regime, therefore, multiple vertical strands bind the villagers to the government, rather than one, the pho ban, as was the case formerly. In this respect developments at the local level in Laos have followed the course outlined by Michael Moerman in his essay on Thai village headmen as "synaptic leaders" who stand at the interface between the local community and the state, under pressure from and mediating the interests of both. He writes, "One process of Thailand's modernization is for the complementarity of primordial groups to become less important than career lines that cross such groups, organizations that penetrate them, and ideas that homogenize them. Another is for identification with such primordial groups . . . to become less important than the specific interests of individuals and social categories. . . . This articulation of interests frequently involves replacing a single multipurpose synaptor by specialized or competitive synaptors, or by individual accessibility between national and rural persons."[9] But Laos is in the very early stages of this evolutionary process, and primordial loyalties remain strong.

The Buddhist Sangha

The only institutional form that reached from the pinnacle of national power into the heart of the lowland villages under the RLG was the Buddhist sangha. It provided the core of RLG nationalist ideology in the absence of a modernizing ideology projected by a nationalist elite. The RLG elite, however, found it increasingly difficult to even promote themselves as the protectors of the faith and of "Lao tradition," given their dependence on U.S. support and adopted Western life-styles. This was exploited by Pathet Lao propaganda, and the RLG responded in 1959 by placing stricter government controls on the organization of the sangha. Thus Royal Ordinance No. 160 gave the government "implicit right of veto over the election of abbots and elders to positions in the sangha administration [which] was vested in government officials at the next highest rank of the parallel-government sangha hierarchy; higher sangha dignitaries might stand for election only with cabinet consent; and all correspondence between different administrative levels of the sangha had to go via official government channels."[10] State-making and Buddhism are fundamental to Southeast Asian political history, and in Sihanouk's Cambodia, Thailand, and Burma Buddhism has played a pivotal role in articulating the modern state's legitimating ideology.[11] In Cambodia and Thailand, however, Buddhism could take a central place in nationalist ideology because the relative ethnic homogeneity of these countries meant a majority of the population were Buddhist. In Laos (as in Burma) this is not the case because Buddhism is the religion of the ethnic Lao population but not of the hilltribe groups. A nationalism in Laos that was dependent on Buddhism consequently risked being seen by other ethnic groups as a form threatening cultural domination rather than a vehicle of national integration. This was one reason RLG nationalism remained peripheral to the lives of many Lao citizens.

By contrast, the major achievement of the Pathet Lao was its ability to project itself as a nationalist force. Its long period in the mountains meant that it not only recruited from among the ethnic minorities, but also had to elaborate a nationalist ideology that clearly recognized them as part of the Lao nation. Accordingly, Buddhism could not continue to play its former central role under the LPDR. The communist government moved swiftly to bring Buddhism under its sway after 1975, although some Pathet Lao militants were openly hostile to the religion. Attributed by many observers to the atheism of communist doctrine, the hostility appears to have had complicated ethnic roots as well. Several informants have claimed that the most aggressive anti-Buddhists were soldiers and militants from ethnic minorities who were not Buddhists and who in fact identified the religion with the former, "oppressive" regime.

Yet Buddhism still plays a vital part in the everyday life of the lowland Lao, and the communists are attempting to mold the sangha to its state-making needs. They see the sangha as part of the "ideological struggle," and there are attempts to reconcile Buddhist and communist doctrine. In December 1976 Kaysone, for example, claimed, "Monks actively contribute in transmitting the policies of the party and the state, educating young people and providing medical care for the population."[12] In 1976 the sangha was reorganized when the supreme patriarch was displaced by a committee of the newly formed Lao United Buddhist Association. Buddhism in Laos, unlike that in Thailand, did not undergo a process of reorganization and modernization in the nineteenth century, and its monkhood was less deeply versed in theology than its Thai counterparts. Thus a fairly rudimentary Buddhism could be spun together with a rudimentary Marxism to provide a popular, syncretic ideology that spoke of equality, brotherhood, and working together for the good of everyone rather than for personal material wealth, and so on. Few peasants understand or are interested in the philosophical differences between the two systems of thought, and in this respect they are not much different from communists elsewhere who happen to be Christians. Such syncretism is virtually condoned by the LPRP, but it is not preached as a form of "Buddhist Socialism" in the manner it was in Sihanouk's Cambodia or in Burma.

Nevertheless, the state's relationship with the sangha was, for a time, fraught with tension. In the early days of the regime militants argued that the monks, who depended on alms, were like the old ruling class, "who didn't work but ate," and they were compelled to till their own gardens. This injunction (along with food shortages in the country in 1976–77) led to an exodus of monks from the vats, some of whom became forest monks. Many believers felt that monks who worked were not really monks, and they stayed away from the vats. This led to a revival and reinvigoration of spirit worship and consultations at the village level. The irony is that the communist "ideological regeneration" of Buddhism in Laos was aimed at purging it of "superstitious practices," but its own practice in fact led to their revival outside the vats. Rumors of discontented spirits circulated, spirits who were believed to manifest themselves in events like, for example, the snapping of the flagpole on top of the presidential palace during a storm in 1979, which was said to signal forthcoming political turbulence. Thus, rather than mobilizing Buddhism for state ends the communists were in fact alienating many lowland Lao.

By 1979 the regime's policy toward Buddhism had softened, and in Hatsayfong, for example, the Lao Patriotic Front attempted to "plan" support for the monks by trying to get household clusters in the villages (nuay) to take rotating responsibility for providing alms for the monks, a practice that can also be found in some areas of Thailand. In the latter areas such official responsibility evolved from grassroots practice; in Laos, attempts to impose even this level of control were met with spontaneous resistance, and people continued to give alms according to individual volition. In recent years popular Buddhism has flourished again in the context of a refurbishing of vats and a significant growth in the number of monks: it is surprising how little has really changed. In ban Thana the head of the vat committee has been the same person for fifteen years. The committee also contains members from the Lao Front for National Reconstruction, which sees support for the vat as one of its main responsibilities. Popular Buddhism persists, although at all major Buddhist ceremonies there are now obligatory references to building socialism and the country. The regime's aims have been made compatible with Buddhism, and the communists are no longer alienating ordinary believers. Nevertheless, one suspects that the old people of the villages who run these committees are more preoccupied with their impending transmutation than with the country's transformation.

Village Political Organization

The communists, in attempting to construct a modern "developmental state," tried to replace the lone, synaptic village leader with committees and specialized functional positions. Yet it is a reorganization that looks more formidable on paper than it does on the ground in the countryside. In many places the various mass organizations are barely functioning simply because of the weak reach of the central organizations. Local solidarity tends to prevail over outside allegiances.

Despite the state's desire to sink administrative roots in the villages, many of its policies (including those already discussed in this book) actually militated against supralocal organization and identification. Restrictions on the movement of people and goods forced people back into their local communities. In a sense government policies caused Lao villages to become less open and more corporate. The interaction between village organization and the state is a central line of thought running through Popkin's study of Vietnamese peasants, in which he argues, "Corporate villages had their origins not in a primitive communal mentality, but in the problems of taxation confronting both peasants and supravillage authorities—be they feudal or bureaucratic."[13] Corporate villages, he suggests, were simply easier to administer in premodern states, and I think there is an important continuity between this premodern arrangement and socialist states like Laos, especially in their commandist phase. One might say there is a continuity between the political superstructure of the natural economy and that of the communist period.

Popkin then turns his attention to the internal workings of the corporate villages, where, drawing on his Vietnamese material, he correctly directs attention to the exercise and abuse of power by village elites toward the less well-off and landless "outsiders" (although I believe his conception of village stratification is too rigid and limits the applicability of his argument). He argues that expressions of village solidarity concealed these divisions and therefore tended to serve the interests of the local elite. The presentation of a united front to outsiders and the state is apparently similar to the situation in Laos, where, as Taillard argued, there was a "confrontation of the power of the village with the power of the state" and the "dissociation of the two centers of power in Laos." However, the important difference between the two situations is that the Lao village and rural landscape were less stratified than in Vietnam, and therefore the solidarity of the Lao village more real. Thus when Taillard writes of village "democracy" and enforced consensus it is not in the interests of an entrenched elite:

> One often hears talk of "village democracy." It is an ambiguous expression. In western style democracy the vote is the source of all authority: the minority is subordinate to the majority, and this implies a quantitative evaluation of the forces involved. In a democracy founded on unanimity, the view of things is essentially qualitative. A debate gathers together all the members of the village community, in the course of which contradictory opinions are expressed and propositions are aired in order to be resolved. All authoritarian attitudes are excluded; agreement must be entered into freely by everyone concerned thereby losing its individual character and consequently there is no victor or vanquished. The role of the chief of the village is to refashion the opinions expressed, to find arguments to convince the doubters. . . . In extreme cases where, after a reasonable delay, agreement is impossible to reach, the unyielding persons are excluded from the community because their obstinacy threatens to break its vital solidarity.[14]

Although, as we saw much earlier in the case of ban Nok, landholders are more clearly village citizens than the landless. However, the majority of Lao villagers have access to land and consequently have rights to be involved in village decision making.

Popkin's main interest is in the transformation of precapitalist relations

189

by a capitalist state. Thus he argues, "The central state is not automatically a threat to the peasantry; on the contrary, it can be an ally in the process" of breaking localized precapitalist restrictions that work in favor of an old rural elite.[15] This process is more complicated when the transformation is being attempted by a communist state because on one side its policies often reinforce corporate tendencies, while on the other it tries to extend modern administration into the villages. It is, therefore, a profoundly contradictory process.

Peasant suspicion of institutions created from the outside is well known and has been the result of the fact that these institutions have usually been controlled by the great and powerful. An ordinary peasant learned to approach such institutions with circumspection, or preferably not at all, for fear of provoking their unpredictable wrath. This attitude has not changed as much as the new communist regime would like to think. Indeed, one could argue that the changes which have cascaded down on the peasants from on high since 1975 have made the state appear even more unpredictable and the peasants even more circumspect. This made some of my research difficult. Some of my encounters with village leaders aroused instant suspicion. One village headman, for example, was shredding tobacco outside his house when I approached him for some information. I recorded the following: "He sat at his work sharpening his machete, shaving some more tobacco and sharpening his knife again. Occasionally he would stop his work while talking to us and look at us with black, suspicious eyes while simultaneously tightening the tobacco leaves into a wad which was fed through a 10cm diameter hole in a piece of wood against which he ran the knife. One could not help feeling he was also tightening himself against us at the same time—presumably to stop 'outsiders' from shredding him."

On the other hand, officials at the local level are now linked to the state by stronger vertical ties, and therefore the pathan ban and pathan tasseng are able, if they wish, to enforce the government's line. Extensive discussions still occur in the village, and "village democracy" is still practiced, but now it often happens in a context in which a special official, in health, for example, will lead the discussion. Debate, moreover, occurs in the full knowledge that officials speak with the ultimate authority of the state. However, because of conflicting loyalties peasants remain reluctant, as in the old regime, to take on official posts or to enforce state decisions.

The rule of impersonal law in a Western, liberal-democratic sense is rarely known or experienced in the villages of Southeast Asia.[16] To deal with powerful institutions beyond the village one has traditionally needed patrons at various levels in the power structure. With patronage went corruption, and in this sense a system built on patronage is one built on pervasive corruption. It personalizes political and social relationships and undermines government claims that it is acting in the "national interest." From the point of view of the least powerful, therefore, those in power are there only to further their own interests, usually at the expense of those below them. The limitations on individual rights in communist systems have served only to keep these attitudes alive.

The communist government in Laos has attempted to surmount these attitudes by establishing a political administration in the countryside that expresses a strong developmental and nationalist commitment. For example, tasseng offices are plastered with ubiquitous nationalist slogans like: "Profoundly congratulate the person who sells paddy to the state"; "Selling rice to the state is an act of Nationalism and of love for socialism." By projecting a sense of national purpose, the government has attempted to supplant impersonal aims for personal ones. The new system is ultimately policed by a political vanguard, the "incorruptible" communist party, in which adherence to party rules and policy is the key criterion for advancement, not patronage in its traditional sense. In this respect it is an attempt to establish a modern, rule-governed political organization in place of entourages. Neither patronage nor corruption is absent, however, and Kaysone has been forced to comment on it many times. At the Congress in 1986 he said cadres were practicing "favoritism: toward one's relatives, friends and those coming from one's own locality or tribe"; and he spoke of "lousy elements . . . abusing the authority entrusted in them and the wealth placed under their management by the people, oppressing the people and carving into their property, thus becoming a privileged and parasitic group."[17] Martin Stuart-Fox has argued that "petty corruption has become so widespread that it is all but institutionalized."[18] However, corruption has not been the principal base on which the communist system functions, and corruption in communist Laos is not a political norm but is risky business, as the almost annual purges for corruption show. But authoritarian systems inevitably produce abuses of power, and in this sense corruption is endemic.[19]

Even so not a great deal of evidence exists concerning serious abuses in the rural areas. This is reflected in peasant, and even refugee, attitudes. While refugees may criticize the authoritarianism and apparent arbitrariness of the new regime, they rarely attack the communists for corruption. Peasants in Laos say it is easier to approach government officials to sign documents than before 1975 because one does not expect to pay a bribe first. The party and government are perceived as distant and powerful, but more rarely seen as rich and corrupt. Nevertheless, the ease with which petty corruption can spring up was demonstrated in early 1985, when Vientiane province attempted, as an effort in administrative rationalization, to abolish the tasseng level, leaving only the muang, ban, and nuay. It was thought that the tasseng had little purpose because the ban was the normal work unit and the muang had the real power to make decisions. People spoke of the ban-muang as a traditional unit and assumed it was a natural unit of administration. However, after the tasseng were abolished the muang level quickly became overloaded with requests for marriage licenses and permission to buy a house. People soon began offering bribes in order to get special attention for their petition, and paid intermediaries sprang up to assist those who felt too intimidated to approach the more remote muang level. Thus after only a year the tasseng level was restored. However, government policy is still to gradually do away with this level of administration.

Cooperatives and the State

Government statements have reflected a desire to see the cooperatives become the key administrative and economic institution in the countryside. The organizational structure of cooperatives on paper usually mirrors that of the village, and no doubt there are some communist planners who would like the cooperative and the village to be isomorphic. But only at the height of the collectivization campaign were whole villages among lowland Lao in a single cooperative, and then only briefly and under duress.

Among the cooperatives examined in this study, only Don Dou even vaguely approached the "ideal" homology of cooperative and village. Yet less than one-quarter of the households in the village were ever in the cooperative. The head of the cooperative, Ngai, was pathan ban until 1984 and remained formal head of the cooperative until 1986. He gained the position of pathan ban in 1975, when the old pho ban was elected to a tasseng People's Committee during the drawn-out institutional "revolutions" of 1975 that consolidated the Pathet Lao's power. The old pho ban said he was given his position in 1973 when, after the ceasefire agreement, the Pathet Lao had insisted that Don Dou become a ban separate from ban

Thana. His *samien* (assistant) at the time was Ngai. He had been elected pho ban because he was the oldest member of the village, he said, but he found the work difficult because he is uneducated and finds public speaking difficult. This man is a very traditional figure, and his house is decorated with large pictures of the old Lao king and the royal family. He does not see anything problematic about this, as he sees little difference between the new and old regime, except that there is less money available for the vat and more committees. Although displaced by Ngai, this man was reintegrated into the administrative structure as a member of the National Front for Reconstruction. He sees the front in a favorable light because it institutionalizes respect for elders in the village and reinforces their capacity to intervene in and mediate village disputes.

Ngai was neither a communist party member nor a member of the front. As samien he would normally succeed to the old pho ban if the latter stepped down or died. Ngai was elected to the position as pathan ban in 1975 and again in 1976. A committee of five was elected in 1976, all of whom had to be approved by the tasseng level. Theoretically reelections are supposed to take place for these positions every year, but the traditional system of electing people as the need arises has reasserted itself: villagers see no point in having yearly elections if no one is going to contest the positions. In 1976 there were representatives from all five "mass organizations" on the village committee. By early 1982 it was decided that this was unnecessary, and the committee was reduced to three: Ngai, Put, a cooperative member and activist, and La, head of the youth league in the village but not in the cooperative. Again, here was an uncanny reassertion of the old system, in which the pho ban normally had two assistants.

There was a significant overlap between cooperative membership and the village mass organizations. Thus the head of the cooperative's women's association, Mayoury, was also head of the village women's organization; her husband organized the self-defense unit for both the cooperative and the village; the youth league functioned only at the village level, while the tasseng office handled educational and cultural services for the village. In the presence of such overlapping between the cooperative organizations and the village organizations, the cooperatives have the potential to act as a corporate group in village politics, especially given the tendency to coalesce around kinship cores. However, in none of the villages of Hatsayfong had the cooperative organization effectively supplanted the village organization, and it appears increasingly less likely that this will happen.

In ban Thana the relationship between the cooperative and the village fluctuated in tandem with the fortunes of the cooperative itself. At its height, between 30 and 40 percent of the households in the village were in the cooperative, and in the beginning five out of seven members of the ban committee were in the cooperative. The pathan ban of ban Thana, Daeng, had joined the cooperative when it was established, but he did not become its head. Nevertheless, there was a strong element of continuity between the village leadership and the cooperative leadership. But as the cooperative disintegrated so too did this relationship. Daeng and two other members quit the cooperative, which meant that by 1982 only two members of the village committee were also members of the cooperative, and the influence of the cooperative on village political affairs was marginalized. The mass organizations really function only at village level. The cooperative at ban Nok had even less impact on village leadership than that at ban Thana, although one member of Maha Houa's cooperative had been on the village committee for many years. In 1987 all of the members of the ban Nok village committee claimed to be members of an agricultural cooperative but in fact were really members of labor-exchange groups and collectives for buying inputs. Two members of the newly formed village trading cooperative committee were also members of the village committee, and this pattern appears to be increasingly common elsewhere. In fact, the trading cooperatives probably stand a much better chance of being isomorphic with the village than the agricultural cooperatives; however, unlike the latter they do not attempt to reproduce the various specialized activities of the village and therefore cannot fulfill the state's dreams of the cooperative being a working and administrative organization able to supplant the village administration.

It is incumbent on communist party members to join their village cooperatives and to spearhead their progress, but the party's presence below muang level is minimal. Thus the Sixth Resolution of the party and Council of Ministers reported in 1988 that "party members in the countryside compose 44 percent, and rural party cadres 41 percent, of the total membership throughout the country."[20] Dtoo Pheng was the only active party member in the cooperatives in Bo-O, and he has since retired. The muang party activists are dispatched to the tasseng to provide advice and to monitor what is happening at the local level. But tasseng Bo-O, for example, had only one such party activist working there during the period of my research. Thus the "building of socialism in the countryside" is largely in the hands of nonparty activists and administrators.

In the first few years after the communist takeover great emphasis was placed on the political qualities of officials selected for the ban and tasseng committees—patriotism and popularity being key virtues. But as the practical realities of economic development have tempered the regime's political zeal so there has been a progressive shift toward persons with technical qualifications. Daeng at ban Thana was a traditional leader who made the transition from pho ban to pathan ban, but his literacy was poor and he was also slightly deaf, and he became increasingly aware that the new government's demands for statistics and reports were beyond his capabilities. A reshuffling throughout the various organizations in the tasseng gradually replaced older officials with people who are at least literate. By early 1984 the deputy head of ban Thana, Phetsavan, had replaced Daeng. Phetsavan talks of the need for planning, which for him means the village leadership disseminating agricultural advice among the farmers concerning multiple cropping, weeding, irrigation, the use of fertilizers. In this perspective the "collectives" are seen as paddy field equivalents of the nuay. They are vehicles for the dissemination of information. Someone from a "collective" group can be called to a seminar about a new rice strain, for example, and be expected to pass the information on to the other members of the "collective."

Some writers have emphasized the political centrality of the vat and its monks in the organization of village life, and one could perhaps expect that the cooperative would have challenged that role. But this has not been the case. In muang Hatsayfong the major village bouns and religious meetings are held in the *sala* in the grounds of the vat, while in Don Dou the building of the cooperative shed led to political meetings being held there, especially as it had electricity. But decisions about where meetings would be held largely depended on what was being planned, and the villagers saw no competition between the vat and the cooperative. The political role of the vat in village organizational affairs possibly has been overstated. One pho ban told a researcher in the mid-1960s, "The meeting is usually held in the nai ban's house if the subject of the meeting is related to the construction of a road, a school or the improved rice programme. . . . The meeting is held in the vat if related to the construction of a sala or the preparation for a *Boun Pravet* or the *Boun Bang Fai*."[21] In a number of other villages it was observed that meetings with agricultural extension officers were also held in the nai ban's house. These secular/religious distinctions persisted in villages in the postrevolutionary period, except that in Don Dou, for example, secular activities moved from the headman's house to the cooperative shed.

Women's Association

Potentially the ALPW is one of the most socially radical organizations set up by the new regime at the ban level. I have already touched on the fact that the status of women in Lao society is relatively low, certainly as compared with standards in Western societies. Of course, the status of women in Laos varies between ethnic groups, and in general it would seem that the status of lowland Lao women is considerably higher than that of women in most hilltribe groups or in neighboring Vietnam or China. Before 1975 women held no official organizational positions in the countryside; men were the exclusive spokesmen at local meetings. Mayoury, the head of the ALPW in Don Dou, said women in the tasseng were first organized through seminars held in the area in 1975 to discuss the status of women in Lao society and their role under socialism. She joined the association after attending some of these seminars. She then applied to the muang ALPW, and after her acceptance she was subsequently recommended to the muang by the ban committee as a good person to head the organization in the village. It should be noted that there was not a wide choice; only one other woman in the village had applied to join the association at the same time. By 1982, however, it had thirty members, all married because unmarried women joined the youth organization.

Consequently, women now have more say in village administration than previously, but the main change, at least in Don Dou, appeared to have been the curbing of actual or threatened male violence against women in the village. Mayoury said that in the past women were afraid to contradict their husband for fear of being beaten. Physical beatings, she claimed, became particularly serious in 1976, presumably as a result of the disruptions to family income following the contraction of the urban economy. (A similar rise in the level of domestic violence is witnessed in the West during recessions.) The role of the association was to mediate disputes and to explain to the husband that he can no longer treat his wife harshly under socialism. If he refused to listen to the association it would then call in the ban committee. In the early period five or six men were sent off to reeducation seminars for refusing to change their attitude toward their wives. Some offending men, she said, had tried to short-circuit the impact of the association. When the husband became aware that he was about to be visited by the association he went straight to the all-male ban committee both because he expected a fairer hearing from them and because he refused to be spoken to in an authoritative way by women. The ban committee refused to accept these approaches, she said, and the association was always called in to discuss the case.

Nevertheless, general cultural intimidation of women continues to take its toll on their political participation. Often, except for the older women or the head of the ALPW, they are too shy to speak up in meetings, both in the village and in the cooperative. These restrictions remain strongest in traditional areas relating to religious affairs. In new institutions like the cooperative, which are formally democratic, women tend to have a little more say and greater positions of responsibility. For example, the woman accountant in Maha Houa's cooperative is also on the village committee. Yet the persistence of a customary division of labor between men and women, which ensures that the latter have continuous work commitments, also ensures a low level of political participation by women.

The status of women in socialist societies matches neither the demands of feminists in the West nor official claims that communism emancipates women. Yet in socialist Laos women do have more significant political and social roles than they had in the past, and the checks placed on male intimidation of women at the local level should not be underrated. Black Tai women, who live in a patriarchal social structure, said the association at least allowed them to be present (however briefly) at formal meetings with outsiders, something they claimed would have been impossible in the past. The dilemma faced by Western liberalism in this situation is that while the extension of mass organizations by communist states into the everyday lives of their citizens is often symptomatic of "totalitarian" controls, it can also extend rights to those sections of the population for whom they have been nonexistent (a point Popkin makes). Thus, in the case of women, these organizations often extend their liberties at the expense of archaic male prerogatives.

Mass organizations in the village also operate in the absence of a properly functioning legal system, and they partly displace the "frontier justice" that was the grim reality of the traditional system. The objective problems faced by poorly integrated political systems, communist or otherwise, means there is always leeway for petty tyrants in the provinces, and centralized, one-party communist states are probably better equipped for wiping out such localized abuses. On the other hand, communist political structures contain the possibility of substituting centralized oppressiveness for petty tyranny.

The Persistence of Patronage

In chapter 3 I noted that a special section for the coordination and guidance of cooperatives had been established in the prime minister's department under Sali Vongkhamsao in late 1978. In the words of one Lao official, it existed as a sort of "pseudoministry" alongside the Ministry of Agriculture, Forestry, and Irrigation. Both bodies were charged with promoting cooperatives. This resulted in institutional competition and, all too frequently, the issuing of contradictory directives. Thus on 1 October 1981, a decision was taken to move the cooperatives section out of the prime minister's department into the Ministry of Agriculture, Forestry, and Irrigation. The change was formalized in January 1982 as part of a general reorganization of ministries and responsibilities in an attempt to induce more rationalization and specialization. Thus forestry moved into another ministry's jurisdiction, and the Ministry of Agriculture, Irrigation, and Cooperatives (MAIC) came into being.

This much is straightforward, but the reorganization disrupted what appears to have been an informal system of bureaucratic patronage practiced toward some cooperatives within the ministry. A high official in the MAIC who was in charge of promoting cooperatives had attempted to establish model cooperatives by channeling considerable resources to them and abundant extension service advice so that they could have a "demonstration effect" on private peasants, who would then become enthusiastic about joining cooperatives. According to officials in the Department of Cooperatives of the MAIC, this strategy created friction with the muang administration, who believed that resources should be channeled through them and that the muang should decide on the priorities for distribution of resources in their area. Following the administrative reorganization of the ministry there was discussion about what should happen to the model cooperatives that had been singled out for special attention and about whether they should remain under the patronage of the official who had moved to another department in the ministry. The cooperatives department insisted that all activities relating to cooperatives be channeled through them and the proper channels of administration at lower levels, and they were successful.

The reorganization had ramifications in muang Hatsayfong, where the peasants had quickly recognized this bureaucratic patronage as the familiar, traditional patron-client system. For example, the leaders of ban Thana cooperative argued in 1983 that the main difference between their cooperative and Don Dou was that the latter was directly under the ministry's control and therefore received better facilities, while ban Thana cooperative was under the responsibility only of the tasseng office. Dtoo Pheng gave a surprisingly frank interpretation of why differences existed between cooperatives, one that shows the persistence of what the regime would certainly call "old ways of thought." He said that in 1979 Don Dou had been under the tasseng, in 1980 under the muang, in 1981 under the khoueng, and at the end of that year it came under the direction of the ministry. There was, he said, a tendency for higher levels in the administration to want to have the better cooperatives in their sphere of influence. Thus one cooperative in the muang had been "demoted" from the ministry level to the muang level, while a cooperative in neighboring muang Saysatane had been elevated for good performance. Muang Hatsayfong, he said, had three cooperatives directly under the ministry—Don Dou, ban Hom, and Tanalang. His perception was that if the cooperatives did well they went up the administrative ladder, and if not they were cast downward.

The obvious attempt by bureaucrats to have only success stories attached to them in the interests of their own and their ministry's or section's fortunes was seen by Dtoo Pheng as a natural tradeoff between bureaucrats and the cooperatives. Predictably Maha Houa was also sensitive to the patronage of Don Dou and its impact on the latter's performance, and, as we have seen, he had run into difficulties with the local administration. According to officials at the cooperatives department, Maha Houa had tried to bypass the lower administrative levels and directly approached them for machinery; he was obviously in search of a patron at the top level. Only after several attempts was he convinced that the system had been reorganized and that he had to work through the muang. Don Dou resisted the reorganization, and its officials continued for some time to try to work through personal contacts rather than through the muang. By 1984, the administrative gaze of the Cooperatives Department had shifted to commercial cooperatives like Dan Sang, who were now receiving special favors in order to get started and become a success to be emulated by others.

No doubt the peasants' familiarity with personalized patronage makes its use attractive to them. But the situation in Hatsayfong arose out of the confusions created by the bureaucratic overlap in the administration of the cooperatives that had followed the creation of ad hoc administrative organizations in the latter phase of the collectivization campaign. Officials charged with making the cooperatives a success tried to vault over administrative levels in an attempt to bypass some of the bottlenecks that had occurred. But by doing so they immediately began to reproduce patron–client structures and created confusion and even disillusionment when peasants observed the selective practice of patronage. Yet the lack of resources to dispense ensured that the patronage system remained limited in its extent and ensured that few local village leaders became locked into dependency on outside sources for dispensing patronage within their villages. Primordial ties of solidarity retained their force.

Cooperatives were to play a key role in the government's strategy of introducing social, economic, and political changes into the countryside. As grass roots institutions, they could mobilize, it was hoped, the mass of the peasantry for rapid social change. The failure of the orthodox communist cooperative strategy in Laos has led to a reformulation of cooperatives' role and a greater reliance on the various front organizations at the village level to promote government policies regarding improved methods of production and irrigation or the curtailing of slash-and-burn agriculture. Resolution No. 6, for example, called for the promotion of groups of "three to seven families, depending on the size of villages, their environment and working conditions: with the aim of leading a common political life, mutual assistance in production and livelihood. Existing solidarity production groups must coordinate with local villagers and must not be set up apart. Each group must have a chief and a deputy chief who will be under the authority of the administration of the village."[22] Such moves are to be accompanied by renewed attempts to phase out the tasseng level of administration in an attempt, first, to redistribute resources—expertise in particular—down to the villages, and second, to consolidate the muang level of administration. The aim is to institute the muang as the key political unit and to charge it with formulating plans that not only take account of the general plans elaborated by the central government as mediated by the khoueng, but also adapt them to local peculiarities. Resolution 6 called on the muang to draw up "detailed directives, quantitative targets and measures to determine the kind of animals to rear, what main plants to cultivate, and how to improve land quality." It also called on the muang to "pay special attention to the organization of forms of cooperation between the farmers." Undoubtedly this attempt to rationalize administration is aimed at placing more cadres in the villages and promoting party growth there as well as consolidating the muang organization of the party. In this way the

LPRP hopes to retain control over the direction of social, economic, and political developments in the countryside.

Theda Skocpol observed in her book *States and Social Revolutions* that all modern revolutions have resulted in the extension and strengthening of the power of the state over society.[23] This occurred in Laos after 1975. The communist government there has succeeded more than any previous government in sinking multistranded organizational roots in the villages and providing a credible nationalist ideology. Yet the limited power and reach of the state, combined with misguided policies and bureaucratic authoritarianism, have ensured the continuation of many traditional political patterns. Indeed, initially they reinforced tendencies toward corporate villages; more recent policies have reversed this trend. However, it is clear that Kaysone, for example, does not understand the sociological roots of these patterns. When he criticizes the problems of bureaucracy in the state apparatus, its causes are not seen to lie in the inherent difficulties of bureaucracy or party autocracy, but as a hangover of the anarchic work style of small producers: "At present we are facing a big obstacle in enhancing the effectiveness of the party leadership, namely, the routinistic, scattered style of work typical of small producers, a style that is widespread in every branch at every level."[24] In other words, centralized direction by the party and bureaucracy requires streamlining and perfecting rather than rethinking. The legacy of Marxist-Leninist theory made the idea of having the agricultural cooperatives as a basic political-economic unit in the countryside attractive. However, the economic failure of producer cooperatives has ruined that vision.

While the LPDR has established closer relations between the government and the villages than previous regimes, it has still not overcome peasants' wariness of states in general or their recognition of themselves as surplus givers to state-based surplus takers. As one peasant remarked to me, "State officials grow cleaned rice (*khao saan*); the people grow paddy rice (*khao bpeuk*)."

9

Peasants and Socialism

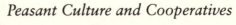

Peasant Culture and Cooperatives

It has been suggested that peasant culture is predisposed to socialist agriculture, or cooperatives. Marx speculated along these lines late in life after he was approached by Vera Zasulich to comment on the compatibility of the Russian peasant commune with socialism. In his various draft replies, Marx first repudiated the idea that the transition to capitalism in Europe outlined in *Capital* provided a suprahistorical model of social change applicable everywhere; second, he thought that the commune may be "able to incorporate the positive achievements of the capitalist system, without having to pass under its harsh tribute." By his final letter, he was "convinced . . . that the commune is the fulcrum for social regeneration in Russia." In contrast to much of his earlier writing, with its stormy literary imagery of socialism as the radical negation of capitalism and all else, here he says the use of the commune as a starting point "may open a new chapter [in modern society] that does not begin with its own suicide." Such a continuity between past, present, and future almost suggests some form of evolutionary socialism outside Europe. The positive features Marx identified in the commune were communal rights over property and the peasants' familiarity with traditional forms of cooperation in labor and production, which he felt "could greatly facilitate their transition from small-plot to collective farming."[1] Capitalism would necessarily wipe out these features, he said, implying that socialism could preserve and further develop them.

In earlier chapters we saw that similar notions were used in Laos to assert a continuity between peasant traditions of cooperation and cooperative farming. It should be recognized, however, that not only members of the LPRP espoused them. One Swedish adviser in Laos claimed that the formation of cooperatives among the hilltribes would be easier than among the lowlanders because they were more egalitarian and "in those ethnic groups where ownership is communal, the steps towards further collectivisation is easier to achieve."[2] There is no empirical evidence on the various minorities in Laos that would support this claim, and chapter 6 above provides an extended critique of simplistic transpositions of traditional cooperation into modern forms in the context of Lao society and explores the practical and organizational disjunctions between the two.

A large body of anthropological evidence accumulated this century has shown that communal tenure in traditional societies is based on principles quite different from the communal tenure socialists have in mind; so are the rationales for cooperation in work. There are fundamental differences in rights of access to productive resources and there are great variations in authority patterns, most of which are ascribed and authoritarian, at least at the level of productive activity. Ideas of modern (socialist) cooperation are founded on *individuals* participating *equally* and *democratically* in collective activity for mutual benefit. These ideas inevitably cut across traditional concepts of authority and, therefore, promotion of modern cooperatives may lead to a breakdown in traditional solidarity through a challenging of preexisting patterns of authority. In other words, modern cooperatives are likely to destroy the very foundations on which some hope to build.

In chapter 7 reference was made to Ronald Dore's important observation concerning the need for institutionalized suspicion in cooperatives, that is, the impersonalizing of key procedures in order to avoid accusations of corruption. He points out that peasant villages operate on a highly personalized level, and people have not been socialized into separating "institutionalized role relationships from total interpersonal relationships. . . . The necessary effort of imagination and control of affect is not one which people in small rural communities anywhere get enough practice to acquire the habit of."[3] Institutionalized suspicion through the audit may cause either distrust or offense, and he suggests that it is virtually impossible to stop wider personal relationships from influencing decisions by cooperative officials, leading inevitably to accusations of favoritism. And, as he remarks, the accuser is "reasonably likely to be right." Such observations are especially damaging for orthodox communist perspectives on cooperatives, which bring a wide range of interpersonal activities under the umbrella of the cooperative. If cooperatives are formed, as in Laos, with the preexisting stratifications in rural society intact, then powerful villagers are likely to be the most influential members of the cooperative and their practices of favoritism, real or imagined, sources of discontent within the cooperative. These can be managed if the cooperatives are made up mainly of kin or if there is a tradeoff to be made between land-short and landed peasants, as occurred at Don Dou for a time. Such "solutions" serve to confirm the vitality of the traditional structure, not the new cooperative structure. In other fully collectivized communist systems local power bases acquired initially through access to the party or the state become subject to interpersonal pressures for favoritism at the village level. Short of making a complete break with preexisting ways, a modern cooperative program for agricultural development may not be viable in developing countries. But where complete breaks have been attempted the process has been so traumatic as to prove counterproductive.

Other arguments have been advanced against the idea of peasant culture's receptiveness to cooperatives. A very influential article by George M. Foster in the mid-1960s, "Peasant Society and the Image of Limited Good," argued that peasants had a cognitive orientation fashioned by their limited subsistence environment which dictated that all goods, from land to love, existed only in limited quantities. Assuming that the peasant community is a "closed system . . . it follows that *an individual or a family can improve a position only at the expense of others.*" In other words, peasants are engaged in a zero-sum game and are therefore "individualistic"; "traditional peasant societies are cooperative only in the sense of honoring reciprocal obligations, rather than in the sense of understanding total community welfare, and that mutual suspicion seriously limits cooperative approaches to village problems."[4] Foster's article has been widely used to explain the failure of cooperatives in developing countries. Peasant cultural conservatism and narrowness were the culprits.

If one leaves aside the simplifications of peasant culture in this article (effectively criticized by other authors),[5] the power of its critique of peasant action derives from an unstated contrast drawn between "pure" self-interested and "pure" altruistic action. Given the rarity of the latter and the fact that egalitarian and altruistic communities have shown themselves to be viable social forms only for short periods,[6] it was not hard for Foster to develop his case. In other words, he used otherworldly, or more plainly, unrealistic, standards for measuring human motivation and action—these are of little use to anthropology and sociology.

James C. Scott in the *Moral Economy of the Peasant* offers an apparently similar approach to the study of peasant values, rooting them, as he does, in a "subsistence ethic." However, Scott's conception of the peasant moral economy is not an abstract and universal one, as some of his critics seem to think. It is situational. The culture of subsistence peasants upholds the right of members of the community to a basic living, and various social mechanisms in the village attempt to ensure this: "There is an entire range of networks and institutions outside the immediate family which may, and often do, act as shock absorbers during economic crises in peasant life. A man's kinsmen, his friends, his village, a powerful patron, and even—though rarely—the state, may help tide him over. . . . In most cases, however, a man cannot count with as much certainty or for as much help from fellow villagers as he can from near relatives and close neighbors."[7] Scott's main aim in this book is to discern when claims by superordinate groups cease to be legitimate, and this, he argues, happens when rights central to the moral economy are violated.

Scott is not especially interested in problems of peasant economic cooperation, although various forms of cooperation are clearly mandatory in a moral economy. He does not offer a pastoral vision of peasants, and he warns his readers not to "romanticize" the cooperative safety nets cast across the peasant community. These, he says, are "not radically egalitarian. Rather they imply only that all are entitled to a *living* out of the resources within the village, and that living is attained often at the cost of a loss of status and autonomy. They work, moreover, in large measure through the abrasive force of gossip and envy." We should also "suppose that there was always some tension in the village between the better-off who hoped to minimize their obligations and the poor who had most to gain from communal guarantees."[8]

Foster's argument is that peasant "culture" inhibits initiative and therefore economic development; Scott, on the other hand, stresses the protective functions of peasant culture in conditions in which peasants have little margin for risk, although he argues that once the risk threshold has been lowered individual peasant households will happily innovate. If subsistence is permanently secured, then key elements of the old moral economy begin to fade, only to be replaced by new theaters of struggle over "basic rights"—a new moral economy.[9] Little in Scott's argument encourages beliefs that peasants are somehow naturally disposed toward cooperation. On the contrary, their cooperation occurs in the context of the severe constraints of a subsistence economy and does not function indiscriminately or universally. Even though the basic morality is held across the community, its application radiates out in a personalized fashion from specific groups and individuals. In chapter 3 I remarked that once the peasants' subsistence defensive perimeter has been secured, then cooperatives may be considered as one way of *improving* the peasants' livelihood. There is little to suggest that the operation of the moral economy spontaneously disposes peasants this way; on the other hand, it does not predict inevitable failure either, as Foster's "image of the limited good" does.

Samuel Popkin criticizes both Foster (correctly) and Scott (incorrectly) for defending a view of peasant culture as having "fixed" norms rather than his own position, which argues that "norms are malleable, renegotiated, and shifting in accord with considerations of power and strategic interaction among individuals. There are always trade-offs between conflicting and inconsistent norms." Many of the arguments in this book conform with Popkin's general statement, but unfortunately, he counterposes to an a priori deductive reasoning concerning peasant values another a priori deductive model of "investment logic": "by applying theories of individual decision making to villages, we can begin to develop a deductive understanding of peasant institutions."[10] In this way Popkin in fact challenges the very idea of "peasant culture" because all culture becomes an epiphenomenon of an all-encompassing logic. As much as I agree with many of the individual observations Popkin makes in his analysis of Vietnamese peasants, his reductionism and methodological individualism must be rejected because of its denial of a relatively autonomous role for social institutions such as kinship organization, classes or ethnic groups, or indeed, states.[11] While anthropology has been committed to studying human universals, it has been equally committed to analyzing cultural and social specificity. It allows the study not only of peasant culture, but also of discrete peasant cultures, such as Lao peasant culture as distinct from Chinese or Mexican peasant culture. It is cultures as institutional complexes, not individual choice, that will determine which values will tend to predominate in the "trade-offs between conflicting and inconsistent norms."

So is there a relatively autonomous role for cultural ideas and values in a cooperative program? Commentators on the Lao or Thai, for example, monotonously remark on how friendly, generous, and happy-go-lucky they are; and it is a common self-perception. Ideologies of generosity and sharing are widely held and expressed in the ubiquitous greeting to passersby to "come and eat!" But what is the significance of these values? It is a basic premise of sociology that socialization of individuals as they pass through various social institutions produces values that in turn help reproduce these institutions. Cooperatives have been seen by some as one more socializing agency. John Bennett, for example, writes, "Cooperation is—or can be—a re-socialization of the human group and personality."[12] And Worsley comments, "A collectivist orientation implies the limitation of self-interest and the institutionalization of altruism."[13]

Several issues follow: Can societies establish organizations that will institutionalize cooperative values? or perhaps further enhance or strengthen those values that already exist in a particular culture? And, if such values already exist, to what extent do they favor cooperative development? The last question suggests an uncanny parallel with the debate initiated by Max Weber concerning the contribution of the Protestant ethic to the rise of capitalism. Is it worthwhile asking whether a "cooperative ethic" is a prerequisite for the rise of socialism? Weber's argument is open to two interpretations: first, that Calvinism was a direct cause of capitalism; second, that there was a mutually reinforcing compatibility between the ideology of Protestantism and that of capitalism.[14] The latter thesis is most plausible, and it has been transferred to reformist movements in other major world religions.[15] Whatever the relative merits of these arguments it is clear that major religions can be "manipulated" to promote either capitalist or socialist development. Buddhism in Laos has been interpreted in a way that serves the secular aims of the socialist government, while in Thailand it is used to legitimize a capitalist state. It would be difficult to argue that Buddhism is more predisposed to one form of social organization than another. In fact, it is most plausible to argue that social, economic, and political contexts provide the basic framework in which either reformist or reactionary interpretations of dogma will be elaborated.

A similar lability is found in the folk world of the everyday proverbs in all cultures. As the following Lao sayings document, these reflect the contending demands of self-interest and broader obligations to kin and community. Not surprisingly, there are injunctions against greed:

> He who eats, eats until he vomits,
> He who desires, wants enough to die.

Rationalizations for self-interest:

>Don't put your faith in a single path,
>Beware of the intentions of others.

Strong feelings are expressed concerning laziness and free-riders:

>Call to dinner and he is instantly there,
>Call to work and he runs away.

Expressions of distrust of strangers:

>People of a different village,
>Herbs of different gardens.

And expressions of social obligations of kinship and friendship:

>If you don't rub a jewel for three years, it will tarnish,
>If you don't visit your relatives for three years, they will be strangers.

And:

>Friends die for us to bury, and live for us to feed.

And so on. Popular culture expresses the real, contradictory pushes and pulls of everyday life, and proverbs provide the raw material that allows rationalizations for the social maneuvers of individuals, families, friends, and communities in specific contexts. Most Lao peasants I have spoken with place a high value on cooperative solutions to problems, and most thought producer cooperatives were "a good idea," they just did not work "in practice." In a sense they were saying that despite their values, cooperation of this sort could not work.

Popular sayings and religious ideas, therefore, are in a sense free-floating elements able to be given more or less emphasis, more or less public expression depending on economic, social, and political contexts. In developed capitalist cultures it is generally acceptable to trumpet blatant self-interest, even though this may be paralleled, as in Australia, by ideologies of "mateship." In Laos both politics and traditional culture make similar public expressions of self-interest impermissible, although they are articulated privately. The reasons for this are easily traced: in Laos people still live in small, face-to-face communities held together by many stranded ties. A public declaration of self-interest is a denial of those all-important, if constraining, ties, and therefore there are strong social pressures or sanctions against making such declarations. Communist ideology further strengthened sanctions against expressions of individualized interests to the point that it smothered initiative. Kaysone tried to redress this imbalance during his Congress speech in 1986, when he attempted a reconciliation of individual and social interests. By the end of 1988 in the context of the radical policy shifts begun in mid-1987, Sompavanh Inthavong, vice-minister of trade, commerce, and external relations told me, "This government authorizes people to become millionaires!" I have not seen similar statements in the Lao media or in official pronouncements. There have been no "shocking" public calls to "get rich," as in China, for example.[16] Few societies, let alone peasant ones, can tolerate such public declarations of economic and social warfare. Even America evinced some ambivalence toward the infamous speech on greed in the film *Wall Street*.

Can cooperatives institutionalize collective values and socialize members through them? The answer must be yes, to a certain extent. But they are unlikely to produce "socialist men" if only because socialization is a problematic process: it cannot be totally closed because there is always some lack of fit between individuals and social institutions. Disjunctions between individuals and institutions and among different institutions are the spaces in which social change can develop or evolve into serious contradictions leading to violent change. For example, even in countries with fully collectivized agriculture a minuscule number of private peasants survived. "One had to be a little crazy to resist the incredible pressure put on people to join cooperatives, and indeed, the few who remained outside the collective sector were usually rather odd fellows. . . . [It was] a sort of asylum where the 'socially mentally handicapped' were allowed to rest."[17] At the level of more fundamental social institutions, it has been suggested by some research that extended families socialize their children so that they will curb expressions of aggression and sexuality and instill in them control of impulses that may disrupt group coordination.[18] No one claims that these families are totally successful or that individuals socialized in this way are more prepared to suppress fractious impulses when confronted with demands made by institutions beyond the extended family. Peasants brought up in villages with long-standing practices of cooperation are likely to accept them. They may, therefore, be more predisposed to suggestions for new forms of cooperative activity than peasants who have never experienced similar collective activity. On the other hand, peasants who have been born and bred into rural communes have recently demonstrated that when given the opportunity they will rapidly forsake them for household-based farming—which is, I suggest, more an expression of the fundamental importance of the family's economic role in peasant agriculture than of the autonomous product of particular values.

Few unambiguous conclusions may be drawn concerning the influence of peasant culture on cooperative development. Some writers have been inclined to connect the relatively successful functioning of cooperatives in Japan, Taiwan, and South Korea with strong group sentiments in such cultures. Yet the real situation is more complex. The requirements of irrigation, of course, provided a solid foundation for cooperative activities in Japanese villages, but the forms of cooperation built on this base have changed over time in response to broader economic and social developments.[19] While some spontaneous cooperative development took place among farmers in the 1920s, widespread participation was primarily a response to state coercion following the rise of Japanese nationalism and fascism. "Agricultural Associations, which existed in every village and in which membership was compulsory, were merely organs for government control of the farmer, the channel for the rationing of materials and household goods, and the channel for enforcing crop deliveries to the government." In the post–World War II period, "Such strength as the cooperatives have at present [1958] depends to a great extent on their involvement in the government rice control system and its ancillary financial apparatus."[20] Even more direct and authoritarian state intervention in cooperatives in South Korea and Taiwan (Gordon White delightfully characterizes the latter as possessing "a capitalist economy and a Leninist state")[21] helps explain their prevalence and mode of operation. As in communist regimes, direct state intervention here has been more important for the establishment and maintenance of agricultural cooperatives than peasant cultural values.

Few people would deny that cooperatives can be mandated or collectivization imposed by a state that is both strong enough and determined to do so. Whether such a strategy is economically beneficial in the long run is debatable, but the costs to democracy and human freedom are not. If coercive collectivization is all socialism has to offer the peasantry, then there is little reason for peasants to choose socialist over capitalist development.

The Possibility of Cooperation

What is clear from this book and from cross-cultural comparisons is that there is no invariant human and social property called cooperation. Although cooperation is always present in human societies its features are correspondingly variable. Human cooperation may be universal and therefore a property of human nature, but this tells us little about particular forms of cooperation in specific social contexts. Because cooperation is a fundamental aspect of human sociability and social solidarity it is also the wellspring for a variety of socialist and quasi-socialist ideas and ideals concerning human "brotherhood" and common interests—indeed, for concepts of "socialist man." Yet humans are also irrevocably individuals, both biologically and psychologically, regardless of similarities in patterns of socialization. Consciousness of individuality and of distinct individual interests must therefore be considered an integral part of human nature as well, and not surprisingly this provides a basis for modern ideologies of "possessive individualism."[22]

Societies are the arena in which the dialectic between the irreducibly social and individual nature of humans is played out. To rephrase a justly famous passage from Louis Althusser on the question of economic determinism, which he said meant "determination by the economy in the last instance": At no point are these attributes ever active in the *pure state*, at no time does His Majesty *the Individual* or His Majesty *the Social* stride alone along the royal road of the Dialectic scattering all in its path. "From the first moment to the last the lonely hour of the 'last instance' never comes."[23] Their interaction is "overdetermined." Similar observations, of course, have been made by Raymond Firth, who said anthropologists must reformulate "the old contrast between 'individualism' and 'communism'. For [the anthropologist], this antithesis is a false one, for he would hold that the two sets of motives, and the two forms of organization, co-exist. Certainly this exists in Tikopia, where individual evasion and 'exploitation' exist side by side with, and manifest themselves in spite of, strong mechanisms of social control and regulations in the interests of community welfare."[24] Firth, unfortunately, writes as if "greed" is somehow an innate, anarchic nature hardly tamed by cultural overlays, rather than seeing individuality and sociability as being simultaneously constitutive of humans.

A superior approach would insist on the social and historical contingency of human sociability and individuality and require empirical research to reveal under what conditions greater play is given to one or the other of these facets of human nature. The contingency of human cooperation is revealed by the fact that, for example, spontaneous human cooperation is very sensitive to scale and that beyond a certain point cooperation is present only in the most formal sense, such as with Durkheim's model of organic solidarity arising out of the ramified division of labor in large industrial societies or state-regulated solidarity. The ever-perspicacious Moore writes, "Reciprocity and cooperation do not develop spontaneously, except perhaps on a limited basis among small groups in fairly continuous personal contact. Otherwise there is a continual tendency for selfish individual and *group* interests to break through. . . . Fissiparous tendencies exist in all cultures and societies of any size. Whatever there is in the way of social cooperation (of which reciprocity is only one form) is under continual threat from such tendencies. Where cooperation exists, it has to be created and continually re-created. Specific and identifiable human beings have to perform this act of creation and re-creation."[25] It is this cultural effort that should be the object of social scientific enquiry.

Peasants in rice-growing societies, for example, respond to the imperatives of their ecological and technical environment by creating various forms of cooperation. Irrigation systems establish obligations to cooperate and are usually paralleled or complemented by forms of labor exchange. The necessity of labor exchange arises from the need to carry out particular tasks speedily and often sequentially. Sequential rice replanting at the beginning of a season will require sequential harvesting and therefore cooperative exchanges at both times, with joint water control in between. Labor exchange in this context is a response to peak labor demands. Such an arrangement can be supplemented by wage labor, and in fact the latter gives the whole system an essential flexibility in cases in which peasants possess differential resources and in which the requirements of reciprocity leave one party short of labor. Labor exchange is especially favored among kin and neighbors because it guarantees help from one season to the next and it is usually high-quality labor owing to the sanctions built into the relationship. Exchange labor also persists because of its compatibility with the peasant natural economy. Provided time is available (that is, there are no better alternatives), it costs the peasant little, only "self-exploitation" in Chayanov's terms, to give and receive labor according to mutual need. The main problem with labor exchange from the individual farmer's point of view is its possible inconvenience. Wage labor is at one's beck and call, whereas exchange labor takes place between equals and may entail compromises. Wage labor, on the other hand, has to be weighed against its cost, the availability of money, and its reliability.

It is not insignificant that peasants often remark that it is more fun to work in groups than alone. Work songs, gossip, mutual complaints about the weather and work, and jokes—such as the one yelled out by a Lao peasant behind his plow: "I'm just a lunatic who plays with buffaloes"—all serve to break the monotony of work and lift morale and probably the efficiency of the field-workers. Portable radios have only partially compensated for the loneliness of isolated work—it is difficult to joke with a radio.

Forms of festive, nonreciprocal labor persist in Laos and elsewhere, particularly among kin and especially for heavy tasks like house building. On these occasions food is commonly the main compensation for those who come to help. Wider village or district work parties—to repair roads or to build schools or indeed, irrigation works—are often a form of state-regulated corvée, a type of labor used extensively in communist systems.[26]

Technological change is obviously a key variable that can intervene to disrupt or transform previously evolved forms of cooperation. As Charles Erasmus noted, "Since limitations of time and weight are predisposing factors in the occurrence of reciprocal labor, it is not surprising to find that technological changes which supplement men's strength and speed modify reciprocal labor patterns and decrease their incidence."[27] Yet such changes may simply lead to a transformation of cooperation to accommodate the new context through, for example, the joint ownership of new technology—a shift from sharing labor to sharing tools and machines.

In this complex and changing interaction among environment, technology, and social organization we are primarily concerned with labor-saving technology such as pumps and tractors and with how cooperative responses may be viable only in the short or medium term. For example, as Hong discovered in Taiwan, group ownership of machinery is a rational option for as long as the cost of machinery is high, labor is scarce, and family income low. "When the price of farm machinery declines [for example, with mass production of small rotary tillers] and family income increases owing to the high level of industrialization, joint farming operations may become impractical. When even small farmers can afford to buy farming machinery, joint farming operations will gradually become unnecessary and individual farming might be restored, especially in places where land value and wages are high and non-farm jobs are easy to obtain."[28] Thus agricultural cooperation is best conceptualized as a mutating adaption by peasant domestic units to a changing ecological and economic environment.

If one considers the processes of change in cooperation and cooperatives in peasant agriculture in, for example, Japan, Taiwan, or South Korea it becomes clear that the crucial variables in the overall process of transformation are an ever-expanding market and rural and urban industrialization.[29] One consequence of successful industrialization is a short-age of labor in the countryside, which initially may intensify peasant needs for exchange labor or collective ownership of machinery or both. Growing affluence may see farmers acquiring their own pumps or rotary tillers, thereby releasing the family from cooperative obligations and also releas-ing labor for part-time employment or assembly operations in urban-based industries. To place such a scenario in the context of Laos is to immediately recognize just how undeveloped the economy really is. As we have seen, it possesses a rudimentary national market that minimizes the circulation of labor and other commodities (disregarding the active obstruction of such movement in the years immediately after 1975), and cooperation in the countryside is largely determined by natural environmental cycles and the natural domestic cycle. Growing commercial activity and even minimal industrialization are likely to intensify the need for exchange labor, and given the low incomes of Lao peasants, they would also make the cooper-ative ownership of machinery a rational option, provided of course that machinery will be made available by the state trading apparatus in the appropriate form. That is, small rotary tillers rather than Kubotas designed for the extensive wheat fields of the Soviet Union. Steady growth of irriga-tion and double cropping (vital technological developments) will also place further demands on the availability of labor and therefore on both social institutions for mobilizing it and means to compensate for it.

A dynamic overview of the place of cooperatives in economic develop-ment calls into question the rather rigid, institutional form of cooperation preferred by communist regimes to date. The view of cooperatives and cooperation given above favors an adaptable, flexible, and potentially innovative form that corresponds not only to the flexibility of the peasant household, but also to the requirements of a rapidly changing social struc-ture. By contrast, production cooperatives are often hobbled by institu-tional rigidities that may inhibit the pace of change and could even prove to be a general brake on the economy by slowing down the release of labor from agriculture.

Laos's relatively low population density and relative scarcity of labor in the countryside make it atypical in Asia. Yet a consideration of its pecu-liarities does not change the overall theoretical argument: an analysis of Thailand, for example, or of the much more populous Red River Delta in Vietnam would simply shift the weight of the variables influencing social change and potential cooperative development.

Collectivization and the Domestic Mode of Production

Throughout the preceding argument I have stressed the centrality of the household in peasant social and economic action. I could hardly do otherwise, given its recognized pivotal role as the basic producing and consuming unit in peasant societies. Of course the household also has a central place in much advanced capitalist agriculture too. A fundamental difference between the modern family farm and the peasant farm is, however, exemplified by the fact that the modern farmer buys his bread and meat from a supermarket, while the peasant directly consumes a considerable proportion of the household's production. In other words, the modern farmer fully participates in the commodity economy, and on-farm decisions are decisively influenced by movements in the wider economy.[30] The peasant economy is still guided by production for use rather than for exchange, and a significant portion of peasant activity lies beyond the direct influence of the economy at large.

The resilience of the household, or of the domestic mode of production, in the face of social change arises from the mutually reinforcing character of its various activities. It provides a framework for socialization, the bestowal of affection, the regulation of sexuality, and economic provisioning. Max Weber clearly grasped the logic of its internal cohesion: "In terms of personal relationships, the household in its 'pure', though not necessarily primitive, form implies solidarity in dealing with the outside and communism of property and consumption of everyday goods within the household (household communism)."[31] Or consider Sahlins' words: "Householding is the highest form of economic sociability," the daily act of eating together consecrating the group as a group. "Pooling closes the domestic circle; the circumference becomes a line of social and economic demarcation. Sociologists call it a 'primary group'; people call it 'home.' "[32] Yet households, as Weber noted, are not some form of "pure" communism: "Nowhere do we find unregulated, amorphous sexual promiscuity within the house. . . . On the contrary any kind of communist sexual freedom is most thoroughly banished from a house in which there is communist property ownership . . . in the interest of safeguarding solidarity and domestic peace in the face of jealousies."[33] By way of contrast and comparison, Marx and Engels were influenced by Morgan's descriptions of primitive promiscuity and communal marriage in their construction of an image of primitive communism.

The multiple bases of domestic solidarity have been a target for the most extreme forms of communizing zeal. Reports from Pol Pot's Cambodia revealed not only ruthless collectivization of agriculture, but also attempts to form communal kitchens and to socialize children against their parents and bond them to the nation and in some areas cadre-sponsored mass marriages (a characteristic puritanism arrested tendencies to promiscuity; that was left for the counterculture in the West). Such state action was a recognition, albeit often spontaneous and unconscious, of the anarchic and socially disloyal tendencies in the domestic mode of production.

To any individual a family presents itself as a "natural" social and economic organization. Family and kinship are ascribed (inescapable) statuses and therefore are ready-made for the mobilization of cooperation. As Wolf writes, "They are the product of social synchronization achieved in the course of socialization. The private relation of trust may thus be translated into cooperation in the public realm."[34] The levels of inclusiveness in kinship relations vary and define the boundaries of claims, but the rejection of legitimate claims of kin is among the most discomforting in human cultures. Claims beyond the "natural" ones of kin require different justifications, such as appeals to community, ethnicity, religious duty, nationalism, or revolutionary duty. To compete with or supersede the primordial imperatives of the household these superior claims must be either compelling or compulsory. Cooperatives fall into the category of superior claims; if they are to be voluntary, what they have to offer must be compelling.

The obstacles faced by cooperatives in constructing a legitimate ideology for voluntary cooperative action can be illustrated through a comparison with the problems faced by corporate kinship groups, which, unlike cooperatives, are able to manipulate the powerful ideology of "natural solidarity." In traditional China the ideal family was one in which all the sons and their families lived as a joint "economic-family" or household. But as Freedman notes, there was a tendency for households to split in each generation, and this was often blamed on the in-marrying daughters-in-law, who felt like strangers in their husband's household. He writes, "Although the process of division may be seen against the background of conflicts between conjugal couples in the ordinary round of domestic and agricultural life, it was more fundamentally grounded on the property rights which, vested in each son, tended to pull the component elementary families in a joint establishment apart. The head of a household held its property in trust; his control of it did not obliterate the individual rights of the men under his hand. . . . The strength of the insistence in Confucian ethics on the solidarity of brothers was matched by the pressure forcing them apart."[35] Only particularly powerful families could override these centrifugal tendencies because the benefits of continued association outweighed the costs of separation. We see similar tensions inside the multi-household compounds in Laos, where the pressures for fission come primarily from the affinally related men—although there is no ideology of household and lineage solidarity equivalent to that in China.

Cooperatives are unable to make similar appeals to legitimating ideals of "naturalness," except perhaps to assert that cooperatives correspond to human nature or "socialist man." Cooperatives are formulated in terms that identify them as unmistakably cultural constructions; they are modern, rational, rule-governed organizations ideally made up of equal individuals. Cooperatives are voluntary associations—in Weber's terms "organizations with rationally established rules"—and to that extent they contrast with traditional associations, which operate by rule of custom. These terms, of course, are ideal types whose aim is to highlight differences rather than to indicate the degree to which, for example, formal and customary rules may overlap and intermingle in any empirical situation. In communist cooperative strategies there is considerable overlap and perhaps a basic confusion between the formal and substantive rationalities of economic action. The former indicates the degree to which "the provision for needs, which is essential to every rational economy, is capable of being expressed in numerical, calculable terms," whereas substantive rationality will "measure the results of the economic action, however formally 'rational' in the sense of correct calculation they may be, against these scales of 'value rationality' or '*substantive* goal rationality." There are an infinite number of possible value scales for this type of rationality, of which the socialist and communist standards constitute only one group. The latter, although by no means unambiguous in themselves, always involve elements of social justice and equality."[36] Once again speaking in ideal type terms, one could say that the cooperative program in Laos in its initial stages emphasized the substantive nature of cooperative economic action over the formal aspects, and only gradually did the latter come to predominate; this development in turn called the "rationality" of the cooperatives into question through an assertion of the substantive claims of the household.

Anthropologists are inclined to emphasize that "no form of cooperation can exist on the basis of purely rational, economic exchange relationships. All must have elements of social and symbolic exchange in order to persist."[37] In other words, it is impossible to entirely expel substantive calculations from economic action.[38] Communists attempt to introduce into their cooperative program a new order of social and symbolic exchange in the form of the morality of the "new socialist man" and a developmental nationalism. These ideologies, however, are very abstract and are not compelling in the context of competing substantive claims, namely, those of family and kinship and the ritual reinforcements of the latter.[39] As cooperatives in Laos, for example, moved toward a greater insistence on formal rationality in their calculation of member participation, so these competing substantive claims reasserted themselves to the point where the original rationale for the establishment of the cooperatives was mortally weakened, especially in the absence of compensating economic benefits. In other communist countries commitment, at least publicly, to abstract substantive rationalizations for collectives has been maintained by coercion and has bred subterranean cynicism and a form of "amoral familism."[40]

References to the "naturalness" of family bonding do not mean to imply that peasant households live in rural bliss and fraternal harmony. The evidence from a wide range of peasant societies demonstrates the contrary. Barrington Moore has argued in his intriguing cross-cultural exploration of human needs for privacy that "intimacy can generate friction, hostility and the desire to escape the fetters of intimacy to life in the larger community. Several non-literate societies display a rhythmic alternation between life in a private context and life in a public one."[41] The family is sometimes a haven from community obligations, and the community and friendship a haven from family obligations. In the little world of the peasant village these alternations are vital to human sanity, especially in cultures like the Lao and Thai, which are so strongly regulated by an everyday sensitivity to social hierarchy. Permanent sociability, whether in the family or the community, is oppressive.

Max Weber speaks of "familial communism," yet a closer look at specific inheritance patterns or the division of labor within households reveals distinct interests and tensions: not only between sons-in-law and fathers-in-law in the Lao household or between mothers-in-law and daughters-in-law in the Chinese lineage, but between husbands and wives. In systems with bilateral inheritance or, as in the Lao or northern Thai cases, in which preferred matrilocal residence means land has a tendency to accumulate in the hands of women, distinct rights are exercised over particular pieces of household property by men and women. In Laos, as I observed in chapter 6, this caused female resistance to cooperatives because they would mean conceding these rights to men. Women in many peasant societies also play an important role in trade: in Laos they engage in petty trade. In the new trading cooperatives in Laos men tend to be the key officials, and it is not clear to me how this has affected female control of trade there. So, even in these apparently more acceptable forms of cooperative activity, men and women in specific households may see the costs and benefits of participation in quite different terms.[42]

These observations do not dissolve the importance of the household for peasant economic action. They are designed to problematize the workings of even this "communist" institution and to draw attention to the fact that cooperative programs may affect the lives of men and women in peasant households in distinct, possibly harmful ways.[43]

Household Flexibility

As we have seen, members of the peasant household engage in a wide range of economic activities in order to make ends meet. In the natural economy this entails a high level of self-provisioning—basket weaving, cotton spinning, salt manufacture, even the manufacture of rifles and the various activities are often redirected with the growth of a market economy and increasing involvement in a supravillage division of labor. The command economy and collectivization restrict the range of extralocal activities. In their most extreme forms, as in Cambodia under Pol Pot, the degree to which peasants could retreat even into the self-provisioning and barter of the natural economy was suppressed, which accounted for many of the hardships suffered by the peasants under that regime. Meanwhile, collectivization attempts to redirect the peasants' "free time" toward state-designated activities. The history of collectivization, therefore, can be written as a story of the tug-of-war between collective institutions and household economies. Even during the period of high Stalinism compromises had to be made with peasant households, and the family plot confirmed the persistence of the peasant economy. At times in the Soviet Union under Stalin the household economy began to roll back the collective economy,[44] and in chapter 7 I noted a similar occurrence in northern Vietnam in the mid-1960s.

This persistence is rooted in the flexibility of the family, which, as Eric Wolf has noted, makes it highly adaptable and cost-efficient (because of its capacity for "self-exploitation") compared with specialized modern organizations. "Maximally efficient for the least amount of cost . . . the family is also maximally adaptive to changes in the conditions that define and circumscribe its existence. . . . The family remains the multi-purpose organization *par excellence*."[45] Communists have only slowly grasped the degree to which collectivization has restricted the potential multipurpose economic activities of their peasant populations. This realization has led to the contract system in fully collectivized agriculture and in the Lao case to Kaysone declaring that the "household economy" is "one sector of the socialist economy."[46] Mihail Cernea has argued that the cooperative as a complex and bureaucratic organization is unable to mobilize fragmentary family labor resources that are available on an irregular basis, while family contracts can: "*The family is the only 'organization' capable of doing this for the collective farm.* The [cooperative] is unable to measure . . . irregular contributions in order to reward them, whereas the family is not even concerned with such problems. . . . [Furthermore] intrafamily connections operate as a *micro-network that collects and directs* fragmentary and variable labor resources which would otherwise be wasted."[47] Among the Lao peasants tensions arose in the early stages of collectivization over how the work of children, say, before and after school, could be incorporated into collective calculations. Or, as we saw around Don Dou, some men were engaged irregularly in work in either the abattoir or the fields. The contract system was an attempt to grapple with this in the early 1980s, and in the initial period of my research I regularly came across peasants on contract who were being helped by relatives or friends who normally engaged in other work. The use of contracts in Laos—as compared to that in fully collectivized systems—only accelerated the dissolution of the producer cooperatives and led to a reassertion of an independent peasantry.

Re-posing the Agrarian Question

The opening chapter outlined the three principal reasons given for collectivizing agriculture: economies of scale, avoidance of capitalist class polarization in the countryside, and command planning, which cannot tolerate "unplanned" resistance to surplus transfers from agriculture. The subsequent discussion showed that there are no clear economies of scale in agriculture, especially in rice agriculture, and that capitalist social relations do not spring up inevitably and spontaneously out of peasant agriculture; and finally, it suggested that if the assumptions of command planning are suspended, then collectivisation is not a necessary corollary of socialism. What are the possibilities offered by market style socialism?

In the original debate over collectivization various contributors attempted to outline alternative strategies. Bukharin, the most vocal of these, contended that "collective economics is not the main highway, not the high road, not the chief path by which the peasantry will come to socialism." He argued that the market would play a central role and that marketing and consumer and credit cooperatives would be vital vehicles of socialist development in the countryside. So long as state power remained in socialist hands to direct the economy at a macro level the peasants, "independent of their will," must "grow into socialism." He argued by analogy with capitalist societies that "through the struggle on the market . . . through competition, state and cooperative enterprises will oust their competitor, i.e. private capital. In the end, the development of market relations destroys itself. . . . It turns out that we will come to socialism precisely through market relations."[48] Bukharin's ideas remained orthodox because he expected the market to disappear ultimately.

Both Bukharin and Trotsky vented their sarcasm on Stalin's plans for collectivization. In 1928 Bukharin jibed, "No collectivization is possible without a certain amount of accumulation in agriculture, because you cannot get machines for nothing, you cannot ever assemble one tractor from a thousand wooden ploughs."[49] Writing from exile in 1930, Trotsky quipped, "It is impossible to create large-scale agriculture out of peasant wooden ploughs . . . just as it is impossible to create a ship by adding up fishing boats."[50] In the same spirit as that shown in Marx's and Engels's epigraph to this study, Bukharin and Trotsky focused on the technical preconditions required for horizontal integration by arguing that there are no productivity advantages to be gained by simply expanding existing capital/labor ratios in agriculture—the scientific management of labor notwithstanding. They continued to assume (along with most writers on the subject at that time) that large-scale, mechanized agriculture is most efficient and, therefore, should be the aim of socialist agriculture.

Chayanov and his coworkers were much more aware than the upper echelons of the Soviet government (which both Bukharin and Trotsky had inhabited) of the fundamental reasons for peasant resistance to collectivization. Chayanov was not opposed to change, but he advocated a line of development that would encounter the least resistance from peasants because it did not intrude directly into the heart of the peasant family, as collectivization did. It was also a strategy that was compatible with a market socialist orientation. He argued a case for vertical integration by analogy with developments in capitalist economies. One mode of capitalist penetration of the countryside, he suggested, approximated an elaborate system of subcontracting that left the production of the required commodities in the hands of the farmers. He noted that some "trading machines" had begun "to actively interfere in the organization of production, too. They laid down technical conditions, issued seed and fertilizers, determined the rotation of crops, and turned clients into technical executors of its designs and economic plan." Other forms of penetration included splitting off from the peasant farm particular processes, especially mechanical ones, and he gives as an example the use of mobile steam threshers in the south of Russia. From North America he cites the use of credit forms, the domination of transport, and so on as means by which capitalism converts agriculture "despite the evident scattered and independent nature of the small commodity producers." In the face of classical Marxism and orthodox economics, he argued that capitalism does not require horizontal integration (large-scale farms) because vertical integration can yield a higher profit for capital. He offers an example from the United States, where 65 percent of the wholesale farm exchanges went to the various forms of capital superimposed on the individual farm. He comments, "Compared with this vertical capitalist concentration, the transfer of farms from 10 to 100 or 500 hectares, with the corresponding transfer of a considerable number of farmers from a semi-proletarian to a clearly proletarian position, would be a small detail."[51]

But even under capitalist conditions, Chayanov observed, vertical integration can take cooperative forms for many and varied reasons—weakness in local capital, for example—and involve the peasants in running either production or transport facilities that otherwise would have been dominated by capitalists. This is a "deep" process of vertical integration, he claims, because "the peasant himself hands over to cooperative forms of concentration sectors of his farm that capitalism never succeeds in detaching from it in the course of their struggle."[52]

Chayanov then asks, What is the best way of tieing the peasant economy "into the general system of our state planned economy"? He rejects horizontal integration of peasant farms on the grounds that "classic" social differentiation had not occurred and capitalism had not created "large and technically quite well organized farms to be nationalized": "Therefore, the main form for the concentration of the peasant farms can only be vertical concentration and, moreover, in its cooperative forms, since only in these forms will it be . . . possible in our conditions to introduce into peasant farming the *elements* of the large-scale industrialization and the state plan. This means gradually and steadily splitting off particular sectors from individual farms, and organizing them in higher forms of large-scale social undertakings." While the phrasing of this passage makes concessions to the political milieu of Soviet Russia in the mid-1920s, Chayanov's vision of vertical integration under socialism meant it could take the form, for example, of cooperatives being established for purposes of milling or the purchase and use of threshing machines or even tractors. Such cooperatives would split off activities from the individual peasant farm and industrialize them. The same cooperative could also "split off" the traditional marketing activities carried out by the individual farmer. Such a development then "obliges the small producer to change his farm's organizational plan according to cooperative selling and processing policy, to improve his techniques, and to transfer to approved methods of tillage and livestock farming, insuring a fully standard product, subjecting it to careful sorting, processing, packing and canning according to the world market demand."[53] Meanwhile, the peasant household remains in charge of the land and the labor process on it, and thus the dense web of relations within the peasant family farm is neither directly antagonized nor challenged. A further advantage of vertical integration and cooperation is their flexible solution to the problem of optimal size. Simply through the concentrating and integrating of certain activities according to need, various scales for different activities can be achieved—from group to village, even to intervillage cooperation.

The feasibility of Chayanov's model for developing a peasant agriculture is demonstrated by the spontaneous preferences of peasants in muang Hatsayfong. They were receptive to "collectively" buying certain inputs and selling some of their output collectively. They were prepared to cooperate in specific activities for specific ends—such as the irrigation "collectives." For peasants who own land, such as those in Ban Nok 1 cooperative, the "natural" tendency is toward the formation of a cooperative for marketing or for purchasing machinery. Where peasants did not own much land but owned machinery, as at Don Dou, the spontaneous development of the cooperative was toward vertical integration of the surrounding private peasants by carrying out tractor plowing and rice threshing and milling for them. Progress in this direction stalled because of problems associated with the original formation and aims of the cooperative and government confusion, among other things. The trading cooperatives promoted in the countryside since 1984 have been encouraged to establish backward linkages with peasant farmers and forward linkages with processors or buyers of farm produce. It is still too early to gauge the success of these attempts at vertical integration; the purely commercial profits to be gained by expanded trading opportunities in the new market-oriented environment have absorbed much of the energy of cooperative officials to date. As one Cooperative Department official lamented in discussing the management problems associated with a floundering producers' cooperative in early 1987, the manager spent most of his time in now-legitimate trading activities rather than management.

Any system of socialist vertical integration will clearly have much to learn from the experience of agribusiness in capitalist countries, considerably expanded since Chayanov's time. One thing it has shown is that vertical integration can be initiated either from above or from below. Rice agriculture would appear to be most amenable to vertical integration from below via some form of cooperative, because few agribusinesses in developing countries are interested in staple foodgrains: they entail minimal processing and therefore offer few possibilities for adding value upstream from the direct producer.[54] Irrigation systems already compel a certain degree of cooperation among rice farmers, and other forms of cooperation can be built on the already established framework. A minimal form of cooperation beyond this could take the form of a "bargaining cooperative," one that bargains "with buyers, backed by the threat to withhold its members' output from the market in order to obtain a better price[;] its function is analogous to that performed by a labor union for its members."[55] Extra activities such as the buying of inputs or consumer goods, insurance, loans, or services can be added. Cooperatives could lobby for government provision of extension services for its members and insist that its members adopt changes in cropping patterns suggested by such extension; sometimes changes are the direct outcome of the incorporation of farmers into irrigation schemes. Vertical integration from below appears to be best adapted to the skill-intensive nature of rice cultivation because, as Francesca Bray writes, "technical choices and management decisions are in the hands of not a few landlords [or commissars] but of a vast number of family farmers." This is particularly important for innovation: "R & D is frequently regarded as a process by which the results of specialized scientific research are popularized through extension work. . . . Yet such research activities as crop breeding were practiced by peasant farmers for millennia before falling into the hands of the scientists. . . . The extent of popular participation in agricultural development depends to a large extent on how innovation is advocated or imposed, and by whom. Not surprisingly, farmers tend to be suspicious of official intervention and respond more positively to the example of successful peers."[56] Given that the majority of peasants in Laos (as elsewhere) are involved in foodgrain production, cooperatives established from below in a system of vertical integration are likely to be the most common and perhaps most desirable form. The extensiveness of the activities of these cooperatives inevitably must vary from village to village or district to district, depending on the peculiarities of the area—for example, the presence or absence of long-standing local rivalries or of strong local leaders. Just how much communist governments will be prepared to tolerate independent "collective" action of this sort by cooperatives remains to be seen. They may come to prefer atomized, individual peasants, especially if, as in Poland, they move to form an agricultural union.[57] Liberal capitalism in the United States was hostile to the radical populism of the cooperative movement in the early twentieth century because of its anticapitalist, allegedly "Bolshevik" rhetoric and effectively suppressed it.[58] Atomized individualists were easier to deal with. Communist states have been extremely reluctant to recognize group interests as distinct from 'general interests' (defined by the state). Any democratic socialist program would have to recognize that social institutions have a tendency toward social closure— "the process by which social collectivities seek to maximize rewards by restricting access to resources and opportunities to a limited circle of eligibles"[59]—and cooperatives are no exception, as we saw among the Lao peasants. Group conflict occurs covertly in most communist countries, but in any democracy institutions would have to be developed to mediate the inevitable conflicts between cooperatives and other social institutions.

Vertical integration from the top down in the manner of capitalist agribusiness probably strikes a more responsive chord among state-based officials and state-owned trading organizations. In agribusiness farmers often no longer confront buyers in the impersonal market, as in the model of a pure free-market capitalism. "In the new forms, which are predominantly micro-economic, the incorporation of agricultural output takes place outside the market. . . . Each agribusiness concern has its own farmers, who produce exclusively on the basis of production programmes drawn up by the industrial company. . . . All the activities making up the network are supervised and planned outside the market. . . . The relations between the production stages within the network thus become less com-

225

petitive, having been settled outside the market by an economic structure in the form of a cartel."[60] Risks, however, are still borne by the direct producer. Except perhaps for this last feature, such a structure seems a perfect example of capitalism allegedly prefiguring certain socialist forms of organization. As we saw at the end of chapter 5, a similar structure and strategy have been advocated by the Lao leadership in recent years.

The possibilities for the expansion of such a system in Laos are limited by the lack of agricultural diversification in the country, and only certain kinds of crops are technically most suitable to agribusiness-type activity[61]—capitalist or socialist. Diversification is in turn dependent on more general trends in the economy and macroeconomic decisions by the government. However marginal the activities of socialist agribusiness may be initially in Laos, it is unquestionably one model of development that will expand in importance both there and elsewhere. It also holds out the possibility of allowing the devolution of government responsibility for extension services, from its already overextended extension department in the Ministry of Agriculture to trading companies and cooperatives, thus freeing state resources for grass-roots rice growing cooperatives.[62] Vertical integration from above may also facilitate the formation of cooperatives from below in that contracts with groups of farmers may ease problems of communication, save on supervisory costs, and so on.

Negative outcomes are also possible. Socialist agribusiness could produce domination and alienation of farmers just as capitalist agribusiness does. A small landowner in the Thai northeast who grew sugarcane for a local, mainly Japanese-owned factory explained his predicament by saying it was like "being hired for wages on your own land."[63] If socialist agribusiness stimulates the formation of local farmers' cooperatives, it may also unwittingly provide a solution to problems associated with overpersonalized authority in peasant villages. As relatively impersonal organizations exercising limited but significant power in the countryside, socialist agribusiness could provoke a basis for farmer solidarity that is located at a supravillage level. Such solidarity could then draw on those features in the village that attract the attention of advocates of cooperatives—bonds of friendship and trust, community loyalty—in the construction of the appropriate form of cooperative. The resulting organization would obviate such feelings of powerlessness as those expressed by the northeastern Thai peasant above.

The various forms of cooperative possible within a market socialist context in Laos—as in China and elsewhere—remain to be worked out.

One can be certain, however, that this process of identification will severely test communist tolerance of group conflict arising from the pursuit of group interests and bargaining by autonomous "collective" organizations.

An Anthropology of Socialism

Oddly, anthropology has had a profound impact on the Marxist conception of socialism. It allowed Marx and Engels and many of their followers to construct a model of communism that was the opposite of capitalism out of the materials supplied by anthropologists on so-called primitive communism. Marx and Engels did not see a future communist society as a simple return to primitive communism; nevertheless, the embargo they placed on speculating about a future society left in their followers' hands a series of principles and propositions derived from the contrasts they drew between primitive communism and capitalism. Although the notion of primitive communism has been challenged by subsequent anthropological research—there are no Western Marxist anthropologists who defend the idea as far as I am aware[64]—the image of socialism as being the *opposite* of capitalism persists. Adam Kuper has recently questioned whether even mainstream anthropology really gave up the original conception of primitive society. He writes, "The idea of primitive society probably could not have persisted within anthropology if it had remained static. But it did not. On the contrary, it lent itself to a most dazzling play of variations."[65] He argues that these were all variations within a single *problématique*. Perhaps there is an unacknowledged affinity between Marxist anthropology and mainstream anthropology, although Kuper does not recognize how fundamentally the "illusion" of primitive society has influenced conceptions of socialism. Recently, alternative models of socialism have begun to gain ground,[66] but so far these have found little reflection in either mainstream anthropology or in Marxist-inspired anthropology, where one would expect to find at least some cognizance of them.

Radical anthropology's critique of capitalism is still launched from the perspective of precapitalist culture. In what often appears as a strange marriage of cultural relativism and Marxism, precapitalist cultures are presented as resolutely "other" and opposed to capitalism's "commodification" of social relations. A central concept in this critique is the notion of commodity fetishism, wielded so inventively by Michael Taussig in *The Devil and Commodity Fetishism*. In a more recent argument against scholastic versions of Marxist anthropology, he reasserts the centrality of this concept: "Fetishism alerts us to the radical potential in the old figures of the world's torment as they come to recast the modern, and it encourages us to see and even empathize with the repressed desires for a socialist world in the 'irrational' manifestations of capitalism."[67] The concept of fetishism in Marx analyzes a situation in which relations between people are represented as relations between things. Universal commodity production is impersonal and obscures not only the relations between people embodied in commodity production, but also the social relations in which the commodities are produced. "In capitalist society the phenomenon of fetishism imposes itself on men (a) as mystification and (b) as domination."[68] Abolish capitalist commodity production, the argument runs, and one thereby abolishes mystification and domination. Jonathan Friedman, in an essay on the importance of the concept of fetishism for a Marxist anthropology, spells out the contrast between mystification, or "opacity," and demystification: "The concept of opacity is a fitting one to characterize the nature of relations of production, and it forms a significant opposition with Marx's concept of 'transparency' which is the prerequisite for the operation of a communist economy, i.e. where the social mechanisms which distribute social labor contain within them the true representation of their material effects. A fetish is simply a structure which does not contain this information."[69] Here one can see a desire by anthropologists to extend the concept of fetishism to precapitalist social relations as well, where human work may be seen as the "work of the gods," in contrast to the transparency of communism. Taussig too recognizes the existence of precapitalist fetishism but says "for all its fantasies [it] does not disguise economic relations as relations between things in themselves."[70] Because radical, Marxist anthropology reproduces by *default* older notions of communism or socialism as the opposite of capitalism, a coherent statement of this position cannot be produced. Indeed, because it has been unintentional, most authors would probably deny that this is the logical outcome of their arguments. I think enough has been said to show how it occurs.

It would be fair to say that Marx's concept of fetishism has been overworked. Late in his life Marx was mainly concerned to use it as a critique of the political economy of his day. However, he never entirely freed it from the definition it had gained in his earlier work, in which the concept implied that somehow humans had been alienated from their *essence* under capitalism, epitomized in the fetishism of commodities, and that this essence could be regained only through the supersession of capitalism and commodity production.[71] From this perspective to concede that socialism will involve commodity production (on a scale that is impossible to determine a priori) means admitting that socialism must also entail fetishism and alienation and cannot be "transparent." Such recognition does not necessarily cripple Marx's critique of the theories of political economy of his day, but it does weaken the Marxist critique of capitalism and of capitalism's impact on precapitalist societies. It also reveals an inescapably utopian component in Marxism. It can be argued that fetishism is an inevitable feature of human societies, merely varying according to social structure.[72] No doubt Taussig would see this as a capitulation to modern rationality and "terror." In his latest book, *Shamanism, Colonialism and the Wild Man,* we find him paddling furiously upstream into the South American jungle away from modern anthropology's claim to be a science of man: "Before there can be a science of man there has to be the long-awaited demythification and reenchantment of Western man in a quite different confluence of self and otherness. Our way lies upstream, against the current, upriver near the foothills of the Andes where Indian healers are busy healing colonists of the phantoms assailing them."[73] It is the logical route for a radical theory of fetishism.

While most anthropologists would probably agree that the discipline aims to be a science of all human societies, it has to date concentrated largely on premodern societies and given little attention to socialist societies. One basic reason for this neglect has been anthropology's emphasis on fieldwork, and opportunities for fieldwork in communist countries have been few and far between until recently. This lacuna has had consequences for the development of theory, especially critical theory whose *prise de position* has almost inevitably been on the terrain of precapitalist culture. A decline in the influence of social evolutionary theory, I would suggest, also accounts for the lags in theory. The "stages" of societal development subscribed to by nineteenth-century evolutionary anthropology (including Engels) were rejected outright by all modern schools of anthropology—structural functionalism, cultural relativism, structuralism, and Marxism—and then they discarded all interest in evolution. The cultural materialist strategy proposed by Marvin Harris, which discards nineteenth-century teleological assumptions, is almost alone in its interest in social evolution. This strategy has been assailed from all sides, perhaps most vigorously by modern structuralist-Marxists.[74] Whatever the specific merits of Harris's work, one thing is certain: attention to the problems posed by social evolution would have made it obvious that it is impossible to derive a model of socialist society from a model of primitive society. This book has outlined some of the consequences of such a procedure. It has shown that attempts to implement an orthodox communist model in the context of a peasant society has the paradoxical result of reinforcing many features of the natural economy that socialists claim they want to transform. It has been argued that the inevitable frustration of the state's aim as a result of its own policies leads to an assault on the peasantry by the state (assuming it is powerful enough) and an escalation of coercion, often under the rhetoric of building on traditional relations of solidarity and cooperation. Successful peasant resistance to these communist misconceptions has led to a grudging reappraisal of many of communism's basic beliefs. An evolutionary perspective that eschews inevitable stages would have, on the other hand, alerted theorists to the fact that socialism has more in common with advanced capitalism than it does with the natural economy.

It may come as a surprise to many anthropologists to learn that some elements of a critique of socialism were set out by Marcel Mauss. An enthusiast of the cooperative movement, he wrote at the turn of the century, "Le syndicat et la coopérative socialiste sont les fondements de la société future."[75] Despite his trenchant criticisms of the Bolshevik Revolution, he was "fascinated" by the attempts to form soviets—that is, "an intermediary echelon, vested with property, wealth, disciplinary rights and powers, moderating the individual, but also the state"—which he (and Durkheim) saw as essential for any democratic socialism. The very existence of the Bolshevik regime, he argued, broke the embargo on constructing "plans for future societies," and one could commence an analysis of "actually existing socialism." The Russian "experiment" will have served one purpose, he wrote, by teaching

> nations who want to reform how they should go about it and how they should not go about it. They must retain the market and money; they must develop all possible collective institutions; they must avoid incompatibilities between free associations and collectivism, and between the right of association, including the right of the majority and individualism. Hence this sociological assessment has the dual value I wish to attribute to it: a scientific value, because it is a description of our modern societies and in one of them reveals the essential components that none today can do without; a practical value, because it helps to purge socialist doctrines of a certain number of peremptory aphoristic formulae, a certain number of utopian views.[76]

Anthropologists have been almost exclusively preoccupied with Mauss's study of primitive exchange in *The Gift*.[77] Or Lévi-Strauss, for example, was simply concerned to establish Mauss as a precursor of structuralist theory.[78] But even in *The Gift* Mauss's conclusions are interested in what modern societies can learn from others about social exchange: "the joy of giving in public," "the solicitude in mutuality or cooperation," from which "we can visualize a society in which these principles obtain."[79]

Radical or Marxist anthropologists have tried to counterpose Mauss's "spirit of the gift" in precapitalist societies to the cold, hard calculation of capitalism. And in Mauss we would seem to find more than just a "negative" critique of capitalism when he says, "We should return to the old and elemental. Once again we shall discover those motives of action still remembered by many societies."[80] Yet unlike most contemporary radicals, Mauss demonstrated an understanding of the complexity of modern societies and their bases of social solidarity, and significantly, he is not hostile to the market. For example, he writes, "For as long as one can foresee, *socialism—communism—must seek its path in the organization and not the suppression of the market*."[81]

In contrast to many Marxist socialists, Mauss was not inclined to see socialism as the "dialectical opposite" of capitalism. He presented a more fluid evaluation of social change and of the component parts of societies: "There are no exclusively capitalist societies and there will no doubt be no exclusively socialist ones. There have been no societies that were only feudal, or only monarchic, or only republican. There are only societies which have a regime, or rather—what is even more complicated—systems of regimes, which are more or less characterized, regimes and systems of regimes of their economies, of their political organizations; they have customs and mentalities that can be more or less arbitrarily defined by the predominance of one or other of these systems or institutions. That is all."[82] In these "impure" societies we do not find pure "capitalist man" or pure "socialist man." Instead, we find people active in capitalist social relations, socialist social relations, and still others embedded in the social relations of the peasant natural economy, and all of these people are likely to conduct their lives largely in accordance with the dictates of the specific social and economic relationships in which they are engaged. Of course, their actions are modified by the way the various structures interact, and the precise outcome is an empirical question. The forms of cooperation extant, for example, will vary according to the "systems of regimes of their economies" and be determined by the one that is predominant. But even this structure will vary over time and shift the weight between the different elements in the social structure and perhaps thereby encourage different forms or patterns of cooperation.

In the social sciences Marxist and Weberian theory has emphasized issues of power and social conflict, especially in their analyses of capitalist societies, about which they have written most. Unlike Weberians, Marxists find themselves suddenly disarmed when they analyze socialist societies. Their critique of power and privilege in socialist societies is substantially the same as that of the Weberians, except the latter are less alarmed by what they find in socialist societies; they always expected socialism to be little more than an extension of the "iron cage" of capitalism. Marxists have generally been at a loss when attempting to formulate an alternative, credible theory of noncoercive social cohesion under socialism. Durkheim is one of the few classical thinkers who offers another line of inquiry. Generally he has been dismissed by Marxists because of his preoccupation with social solidarity rather than conflict and because of his myopia about power.[83] He tried to understand how complex modern societies—capitalist or socialist—could cohere. One writer has suggested that Durkheim's vision of social solidarity as outlined in *The Division of Labor in Society* found its "most explicit expression" in Stalin's Russia of the 1930s.[84] This mischievous observation highlights the naivete of Durkheim's conception of state power, but it also points to the applicability of some of Durkheim's ideas to communist-type societies. As Gouldner observed, Durkheim's project was guided by the belief "that *some* degree of moral consensus is indispensable to social solidarity in a capitalist or a socialist society."[85] Durkheim, as Bottomore remarks, has been "the anthropologists' sociologist," and therefore anthropologists should be well placed to adapt some of the insights they have gained from him to an analysis of socialism.

Mauss, like his mentor Durkheim, was interested in the bases of social solidarity in all societies, including socialist societies, and at the end of *The Gift*, where he notes that modern society is still "far from frigid utilitarian calculation," he signals that there are still many forms of "expenditure and exchange other than economic ones."[86] This observation in itself is a charter for anthropology's survival beyond the "decline of the primitive," for it draws attention to the values and meanings surrounding all social interaction. Reciprocity, shared social values, and so on are not the exclusive preserve of premodern societies. As Barrington Moore observes, "Without the concept of reciprocity—or better, mutual obligation, a term that does *not* imply equality of burdens or obligations—it becomes impossible to interpret human society as the consequence of anything other than perpetual force and fraud."[87] At the end of *The Gift* and elsewhere Mauss discusses the motivations of people at work, their need for "recompense," a problem that remains at the heart of socialist economic organizations, be they agricultural cooperatives, factories, or bureaucracies.

One of anthropology's most valuable contributions to modern knowledge has been to show the diversity of human cultures, to show that contemporary social arrangements are not immutable. It thereby provides a glimpse of the breadth of human potentialities. This was the reason Marx and Engels delved into anthropology in the first place. But knowledge of the diversity of humankind also provides a sober understanding of the *limits* of human possibilities. Our knowledge has grown fantastically since the time of Marx and Engels and must now encompass attempts to construct socialist societies as well. Given the degree to which Marxism was misled by early anthropology, the latter's understanding of its early failures should make it well equipped to provide a critique of contemporary socialism. This book has been an attempt to apply some of that accumulated knowledge in the service of such a critique.

Appendix

Exchange Rates, 1981–87

(Kip per $US)

	Official	Commercial	Import Valuation	Private Remittance	Import/ Export	Parallel Market
December 1981	10	30	—	—	—	56
December 1982	10	35	—	—	—	105
December 1983	10	35	—	108	—	140
December 1984	10	35	—	108	—	250
December 1985	10	35	95	108	—	380
June 1986	10	35	95	270	300	440
February 1987	10	35	95	270	300	390
September 1987	350	350	350	350	350	350–70
May 1988	350	350	350	350	350	345

Notes

Preface

1. Claude Lévi-Strauss, *Tristes Tropiques* (New York: Atheneum, 1975), 38.
2. E. E. Evans-Pritchard, *Social Anthropology*, (London: Cohen and West, 1951).

CHAPTER ONE: *New Socialist Man*

1. *Political Report of the Central Committee of the Lao People's Revolutionary Party Presented at Its Fourth Party Congress by Comrade Kaysone Phomvihane, General Secretary* (Vientiane, November 1986) (hereafter *Political Report*).
2. *Political Report.*
3. Karl Marx, *Grundrisse* (London: Penguin Books, 1973), 83.
4. Norman Geras, *Marx and Human Nature: Refutation of a Legend* (London: Verso, 1983).
5. Edmund Leach lampoons the claims of sociobiologist Robert Ardrey: "Relations of solidarity and opposition, amity and hostility, gift exchange and war constitute the basic subject matter of sociological enquiry, and only a very simpleminded man could suppose that such complex matters might be readily understood by simple analogy with the habits of the prairie dog. But this is what Ardrey implies. It is perfectly true that, as members of a common species *Homo sapiens,* we are all predisposed to behave in certain fixed ways which reflect our biochemical constitutions. But this in itself does not tell us very much." E. Leach, "Don't Say 'Boo' to a Goose," in *Man and Aggression,* 2d ed., ed. A. Montagu (London: Oxford University Press, 1973), 157.
6. See Marvin Harris, *Cultural Materialism* (New York: Random House, 1979), chaps. 5, 9; Marshall Sahlins, *The Use and Abuse of Biology* (London: Tavistock, 1977). See also the views of evolutionary biologist Stephen Jay Gould,

"Biological Potentiality vs. Biological Determinism," in his *Ever Since Darwin* (London: Penguin, 1980).

7. Patrick Bateson, "The Biological Evolution of Cooperation and Trust," in *Trust: Making and Breaking Cooperative Relations*, ed. Diego Gambetta (London: Basil Blackwell, 1988); Gerhard Lenski and Jean Lenski, *Human Societies*, 5th ed. (New York: McGraw-Hill, 1987), chap. 1.

8. *Political Report.*

9. On the ethnic Lao in northeastern Thailand see, for example, "The Ideal Villager: A Portrait," in William J. Klausner, *Reflections on Thai Culture* (Bangkok: Suksit Siam, 1981).

10. Cited in Trevor Ling, *Buddhism, Imperialism and War* (London: George Allen and Unwin, 1979), 149.

11. *Political Report.*

12. Alec Nove, *The Economics of Feasible Socialism* (London: George Allen and Unwin, 1983), 10.

13. Materialist research strategies have remained most committed to establishing hierarchies of causality. For a good, concise statement of a historical materialist strategy and its many unresolved problems see Eric Hobsbawm, "Marx and History," *New Left Review* 143 (January–February, 1984). In anthropology the most uncompromising materialist position has been argued by Marvin Harris in his *Cultural Materialism.*

14. George Condominas, for example, in his *Essai sur la société rurale lao de la région de Vientiane* (Vientiane: UNESCO-Commissariat general aux Affaires Rurales, 1962), elevates the everyday Lao saying *bo pen nyang* ("no matter," "never mind"), to the status of a "philosophy" to explain the character of Lao society.

15. Nove, *The Economics of Feasible Socialism*, 62.

16. Frederick Engels, "Origin of Family, Private Property and State," in Karl Marx and Frederick Engels, *Selected Works* (Moscow: Progress Publishers, 1968), 466.

17. Ibid., 593. Marx alludes to this passage in draft letters to Russian socialists late in his life. See *Late Marx and the Russian Road: Marx and 'the Peripheries of Capitalism,'* ed. Teodor Shanin (New York: Monthly Review Press, 1983), 107.

18. Ibid., 589–90.

19. Raymond Firth, "The Sceptical Anthropologist? Social Anthropology and Marxist Views on Society," in *Marxist Analyses and Social Anthropology*, ed. Maurice Bloch (London: Malaby Press, 1975), 37.

20. Maurice Bloch, *Marxism and Anthropology* (London: Oxford University Press, 1983), 10, 11, 26.

21. Michael Taussig, *The Devil and Commodity Fetishism in South America* (Chapel Hill: University of North Carolina Press, 1980), 4, 11.

22. Barbara Bradby, "The Destruction of Natural Economy," in *The Articulation of Modes of Production*, ed. Harold Wolpe (London: Routledge and Kegan Paul, 1980), 93–94. This essay relies heavily on Rosa Luxemburg, *Accumulation of Capital* (London: Routledge and Kegan Paul, 1963). See esp. chaps. 17, 18, 19.

23. Marshall D. Sahlins, *Tribesmen* (Englewood Cliffs: Prentice-Hall, 1968), 9.

24. Mary Douglas, "Primitive Rationing: A Study in Controlled Exchange," in

Themes in Economic Anthropology, ed. Raymond Firth (London: Tavistock, 1967), 131. See also Paul Bohannan, "The Impact of Money on an African Subsistence Economy," in *Tribal and Peasant Economies,* ed. George Dalton (New York: The Natural History Press, 1967).

25. Maurice Godelier, *Perspectives in Marxist Anthropology* (London: Cambridge University Press, 1977), 150.

26. George Dalton, "Primitive Money," in *Tribal and Peasant Economies,* ed. George Dalton (Austin: University of Texas Press, 1976), 266. See also George Dalton, "Peasant Markets," *Journal of Peasant Studies* 1, no. 2 (1974).

27. Eric R. Wolf, *Peasants* (Englewood Cliffs: Prentice-Hall, 1966), 4–11.

28. A. V. Chayanov, *The Theory of Peasant Economy* (Madison: University of Wisconsin Press, 1986), 4.

29. N. I. Bukharin and E. Preobrazhensky, *The ABC of Communism* (Ann Arbor: Ann Arbor Paperbacks, 1966), 72.

30. Chayanov, *The Theory of Peasant Economy,* 23.

31. Bukharin and Preobrazhensky, *The ABC,* 73.

32. Chayanov, *Theory of Peasant Economy,* 24.

33. For the chaos caused by attempting such a step during the Great Leap Forward in China at the end of the 1950s, see G. William Skinner, "Marketing and Social Structure in Rural China," *The Journal of Asian Studies* 24, no. 3 (1965); Geoffrey Shillinglaw, "Traditional Rural Cooperation and Social Structure: The Communist Chinese Collectivisation of Agriculture," in *Two Blades of Grass,* ed. P. Worsley (Manchester: Manchester University Press, 1971).

34. Agness Heller, *The Theory of Need in Marx* (London: Allison and Busby, 1976), 98.

35. Marshall Sahlins, *Stone Age Economics* (London: Tavistock Publications, 1974), 1–2, 13, 39.

36. Ibid., 95.

37. See the discussion by Ali Rattansi, *Marx and the Division of Labor* (London: Macmillan, 1982).

38. E. H. Carr, *The Bolshevik Revolution, 1917–1923* (London: Pelican, 1966), 383.

39. V. I. Lenin, "Left-Wing Communism—An Infantile Disorder," *Selected Works* (Moscow: Progress Publishers, 1967), 3:339, 357.

40. See, for example, Moshe Lewin, *Russian Peasants and Soviet Power: A Study of Collectivisation* (New York: W. W. Norton, 1975); Moshe Lewin, *Political Undercurrents in Soviet Economic Debates* (London: Pluto Press, 1975); Stephen F. Cohen, *Bukharin and the Bolshevik Revolution: A Political Biography, 1888–1938* (London: Oxford University Press, 1980).

41. Alec Nove, "The 'Logic' and Cost of Collectivisation," *Problems of Communism* (July–August 1976): 55.

42. Paul A. Baran, *The Political Economy of Growth* (New York: Monthly Review Press, 1968), 266.

43. Ibid., 267–68.

44. Ibid., 272.

45. In the 1962 foreword Baran begins to acknowledge some problems with his

perspective when he writes that the "mechanical revolution . . . did *not* lead to the spectacular increases of agricultural output per acre of land that was expected by many economic theorists—Marxist and non-Marxist alike. The increase of productivity per acre depends apparently much more than was anticipated on the *chemical* revolution in agriculture" (ibid., xxxii). This observation is especially important for rice production.

46. Ibid., 277, 281–82.

47. Alec Nove, *An Economic History of the USSR* (London: Pelican Books, 1972), 186.

48. Baran, *Political Economy of Growth*, 276.

49. For agriculture's share in overall investment in Eastern Europe and the USSR see Robert Bideleux, *Communism and Development* (London: Methuen, 1985), table 10:249; and on China, P. Nolan and G. White, "Urban Bias, Rural Bias or State Bias? Urban–Rural Relations in Post-Revolutionary China," *Journal of Development Studies* 20, no. 3 (1984).

50. See Robert F. Miller, *One Hundred Thousand Tractors* (Cambridge: Harvard University Press, 1970).

51. Baran, *Political Economy of Growth*, 278.

52. Ibid., 289, 290.

53. The Chinese boasted they had achieved 10 tons of paddy per hectare simply by reorganizing the relations of production, compared to a Vietnamese yield of 3.5 tons per hectare on two-crop land. Naturally the Vietnamese leaders desired 10 tons, but the Chinese claims were no more than a revolutionary fantasy, as the Vietnamese soon discovered themselves. See Andrew Vickerman, *The Fate of the Peasantry*, Monograph Series no. 28 (New Haven: Yale University Southeast Asia Studies, 1986), 141–42.

54. Chayanov, *Theory of Peasant Economy*, 68, 69, 112.

55. Ibid., 89, 236.

56. Ibid., 246, 247, 248, 249. *Peasant Farm Organization*, originally published as a separate book, is reproduced in its entirety in *Theory of Peasant Economy*.

57. Francesca Bray, *The Rice Economies* (London: Basil Blackwell, 1986), 27.

58. Ibid., 115.

59. Boguslaw Galeski, *Basic Concepts of Rural Sociology* (Manchester: Manchester University Press, 1972), 190.

60. For a discussion of some of the theoretical issues and debates see Grant Evans, "The Accursed Problem: Communists and Peasants," *Peasant Studies* 15, no. 2 (1988).

61. Teodor Shanin, "Chayanov's Message: Illuminations, Miscomprehensions, and the Contemporary 'Development Theory,'" introduction to A. V. Chayanov, *Theory of Peasant Economy*, 2–3.

CHAPTER TWO: *The Sociology of Isolation*

1. *Bangkok Post* (7 June 1988).

2. David K. Wyatt, *Thailand: A Short History* (New Haven: Yale University Press, 1984), 89.

3. David Feeny, *The Political Economy of Productivity: Thai Agricultural Development, 1880–1975* (Vancouver: University of British Columbia Press, 1982), chap. 6.

4. Paul Lévy, *Histoire du Laos* (Paris: Presses Universitaires de France, 1974), 75.

5. Joel Martin Halpern, "The Economies of Lao and Serb Peasants: A Contrast in Cultural Values," *Southwestern Journal of Anthropology* 17 (1961).

6. Wolf Donner, *The Five Faces of Thailand: An Economic Geography* (St. Lucia: University of Queensland Press, 1982), 792.

7. Martin Barber, "Migrants and Modernization: A Study of Change in Lao Society" (Ph.D. diss., University of Hull, 1979), 57. There is no agreement on the actual size of Luang Prabang at this time.

8. Eric R. Wolf, *Europe and the People without History* (Berkeley: University of California Press, 1982), 80.

9. See, for example, "Essai sur l'évolution des systèmes politiques thaïs," in George Condominas, *L'Espace social à propos de l'Asie du sud-est* (Paris: Flammarion, 1980). The term *Tai* usually denotes a common linguistic and cultural entity in Southeast Asia that includes the Thai, the Lao, the Lu, the Black Tai, and others.

10. Wyatt, *Thailand: A Short History*, 7.

11. Wolf, *Europe and the People without History*, 88–100.

12. Louis de Carné, *Travels in Indo-China and the Chinese Empire* (London: Chapman and Hall, 1872), 158–59.

13. Yang Dao, "Les difficultés du développement économique et social des populations Hmong du Laos," Thèse de Doctorat de Troisième Cycle (Université de Paris, 1972).

14. Karl Gustav Izikowitz, *Lamet: Hill Peasants in French Indochina* (Etnografiska Museet, Göteborg: 1951), 346.

15. Alfred McCoy et al., *The Politics of Heroin in Southeast Asia* (New York: Harper and Row, 1972), 75.

16. Wolf, *Europe and the People without History*, 97.

17. McCoy, *The Politics of Heroin*, 83–84.

18. See ibid. for details.

19. Fred Branfman, "Presidential War in Laos, 1964–1970," in *Laos: War and Revolution*, ed. Nina S. Adams and Alfred W. McCoy (New York: Harper Colophon Books, 1970), 226.

20. Joel Martin Halpern, *Government, Politics, and Social Structure in Laos*, Monograph Series no. 4 (New Haven: Yale University Southeast Asia Studies, 1964), 5–8.

21. Jean Pierre Barbier, "Objectifs et résultats de l'aide économique au Laos: Une évaluation difficile," *Revue Tiers Monde* 16, no. 62 (April-June 1975).

22. Branfman, "Presidential War," 225.

23. Inpheng Suryadhay, G. Condominas, J. Granier, Ch. Taillard, "La propriété foncière selon les pratiques coutumières lao," *Bulletin des Amis du Royaume Lao* 6 (1971): 109.

24. Howard Kaufman, *Village Life in Vientiane Province (1956–57)*, Laos Project Paper no. 12 (Brandeis University, Mass., 1961), 23.

25. Ministère du Plan et de la Coopération, *Etude du périmètre de Tha Deua*, Annexe 1, Socio-Economique (Vientiane, September 1973), 42.

26. Christian Taillard, *Les berges de la Nam Ngum et du Mékong* (Commissariat Général au Plan, Vientiane, November 1971), 59.

27. Besides the abovementioned studies by Barber, Condominas, Kaufman, Halpern, Taillard, see also Tseuno Ayabe, *The Village of Ban Pha Khao, Vientiane Province*, Laos Project Paper no. 14 (Brandeis University, Mass., 1961); Fred Branfman, *The Village of the Deep Pond, Ban Xa Phang Meuk, Laos*, Asian Studies Committee, Occasional Paper Series no. 3 (University of Massachusetts at Amherst, May 1978).

28. Christian Taillard, "Les berges de la Nam Ngum et du Mékong," *Etudes rurales*, nos. 53-54-55-56 (January–December 1974): 143.

29. Ibid.

30. John L. S. Girling, *Thailand: Society and Politics* (Ithaca: Cornell University Press, 1981), 69–70.

31. Joel M. Halpern, "Capital, Savings and Credit among Lao Peasants," in *Capital, Savings and Credit in Peasant Societies*, ed. Raymond Firth and B. S. Young (London: George Allen and Unwin, 1964), 88.

32. Cited in Judith W. Cousins and Alfred W. McCoy, "Living it up in Laos: Congressional Testimony on United States Aid to Laos," in Adams and McCoy, *Laos*, 348.

33. Kaysone Phomvihane, *La révolution lao* (Moscow: Editions du Progrès, 1980), 68–69.

34. MacAlister Brown and Joseph J. Zasloff, *Apprentice Revolutionaries: The Communist Movement in Laos, 1930–1985* (Stanford: Hoover Institution Press, 1986).

35. For a discussion of these issues see chapter 1 of Grant Evans and Kelvin Rowley, *Red Brotherhood at War: Indochina since the Fall of Saigon* (London: Verso, 1984).

36. Halpern, "Capital, Savings and Credit," 12.

CHAPTER THREE: *The Campaign and After*

1. For a detailed discussion of the issues raised in this chapter see Grant Evans, *Agrarian Change in Communist Laos* (Singapore: Institute of Southeast Asian Studies, 1988).

2. *Documents du Congrès National des Représentantes du Peuple* (Vientiane: Editions Lao Hak Sat, 1976), 72.

3. For a discussion of the economic problems faced by the Lao government see Grant Evans, "Planning Problems in Peripheral Socialism: The Case of Laos," in *Current Developments in Laos*, ed. Leonard Unger and Joseph Zasloff (London: Macmillan, 1989).

4. BBC *Summary of World Broadcasts: Far East* (4 April 1977). Hereafter cited in text as *SWB*.

5. *Foreign Broadcast Information Service,* supplement no. 1, Asia and Pacific (17 March 1978), 7 (my emphasis). Hereafter *FBIS*.

6. *FBIS* (17 March 1978), 31.

7. Ibid., 30.

8. James C. Scott, *The Moral Economy of the Peasant* (New Haven: Yale University Press, 1976), 24.

9. For a summary of what is known of the overall situation see Evans, *Agrarian Change in Communist Laos,* 39–46.

10. *Political Report* (1986).

11. *Political Report.*

12. The standard definitions are: Level 1: Loose voluntary associations or mutual aid teams of a few farmers who pool assets and work but retain individual ownership rights and decision making. Level 2: Assets under cooperative control but with some rental paid to original owners of land, draft animals, and major equipment. Members are free to enter or leave, taking their assets with them. Level 3: Full cooperatives, in which all assets are owned by the cooperative and no rentals are paid. Cooperative members share returns in proportion to work points allocated by the cooperative management committee.

13. Interview with the author, 24 February 1983.

14. *Political Report,* 25.

15. Economist Intelligence Unit, *Indochina,* no. 3, (1987): 18.

16. *Political Report.*

17. He also makes an interesting addition to this sector later in his speech, when he says the "household economy" is "one sector of the socialist economy" (ibid.).

18. *Political Report.*

19. "Resolution of the Joint Conference between the Party Central Committee and the Council of Ministers on the Expansion of Commodities Producing Agriculture and Improvement of Agricultural Management" (Vientiane, 15–22 June 1988).

20. Interview, 17 December 1988. Much of this interview is reproduced in the *Asian Wall Street Journal* (14 February 1989). See also the accompanying articles by the author in *ibid.* (14, 15, 17 February 1989).

21. *Political Report.*

CHAPTER FOUR: *Peasant Society under Socialism*

1. *SWB,* 13 October 1984.

2. *SWB,* 5 February 1987.

3. Azizur Rahman Khan and Eddy Lee, *Employment and Development in Laos: Some Problems and Policies* (Bangkok: ILO-ARTEP, 1980), 37–38.

4. Hans U. Luther, *Socialism in a Subsistence Economy: The Laotian Way* (Chulalongkhorn University Social Science Research Institute, January 1983), 26.

5. Athar Hussain and Keith Tribe, *Marxism and the Agrarian Question* (London: Macmillan, 1981), 1:61.

6. Ibid., 2:100.

7. Chayanov, *The Theory of Peasant Economy,* ed. Daniel Thorner et al. (Homewood, Ill.: Richard D Irwin, 1966), 171.

8. Ibid., 159.

9. The category "member of cooperative" is highly problematic in this survey, which was conducted as part of a government training program. The survey was unlikely to question a peasant's reported status. As I discovered, most peasants who were in fact private peasants invariably reported they were in a "cooperative." I shall return to this in the next chapter. It is more realistic to consider most of those reported in the above survey independent peasant cultivators.

10. The proximity of the cooperative to Vientiane meant that it was used as a "model" cooperative (see next chapter) and provided a showcase for one-time journalistic or official visitors. An example of one visitor is given in Murray Hiebert, "Laos: Flexible Policies Spark Tenuous Recovery," *Indochina Issues* (May 1983): 4. The director's initial response to me was his standard one; he didn't believe I would be around for months to check out the story.

11. Lucien M. Hanks, *Rice and Man* (Chicago: Aldine, 1972), 88.

12. Ministère du Plan et de la Coopération, *Etude du périmètre de Tha Deua,* Annexe 1, Socio-Economique (Vientiane, September 1973), 66.

13. Personal communication, Vientiane, November 1988. Ireson was carrying out a study for the Swedish International Development Agency on women's use of forest products.

14. Howard Kaufman, *Village Life in Vientiane Province, (1956–57),* Laos Project Paper no. 12 (Brandeis University, Mass., 1961), 9.

15. Karl Marx, *Capital* (London: Penguin Books, 1976), 1:456.

16. For good discussions of petty commodity production in peasant communities see Joel S. Kahn, *Minankabau Social Formations* (Cambridge: Cambridge University Press, 1980); Jennifer Alexander, *Trade, Traders and Trading in Rural Java* (Singapore: Oxford University Press, 1987), chap. 4.

17. Christian Taillard, "Le village lao de la région de Vientiane: Un pouvoir local face au pouvoir étatique", *L'Homme* 17, nos. 2–3 (April-September 1977): 78.

18. For example, in August 1977 *Sieng Pasason* ran an editorial entitled "Build a line of conscientiously practicing thrift and make it a national habit." Thrift, it said, must be a "main policy of our Party and state" *SWB* (3 September 1977).

19. Francesca Bray, *The Rice Economies* (London: Basil Blackwell, 1986), 135.

CHAPTER FIVE: *"The System of Civilized Cooperators"*

1. V. I. Lenin, "On Cooperation," *Selected Works,* (Moscow: Progress Publishers, 1967), 3:761.

2. *FBIS,* (30 April 1979).

3. "Some Ideas Concerning the Provisional Regulations for the Cooperatives" (Vientiane, c. 1980).

4. Translated for this book by Pralomvong Sinbandith.

5. For a discussion of the issue of "exploitation" in the cooperatives see Grant Evans "'Rich Peasants and Cooperatives in Socialist Laos," *Journal of Anthropological Research* 44, no. 3 (Fall 1988).

6. Khan and Lee observed the following for 1979–80: "The cooperative makes no payment for land contributed by members. In this respect the system of payment [*sic*] is more advanced than in many other cooperatives. However, the cooperative also rents land from non-members. . . . The payment is very small, only one and a half per cent of the yield" (*Employment and Development*, 49). This sounds extremely suspect, but if it is true it accounts for some of the dissatisfaction private peasants felt with the cooperative.

7. "Some Ideas Concerning the Provisional Regulations for the Cooperatives."

8. I encountered a similar logic in a discussion among peasants in a village north of Vientiane. An old ex-soldier who had been sent off to reeducation in Xieng Khouang was scoffing at the claims that cooperatives existed in the district. They were, he said, nothing like "real" cooperatives as they existed in the old liberated areas, and therefore he would not join until they were real cooperatives with hospitals, schools, machinery, etc. Thus did he rationalize his nonparticipation in cooperatives in his home village.

9. See Kaysone Phomvihane, *SWB* (25 February 1988).

10. Since I visited this cooperative it has expanded its nonagricultural activities extensively and in 1988 established a joint clothes manufacturing venture with a Thai businessman.

11. Jack Potter, *Thai Peasant Social Structure* (Chicago: University of Chicago Press, 1976), 180.

12. See R. F. Miller, *Socialism and Agricultural Cooperation: The Soviet and Yugoslav Cases,* Occasional Paper no. 9 (Canberra: Department of Political Science, Research School of Social Sciences, Australian National University, 1974), 22.

CHAPTER SIX: *Peasant Economy versus Collective Economy*

1. *FBIS* (30 April 1979).

2. Koichi Mizuno, "Multihousehold Compounds in Northeast Thailand," *Asian Survey* 8, no. 10 (October 1968).

3. Jack M. Potter, *Thai Peasant Social Structure* (Chicago: University of Chicago Press, 1976), 125.

4. Sulamith Heinz-Potter, *Family Life in a Northern Thai Village: A Study in the Structural Significance of Women* (Berkeley: University of California Press, 1977).

5. George Condominas, *Essai sur la société rurale lao de la région de Vientiane* (Vientiane: UNESCO-Commissariat general aux Affaires Rurales, 1962), 10.

6. In an interesting survey of what she calls northern Thai matrilineages, Ann Hale argues that the land factor has become a key one in the modification of the

family development cycle there. One effect of land pressure is that land available for subdivision diminishes to a point where "not all daughter households would receive an inheritance, which means that group fission would be decreasingly likely to follow a development cycle" (Hale, "A Reassessment of Northern Thai Matrilineages," *Mankind* 12 [1979]: 145). Hale also notes that the commercialization of land tends to be a solvent of "matrilineal" inheritance, and she observes further that the wealthy landowners in this region have the highest rates of patrilocal residence (this observation is not especially pertinent to Laos under the communist regime).

7. My investigations in a neighboring tasseng, where ban Hat Kansa is situated, revealed that officials there had registered all land in the name of the male household heads. The women, on the other hand, said they knew exactly who inherited the land and who did not. This discrepancy between official descriptions of ownership and actual ownership could lead to clashes over rights in the future.

8. Christine Pelzer-White, "Socialist Transformation of Agriculture and Gender Relations: The Vietnamese Case," Institute of Development Studies, *Bulletin* 13, no. 4 (1982): 47.

9. Alexander Woodside, *Vietnam and the Chinese Model* (Cambridge: Harvard University Press, 1971).

10. Edwin E. Moise, *Land Reform in China and North Vietnam* (Chapel Hill: University of North Carolina Press, 1983), 223, 256.

11. Kay Ann Johnson, *Women, the Family and Peasant Revolution in China* (Chicago: University of Chicago Press, 1983), 112; see also Norma Diamond, "Collectivisation, Kinship, and the Status of Women in Rural China," in *Toward an Anthropology of Women*, ed. Rayna R. Reiter (New York: Monthly Review Press, 1975).

12. Quoted in Elizabeth J. Perry, "Rural Violence in China," *China Quarterly*, no. 103 (September 1985): 426; for a similar observation see Elizabeth Croll, *The Politics of Marriage in Contemporary China* (London: Cambridge University Press, 1981), 176.

13. Elizabeth Croll, *Chinese Women after Mao* (London: Zed Press, 1983), 12. For an interesting discussion of labor recruitment in the traditional Chinese family see James P. McGough, "The Domestic Mode of Production and Peasant Social Organization: The Chinese Case," in *Chayanov, Peasants, and Economic Anthropology*, ed. E. Paul Durrenberger (London: Academic Press, 1984).

14. Martin Stuart-Fox, "The Initial Failure of Agricultural Cooperativization in Laos," *Asia Quarterly*, no. 4 (1980): 286. For a critique of the "loose structure" concept see Potter, *Thai Peasant Social Structure*, chap. 1.

15. Suryadhay, cited in Martin Barber, "Migrants and Modernization: A Study of Change in Lao Society" (Ph.D. diss., University of Hull, 1979), 324.

16. Maxine Molyneux, "Socialist Societies Old and New: Progress Towards Women's Emancipation?", *Monthly Review* (July–August 1982), 61.

17. For a more detailed presentation see A. V. Chayanov, *The Theory of Peasant Economy* (Madison: University of Wisconsin Press, 1986), chap. 1.

18. The economic importance of child labor in peasant farming is still under-researched. No study of the problem in Laos remotely compares with that of Ben-

jamin White for Java. See Benjamin White, "The Economic Importance of Children in a Javanese Village," in *Population and Social Organization,* ed. Moni Nag (Paris: Mouton Publishers, 1975).

19. Condominas, *Essai sur la société,* 2.

20. See, for example, John W. Bennett, "Reciprocal Economic Exchanges among North American Agricultural Operators," *Southwestern Journal of Anthropology* 24 (1968): 276–309.

21. Alvin W. Gouldner, "The Norm of Reciprocity: A Preliminary Statement," *American Sociological Review* 25, no. 2 (1960): 175.

22. In a different context Maurice Bloch has made similar observations: "The value of real kinship by contrast with artificial kinship lies in the fact that the motives of individuals in cooperative activities go beyond the economic uses to which they are put at any particular time and it is this which gives them their economic significance. Such relationships provide potential cooperation continuing through the vicissitudes of time. It is the knowledge of this effect of the morality of kinship which governs the planning of labor teams. . . . It is the presence of moral cooperators which enables a man to afford to concentrate on manipulating short-term links" ("The Long Term and the Short Term: The Economic and Political Significance of the Morality of Kinship," in *The Character of Kinship,* ed. Jack Goody (London: Cambridge University Press, 1973), 79–80.

23. There appears to be some well-concealed disagreement over his right to land of his original mother. He insisted that it had not been divided up, but in practice it had been, and his older brother who lived in the maternal house had received a larger inheritance than he. One suspects that the head of household 3 continued to insist that the land had not been divided up because it gave him some rights, to labor at least, on that land. And no one was insisting on clarification of the issue. He had missed out on a larger share, it seems, because he spent the late sixties and early seventies away in the army, then three years in Xieng Khouang province in "reeducation." His absence also seems to be the reason why his older sister, who looked after his adopted mother, also inherited a larger share from the adoptive mother. He was, of course, provided with land by the latter to build a house. His wife, however, added little to their resources because she came from Vang Vieng to the north.

24. Alvin Gouldner writes, "Although compliance with the norm of reciprocity may foster complex, long-linked social interactions over time, each act inducing another and each return requiring a new return, it is nonetheless sometimes possible for people in a relationship governed solely by the norm of reciprocity to be 'even' with one another at some point—or at least, to view their relationship in this way and call it 'quits'. This is a dangerous moment in the life of social systems. Indeed, when we hear men talk about 'balancing' or 'squaring' accounts with one another we commonly suspect an aggressive intent, and rightly expect that there is trouble ahead" ("The Importance of Something for Nothing," in *For Sociology* [London: Penguin Books, 1975], 274).

25. John Wong, "The Group Farming System in China: Ideology versus Pragmatism," in *Group Farming in Asia,* ed. John Wong (Singapore: Singapore University Press, 1979), 100.

26. Andrew Vickerman, *The Fate of the Peasantry,* Monograph Series no. 28 (New Haven: Yale University Southeast Asia Studies, 1986), 126.

27. Robert Bideleux, *Communism and Development* (London: Methuen, 1985), 199.

28. Moise, *Land Reform,* 221, 252, 257.

29. Peter Worsley, *The Third World* (London: Weidenfeld and Nicholson, 1967), 165.

CHAPTER SEVEN: *Cooperation in the Cooperatives*

1. "Agricultural Problems: (Vol. 5) The Management of Cooperatives," *Vietnamese Studies* 51 (1977): 76.

2. *FBIS* (30 April 1979).

3. *Some Ideas Concerning the Provisional Regulations for the Cooperatives* (Vientiane, c. 1980).

4. See, for example, Adam Fforde, "Socio-economic Differentiation in a Mature Collectivized Agriculture: North Vietnam," *Sociologia Ruralis* 27, nos. 2/3 (1987): 210–13; Jean C. Oi, "Communism and Clientalism: Rural Politics in China," *World Politics* 37, no. 2 (1985).

5. *SWB* (24 June 1978).

6. *Vietnamese Studies* 51 (1977): 98, 102.

7. Women at Don Dou cooperative said, for example, that they preferred bundling the seedlings in the dry season because the lower water level meant they could sit down on small wooden stools as they worked.

8. The following example gives some idea of the complexities as they relate to a Vietnamese commune: "In the district of Hai Van the table of norms comprises 382 different levels: 165 for agriculture; seven for raising livestock; 178 for diverse trades; seven for transport; 25 for afforestation. In each cooperative—and this is the case for Hai Van—a final table is prepared. . . . They comprise, in all, 80 norms" (Francois Houtart and Genevieve Lemercinier, *Hai Van: Life in a Vietnamese Commune* [London: Zed Books, 1984], 30).

9. Ronald F. Dore, "Cooperatives in Traditional Communities," in *Two Blades of Grass,* ed. P. Worsley (London: Manchester University Press, 1971), 54–55.

10. The cooperative no longer exists.

11. It should be recognized that resentment at paying managers has been a contentious issue even in cooperatives in advanced agricultural situations as well, where there is a more obvious need for such functions. For the American case see Richard B. Heflebower, *Cooperatives and Mutuals in the Market System* (Madison: University of Wisconsin Press, 1980), 198.

12. *Characteristics of the Cooperative and their Principles of Organization* (Vientiane, November 27, 1979), 54.

13. Ibid., 50.

14. An analogous system had spontaneously emerged earlier in northern Vietnam in the mid-1960s: "Because of the special nature of agricultural production,

some people thought that it would be a good idea to stimulate production by giving the fixed group certain rights, for instance: 'to really own a certain area of land'. . . . This is what actually happened in a good number of cooperatives, chiefly at the beginning, as production brigades turned into 'small cooperatives' within the mother cooperative. . . . In some cases [it] resulted in the disbanding of cooperatives. This was quite simply a return to private ownership" (*Vietnamese Studies* 51 [1977]: 78–79).

15. Samuel L. Popkin, *The Rational Peasant: The Political Economy of Rural Society in Vietnam* (Berkeley: University of California Press, 1979), 265.

16. Interestingly the Chinese Communists recognized this problem very early on. A Central Committee and State Council directive in 1956, while criticizing the 'commandist' tendencies of some cadres, commented: "Agricultural production differs from industrial production. A greater proportion of agricultural production is self-supporting in nature and is at the same time dependent on natural and geographical conditions. Agricultural producer cooperatives are not State enterprises, but are managed under a collective system. Therefore we cannot draw up agricultural production plans as we draw up industrial production plans" (cited in Marsh Marshall, *Organizations and Growth in Rural China* [London: Macmillan, 1985], 56–57). This insight, unfortunately, was soon swamped by the Great Leap Forward.

17. As J. M. Brewster wrote in 1950, "In agriculture . . . machine methods remain compatible as hand techniques with either (1) family or (2) larger-than-family units. Their compatibility with family units lies in the fact that farm operations are widely separated by time intervals after mechanizations as before; hence, the number of things that must be done at the same time on a farm remains as close as ever to the number of workers in an ordinary family. . . . Technological advance . . . accelerates the functional task forms of specialization in industry, but not in agriculture. In working simultaneously, manufacturing machines so multiply the number of concurrent operations as to (1) wipe out the union of managerial, supervisory, and labor employments in the same individual or family and re-establish them as full-time operations of different classes, and further (2) destroy a similar union of labor operations. But since farm mechanization nowise increases the number of things which must be done at the same time, it provides no new basis whatever for either the functional or task form specialization" (cited in Kenneth L. Bachman and Raymond P. Christensen, "The Economies of Farm Size," in *Agricultural Development and Economic Growth*, eds. H. M. Southworth and B. F. Johnston [Ithaca: Cornell University Press, 1967], 251).

18. *FBIS* (30 April 1979).

19. *SWB* (13 October 1984).

20. *FBIS* (30 April 1979).

21. For an excellent overview see Bachman and Christensen, "The Economies of Farm Size"; see also Marshall, *Organizations and Growth in Rural China*, 52–59.

22. R. Albert Berry and William R. Cline, *Agrarian Structure and Productivity in Developing Countries* (Baltimore: Johns Hopkins University Press, 1979), 1.

23. *FBIS* (30 April 1979). Kaysone has repeated this assertion many times, as

have various government statements, the latest being the Sixth Plenum Resolution in mid-1988: "Resolution of the Joint Conference between the Party Central Committee and the Council of Ministers (June 15–22, 1988) on the Expansion of Commodity Producing Agriculture and Improvement of Agricultural Management," which claims that "farmers use only 30 percent of their working days."

24. For the concept of a "potential" surplus see Paul Baran, *The Political Economy of Growth* (New York: Monthly Review Press, 1968), chap. 2.

25. Marshall, *Organizations and Growth*, 41.

26. Francesca Bray, *The Rice Economies* (London: Basil Blackwell, 1986), 164.

27. Kay Ann Johnson, *Women, the Family and Peasant Revolution in China* (Chicago: University of Chicago Press, 1983), chap. 11.

28. On the other hand, one Lao official complained to me in 1986, "Political speeches tell the Lao people how hardworking they are, yet they are really lazy, and it makes it very difficult for us to encourage them to work hard when they are being congratulated for being hard workers."

29. Christian Taillard, "Les berges de la Nam Ngum et du Mékong," *Etudes rurales*, nos. 53-54-55-56 (January–December 1974), 161.

30. William J. Klausner, *Reflections on Thai Culture* (Bangkok: Suksit Siam, 1981), 36, 51.

31. Christian Taillard, "L'irrigation dans le nord du Laos: L'exemple du bassin de la Nam Song à Vang Vieng," *Peninsule* 4–5 (1982): 26.

32. Ibid., 28, 34.

33. E. Walter Coward, Jr., "Local Organization and Bureaucracy in a Lao Irrigation Project," in *Irrigation and Agricultural Development in Asia*, ed. E. Walter Coward, Jr. (Ithaca: Cornell University Press, 1980), 336.

34. Vientiane, January 1983.

35. For examples see D. S. Thornton, "The Organization of Irrigated Areas," in *Policy and Practice in Rural Development* ed. Guy Hunter et al. (London: Croom Helm in association with ODI, 1976), 149–50.

36. Marshall, *Organizations and Growth*, 76–87.

37. For one discussion see Marie Alexandrine Martine, "La riziculture et la maîtrise de l'eau dans le Kampuchea democratique," *Etudes rurales* (July–September 1981).

38. See Thornton, "The Organization of Irrigated Areas," or Peter Dorner, *Land Reform and Economic Development* (London: Penguin, 1972), chap. 2.

39. Bray, *The Rice Economies*, 162.

CHAPTER EIGHT: *"The New Countryside"*

1. Kaysone Phomvihane, *Political Report* (Vientiane, December 1986).

2. Karl Marx, "The Civil War in France," in *Karl Marx, The First International and After*, ed. D. Fernbach (London: Penguin, 1974), 209.

3. See, for example, Stephen F. Cohen, *Rethinking the Soviet Experience* (Oxford: Oxford University Press, 1985), chap. 1, "Scholarly Missions: Sovi-

etology as a Vocation." I basically concur with Cohen's criticisms of the use of the concept.

4. Barrington Moore, Jr., *Authority and Inequality under Capitalism and Socialism* (Oxford: Clarendon Press, 1987), 36.

5. Nevertheless, it has attempted to control the activities of individuals whom it considers to fall outside its conception of socialist society. Thus the regime has been wary, if not hostile, to *mo phii* (spirit healers) and *nang tiam* (spirit mediums). The latter, for example, have been kept under surveillance, and when I attempted to record a nang tiam ceremony in early 1987 I was chased off following the sudden arrival of a member of the Ministry of Interior, who said I would use the ceremony to make propaganda for the BBC. Why the latter was singled out I do not know, but such "superstition" clearly deviated from the monochrome image the government wished to project. Since 1988, however, considerable liberalization in most spheres of cultural life has occurred.

6. George Condominas, *Essai sur la société rurale lao de la région de Vientiane* (UNESCO, January 1962), 117.

7. *Political Report.*

8. Martin Stuart-Fox, *Laos: Politics, Economics and Society* (London: Frances Pinter, 1986), chap. 3.

9. Michael Moerman, "A Thai Village Headman as a Synaptic Leader," in *Modern Thai Politics,* rev. ed., ed. Clarke D. Neher (Schenkman Books, 1979), 249–50.

10. Martin Stuart-Fox and Rod Bucknell, "Politicization of the Buddhist Sangha in Laos," *Journal of Southeast Asian Studies* 13, no. 1 (1982): 62.

11. See Trevor Ling, *Buddhism, Imperialism and War* (London: Allen and Unwin, 1979); Tin Maung Maung Than, "The *Sangha* and *Sasana* in Socialist Burma," *Sojourn* 3, no. 1 (1988).

12. Cited in Stuart-Fox and Bucknell, "Politicization of the Buddhist Sangha"; see also the statement by Phoumi Vongvichit in the appendix of Ling, *Buddhism, Imperialism and War.*

13. Samuel Popkin, *The Rational Peasant* (Berkeley: University of California Press, 1979), 39.

14. Christian Taillard, "Le village lao de la région de Vientiane: Un pouvoir local face au pouvoir étatique," *L'Homme* 17 (avril–septembre 1977): 84, 80–81.

15. Popkin, *The Rational Peasant,* 77.

16. Lucien Hanks has evoked the powerlessness felt by villagers there: "We are scarcely surprised to learn that here people declare that government, like drought, floods, and famine, is a major evil in this world. Rare is the Southeast Asian village that has received a government official without expecting him to extort money and that does not pay him some fraction of his demand in order to speed him on his way. Angry officials have been known to return to the village with soldiers and massacre the inhabitants. So during edgy days whole villages may be abandoned when some unidentified stranger approaches. Even when an official comes bearing gifts, all anticipate a time when favors will have to be reciprocated" ("Corruption and Commerce in Southeast Asia," *Transaction* 8, no. 3 [May 1971]: 21–22).

17. *Political Report.*

18. Martin Stuart-Fox, "Politics and Patronage in Laos," *Indochina Issues* 70 (October 1986): 7.

19. For a discussion of the degree to which corruption is endemic in certain systems see Larissa Adler Lomnitz, "Informal Exchange Networks in Formal Systems: A Theoretical Model," *American Anthropologist* 90 (1988).

20. "Resolution of the Joint Conference between the Party Central Committee and the Council of Ministers (June 15–22, 1988) On the Expansion of Commodity Producing Agriculture and Improvement of Agricultural Management."

21. Vongsavanh Boutsavath and Georges Chapelier, "Lao Popular Buddhism and Community Development," *Journal of the Siam Society* 61, no. 2 (July 1973): 19.

22. "Resolution of the Joint Conference."

23. Theda Skocpol, *States and Social Revolutions* (London: Cambridge University Press, 1979).

24. *Political Report.* Here Kaysone is clearly adopting Lenin's dubious analysis of the causes of bureaucracy under socialism when he wrote in one of his early NEP articles, "In our country bureaucratic practices have different economic roots [to capitalism], namely, the atomized and scattered state of the small producers with his poverty" (V. I. Lenin, "The Tax in Kind," *Selected Works* [Moscow: Foreign Languages Publishing House, 1967], 3:602).

CHAPTER NINE: *Peasants and Socialism*

1. These various texts of Marx have been gathered in *Late Marx and the Russian Road: Marx and 'The Peripheries of Capitalism,'* ed. Teodor Shanin (New York: Monthly Review Press, 1983), 111, 124, 112, 104.

2. Cited in Azizur Rahman Khan and Eddy Lee, *Employment and Development in Laos* (Bangkok: ILO-ARTEP, 1980), 48.

3. Ronald Dore, "Modern Cooperatives in Traditional Communities," in *Two Blades of Grass,* ed. Peter Worsley (Manchester: Manchester University Press, 1971), 55–56.

4. George M. Foster, "Peasant Society and the Image of Limited Good," *American Anthropologist* 67 (1965): 296–97, 308.

5. See in particular John G. Kennedy, "Peasant Society and the Image of Limited Good: A Critique," *American Anthropologist* 68 (1966).

6. See Barrington Moore, Jr., "Austerity and Unintended Riches," *Comparative Studies in Society and History* 29, no. 4 (1987); see also Charles J. Erasmus, *In Search of the Common Good: Utopian Experiments Past and Future* (New York: Free Press, 1977).

7. James C. Scott, *The Moral Economy of the Peasant* (New Haven: Yale University Press, 1976), 27.

8. Ibid., 5, 43.

9. James C. Scott, *Weapons of the Weak* (New Haven: Yale University Press,

1986), is largely concerned with the shifting parameters of rights among Malaysian peasants.

10. Samuel Popkin, *The Rational Peasant* (Berkeley: University of California Press, 1979), 22, 18.

11. For a critique of similar theoretical approaches see Andrew Levine, Elliott Sober, and Erik Olin Wright, "Marxism and Methodological Individualism," *New Left Review*, no. 162 (March/April 1987).

12. John W. Bennett, "Agricultural Cooperatives in the Development Process: Perspectives from Social Science," *Studies in Comparative International Development* 18, nos. 1–2 (1983): 4.

13. Peter Worsley, "Introduction," in *Two Blades of Grass*, ed. Peter Worsley, 2.

14. For a good discussion of Weber's argument see Frank Parkin, *Max Weber* (London: Tavistock Publications and Ellis Horwood Limited, 1982).

15. For example, Geertz does this with reference to Javanese traders. Clifford Geertz, "Social Change and Economic Modernization in Two Indonesian Towns: A Case in Point," in *Tribal and Peasant Economies* ed. George Dalton (New York: Natural History Press, 1967); see also Maxime Rodinson, *Islam and Capitalism* (London: Penguin Books, 1977), for one of the best discussions of the role of religion in economic and social change, especially chapter 6.

16. Bukharin's call on the peasants in 1925 to "enrich" themselves made him infamous in communist circles for years afterward.

17. Robert Manchin and Ivan Szlenyi, "Theories of Family Agricultural Production in Collectivized Economies," *Sociologia Ruralis* 25, no. 2 (1985): 260.

18. Eric Wolf, *Peasants* (Englewood Cliffs: Prentice-Hall, 1966), 70.

19. Thomas C. Smith, *The Agrarian Origins of Modern Japan* (New York: Atheneum, 1966).

20. R. P. Dore, *Land Reform in Japan* (London: Oxford University Press, 1959), 278, 295.

21. Gordon White, "Developmental States and Socialist Industrialization in the Third World," *Journal of Development Studies* 21, no. 1 (1984): 101.

22. The term is from C. B. McPherson, *The Political Theory of Possessive Individualism* (London: Oxford University Press, 1964).

23. Louis Althusser, "Contradiction and Overdetermination," *New Left Review* 41 (January–February, 1967): 32.

24. Raymond Firth, *Primitive Polynesian Economy* (London: Routledge and Kegan Paul, 1965), 364.

25. Barrington Moore, Jr., *Injustice: The Social Bases of Obedience and Revolt* (London: Macmillan, 1978), 507 (my emphasis).

26. Erasmus, *In Search of the Common Good*, 61–71.

27. Charles J. Erasmus, "Culture Structure and Process: The Occurrence and Disappearance of Reciprocal Farm Labor," *Southwestern Journal of Anthropology* 12 (1956): 455.

28. Hong Pi-feng, "An Outline of Group Farming Experience in Taiwan", in *Group Farming in Asia*, ed. John Wong (Singapore: Singapore University Press, 1979), 64.

29. For an overview of the transformation of traditional cooperation in Japan see Smith, *Agrarian Origins,* chap. 10. More recent developments are discussed by Mitsuru Shimpo, *Three Decades in Shiwa* (Vancouver: University of British Columbia Press, 1976). See also Yoshiharu Kubo, "The Cooperative Farming System in the Mixed Farming Area of Hokkaido, Japan," and Edward Reed, "Two Approaches to Cooperation in Rice Production in South Korea," both in Wong, *Group Farming.*

30. Shanin quotes the opinion of V. Danilov, who wishes to bring the forces of production into the taxonomy of farming systems as a way of deciding when a peasant farm has been eclipsed. Thus a key aspect of "depeasantisation would be when the prevalent 'factors of production' of the family farms become extra-natural (i.e. highly mechanized and capital-bound grain farms of Utah, USA, or meat farms of Holland)" (Teodor Shanin, *Russia as a 'Developing Society'* [London: Macmillan, 1985], 1:169).

31. Max Weber, *Economy and Society,* ed. Guenther Roth and Claus Wittich (Berkeley: University of California Press, 1978), 1:359.

32. Marshall Sahlins, *Stone Age Economics* (London: Tavistock Publications, 1974), 94–95.

33. Weber, *Economy and Society,* 364.

34. Eric R. Wolf, "Kinship, Friendship and Patron-Client Relations in Complex Societies," in *The Social Anthropology of Complex Societies,* ed. Michael Banton (London: Tavistock Publications, 1966), 9.

35. Maurice Freedman, *Lineage Organization in Southeastern China,* London School of Economics Monographs on Social Anthropology, no. 18 (London: Athlone Press, 1965), 22.

36. Weber, *Economy and Society,* 52, 85–86.

37. Bennett, "Agricultural Cooperatives," 4.

38. Weber recognized this; even "formal rationality of money calculation is dependent on certain specific substantive conditions" (*Economy and Society,* 107).

39. For a fascinating discussion of competing symbolic claims see the two articles by Christopher A. P. Binns, "The Changing Face of Power: Revolution and Accommodation in the Development of the Soviet Ceremonial System," part 1, *Man* 14, no. 4 (1979): 585–606, and part 2, *Man* 15, no. 1 (1980): 170–87. And a book whose focus is somewhat different but which attempts to grapple with the moral bases of action in a communist context, Richard Madsen, *Morality and Power in a Chinese Village* (Berkeley: University of California Press, 1984).

40. This potent phrase was coined by Edward C. Banfield in *The Moral Basis of a Backward Society* (New York: Free Press, 1967), a study of southern Italian peasants.

41. Barrington Moore, Jr., *Privacy: Studies in Social and Cultural History* (New York: M. E. Sharpe, 1984), 270.

42. For a good recent discussion of women traders in Asia see Jennifer Alexander, *Trade, Traders and Trading in Rural Java* (Singapore: Oxford University Press, 1987); also Sidney W. Mintz, "Men, Women and Trade," *Comparative Studies in Society and History* 13, no. 3 (1971).

43. Bennett, "Agricultural Cooperatives," is more sanguine about taking the good with the bad in cooperatives formed in a traditional context. M. P. Moore, "Cooperative Labor in Peasant Agriculture," *The Journal of Peasant Studies* 2, no. 3 (1975), provides further evidence of kin manipulation and conflict, particularly in African cooperatives.

44. Moshe Lewin, "The Kolkhoz and the Russian *Muzhik,*" in his *The Making of the Soviet System* (New York: Pantheon Books, 1985).

45. Wolf, "Kinship, Friendship," 7–8.

46. *Political Report.*

47. Mihail Cernea, "The Large-Scale Formal Organization and the Primary Family Group," *Journal of Marriage and the Family* (November 1975): 934.

48. Cited in Stephen F. Cohen, *Bukharin and the Bolshevik Revolution* (London: Oxford University Press, 1980), 195, 197, 200.

49. Cited in Moshe Lewin, *Political Undercurrents in Soviet Economic Debates* (London: Pluto Press, 1975), 318.

50. Quoted in Richard B. Day, *Leon Trotsky and the Politics of Economic Isolation* (London: Cambridge University Press, 1973), 183.

51. A. V. Chayanov, *The Theory of Peasant Economy,* ed. Daniel Thorner et al. (Homewood, Ill.: Richard D. Irwin, 1966), 262. For a discussion of subsequent developments in American agriculture along these lines see John Wilson, "The Political Economy of Contract Farming," *Review of Radical Political Economics* 18, no. 4 (1986).

52. Chayanov, *Theory of Peasant Economy,* 264.

53. Ibid., 265, 266, 267 (my emphasis), 268.

54. Arthur Goldsmith, "The Private Sector and Rural Development: Can Agribusiness Help the Small Farmer?", *World Development* 13, no. 10/11 (1985): 1131.

55. Richard B. Heflebower, *Cooperatives and Mutuals in the Market System* (Madison: University of Wisconsin Press, 1980), 10.

56. Francesca Bray, *The Rice Economies* (London: Basil Blackwell, 1986), 169, 167.

57. Z. T. Wierzbicki and R. Rambaud, "The Emergence of the First Agricultural Trade Union in Socialist Poland," *Sociologia Ruralis* 23, no. 3/4 (1982).

58. E. Paul Durrenberger, "Introduction," in *Chayanov, Peasants, and Economic Anthropology,* ed. E. Paul Durrenberger (Orlando: Academic Press, 1984), 3–7; and Heflebower, *Cooperatives and Mutuals,* 5.

59. Frank Parkin, *Marxism and Class Theory: A Bourgeois Critique* (London: Tavistock Publications, 1979), 44.

60. Kostas Vergopoulos, "The End of Agribusiness or the Emergence of Biotechnology," *International Social Science Journal* 105 (1985): 291.

61. Goldsmith, "The Private Sector," 1132–33.

62. This possibility is explored in a capitalist context also in ibid., 1126.

63. Andrew Turton, "Limits of Ideological Domination and the Formation of Social Consciousness," in *History and Peasant Consciousness in South East Asia,* ed. Andrew Turton and Shigeharu Tanabe, *Senri Ethnological Studies,* no. 13 (Osaka, 1984), 34.

64. The last attempt at a modified defense can be found in Barry Hindess and Paul Q. Hirst, *Pre-capitalist Modes of Production* (London: Routledge and Kegan Paul, 1975), chap. 1. The idea of a "primitive communal" society has persisted among some Thai anthropologists. Thus, Chatthip Nartsupha, drawing on the work of the Thai communist Cit Phumisak, has asserted that "Holy men" revolts in the Thai northeast during the nineteenth and early twentieth centuries were attempts to establish "a new society of village 'socialism' " (p. 123) and were evidence of "the persistence of primitive communal consciousness throughout [a] 300 year period" (p. 128) Chatthip Nartsupha, "The Ideology of Holy Men Revolts in Northeast Thailand," in Turton and Tanabe, *History and Peasant Consciousness*.

65. Adam Kuper, *The Invention of Primitive Society: Transformations of an Illusion* (London: Routledge and Kegan Paul, 1988), 9.

66. The debate has expanded rapidly, so I will list only a stream of it, one that covers the broadest range of issues: Alec Nove, *The Economics of Feasible Socialism* (London: George Allen and Unwin, 1983); Wlodzimierz Brus, "Socialism—Feasible and Viable?", *New Left Review* 153 (September/October 1985); Ernest Mandel, "In Defence of Socialist Planning," *New Left Review* 159 (September/October 1986); Alec Nove, "Markets and Socialism," *New Left Review* 161 (January/February 1987); Ernest Mandel, "The Myth of Market Socialism," *New Left Review* 169 (May/June 1988); Paul Aurbach et al., "The Transition from Actually Existing Capitalism," *New Left Review* 170 (July/August 1988); Diane Elson, "Market Socialism or Socialization of the Market?", *New Left Review* 172 (November/December 1988); Paul Cockshott and Allin Cottrell, "Labor Value and Socialist Economic Calculation," *Economy and Society* 18, no. 1 (1989).

67. Michael Taussig, "The Rise and Fall of Marxist Anthropology," *Social Analysis*, no. 21 (August 1987): 112.

68. Norman Geras, "Essence and Appearance: Aspects of Fetishism in Marx's *Capital*," *New Left Review* 65 (January/February 1971): 72.

69. Jonathan Friedman, "The Place of Fetishism and the Problem of Materialist Interpretations," *Critique of Anthropology*, no. 1 (Spring 1974): 56–57.

70. Michael Taussig, *The Devil and Commodity Fetishism in South America* (Chapel Hill: University of North Carolina Press, 1980), 231.

71. The best statement of Marx's views, in my opinion, is Geras, "Essence and Appearance."

72. Roy Ellen, "Fetishism," *Man* 23, no. 2 (June 1988). This does not necessarily destroy the possibility of scientific analysis. According to Godelier the functional specificity of institutions in modern societies enables the perception of "the role of material activities and economic relations in social evolution" compared with precapitalist societies (Maurice Godelier, *The Mental and the Material* [London: Verso, 1986], 142).

73. Michael Taussig, *Shamanism, Colonialism and the Wild Man: A Study in Terror and Healing* (Chicago: University of Chicago Press, 1987), 135.

74. See Maurice Bloch, *Marxism and Anthropology* (Oxford: Oxford University Press, 1983), chap. 5.

75. Cited by Mike Gane, "Introduction to Durkheim and Mauss," *Economy and Society* 13, no. 3 (1984): 309.

76. Marcel Mauss, "A Sociological Assessment of Bolshevism (1924–5)," ibid., 338, 367.

77. See, for example, "The Spirit of the Gift" in Sahlins, *Stone Age Economics*.

78. Claude Lévi-Strauss, *Introduction to the Work of Marcel Mauss* (London: Routledge and Kegan Paul, 1987).

79. Marcel Mauss, *The Gift* (London: Cohen and West, 1969), 67.

80. Ibid.

81. Mauss, "A Sociological Assessment," 353. See Elson, "Market Socialism or Socialization of the Market?" for an attempt to theorize a similar proposition.

82. Mauss, "A Sociological Assessment," 372.

83. Tom Bottomore, "A Marxist Consideration of Durkheim," *Social Forces* 59:4 (June 1981).

84. J. A. Barnes, "Durkheim's *Division of Labor in Society*," *Man* 1 (1966): 173.

85. Alvin Gouldner, "Emile Durkheim and the Critique of Socialism," *For Sociology* (London: Pelican Books, 1975), 380.

86. Mauss, *The Gift*, 75.

87. Moore, *Injustice*, 506.

Glossary

ban	village
boun	festival/celebration
chao	lord/chief
hai	upland rice field
Khamphaeng Nakhorn	prefecture
kip	Lao currency
khoueng	province
khum	unit of a village
muang	district/city/nation
na	irrigable or wet rice field
nai	chief/headman
nam	small river/water
nuay	unit of a village
faay	dam
pathan	president
pathet	nation/country
phasat	religious offering
rai	field measure equivalent to 0.16 hectares
sala	rest house
samien	assistant
sangha	order of Buddhist monks and nuns
tasseng	subdistrict
vat	Buddhist temple or monastery

Index

abbatoirs, 73–74
ABC of Communism, The (Bukharin and Preobrazhensky), 13, 14, 19
absentee ownership, 71
abundance: notion of, 16
accounting system. *See* mark point system
administrative decentralization, 184
affluent societies, 16–17
agribusinesses, 120, 224, 225, 226
agriculture. *See* collectivization of agriculture: cooperatives; peasants of Laos
aid. *See* foreign aid
alienation, 229
Althusser, Louis, 211
altruistic communities, 204–05
"anarchistic" tendencies, 183
Ancient Society (Morgan), 8
animals, domestic, 35, 78–79. *See also* buffalo; livestock
animals, wild, 83
anthropology, 3, 9, 10; view of cooperation, 217–18; of socialism, 227–33
Ardrey, Robert, 237n5
aristocracy, 28, 29; in Laos, 34, 37, 40–41
Association of Lao Patriotic Women, 184
audit, 162, 203–04
authoritarian regimes, 177, 183, 191–92
Ayudhya, 28

ban, 32, 183, 184
Bangkok Post, 27
Baran, Paul, 19, 20, 21, 22, 173
Barbier, Jean-Pierre, 34
barter, 12, 15
Bennett, John, 207

Berry, R. Albert, 170
Black Tai, 83, 86, 197
blackmarket, 15, 163
Bloch, Maurice, 9, 10, 247n22
Bolshevik experience, 18
"Bolshevik" rhetoric, 225
Bottomore, Tom, 232
boun (ceremony), 82, 86
bourgeois society, 9
Bradby, Barbara, 10
"brainwashing," 2
Branfman, Fred, 35
Bray, Francesca, 25, 88, 224
Brewster, J. M., 249n17
brotherhood, 211
Buddhism, 5–6, 111, 112, 152, 207; *vats*, 80; ceremonies, 86–88; women in, 132; sangha/state relationship, 185–88
buffalo, 72T, 73, 82, 85; rental of, 92, 104
Bukharin, N., 13, 19, 66, 221
Burma, 29, 186, 187
Buruya, 11

cadre training, 60, 63
Cambodia, 15, 46, 48, 49, 216, 219; Buddhism in, 186, 187
capitalism, 3, 21, 25; compared to socialism, 8, 9–10, 12, 16–17; Marxist view of, 17–18; in Laos, 40, 55, 66, 76, 89, 90; "bypassing" capitalism, 65; capitalist division of labor, 85; Marx on, 202–03; Calvinism and, 207; collectivization and, 221, 222; anthropology's critique of, 227–28
"capitalist decadence," 4

Index